Psychology for Professional Groups

D0363337

Psychology for Social Workers
Martin Herbert

Psychology for Professional Groups

Psychology
for Social
Workers

Martin Herbert

M | BPS

First published in 1981
Second, revised edition 1986
Reprinted 1987, 1990

Published by THE BRITISH PSYCHOLOGICAL SOCIETY and
MACMILLAN PUBLISHERS LIMITED.

Distributed by Higher and Further Education Division
MACMILLAN PUBLISHERS LTD., London and Basingstoke.
Associated companies and representatives throughout the
world.

British Library Cataloguing in Publication Data

Herbert, Martin
Psychology for social workers. — 2nd ed.
— (Psychology for professional groups)
1. Psychology.   2. Social service.
I. Title   II. Series
150'.24362   BF131

ISBN 0-333-41924-3
ISBN 0-333-41925-1 Pbk

Printed in Great Britain by Billing & Sons Limited, Guildford,
London, Oxford, Worcester

Contents

PART TWO: PSYCHOLOGICAL THEORY FOR SOCIAL WORK PRACTICE

Foreword

This book is one of a series, the principal aims of which
are to illustrate how psychology can be applied in
particular professional contexts, how it can improve the
skills of practitioners, and how it can increase the
practitioners' and students' understanding of themselves.

Psychology is taught to many groups of students and is
now integrated within prescribed syllabuses for an
increasing number of professions. Most of the existing
texts which teachers have been obliged to recommend are
typically designed for broad and disparate purposes, and
consequently they fail to reflect the special needs of
students in professional training. The starting point for
the series was the systematic distillation of views
expressed in professional journals by those psychologists
whose teaching specialisms relate to the applications of
psychology. It soon became apparent that many fundamental
topics were common to a number of syllabuses and courses;
yet in general introductory textbooks these topics tend to
be embedded amongst much superfluous material. Therefore,
from within the British Psychological Society, we invited
experienced teachers and authorities in their field to
write review chapters on key topics. Forty-seven chapters
covering 23 topics were then available for selection by
the series' Volume Editors. The Volume Editors are also
psychologists and they have had many years of involvement
with their respective professions. In preparing their
books, they have consulted formally with colleagues in
those professions. Each of their books has its own
combination of the specially-prepared chapters, set in the
context of the specific professional practice.

Because psychology is only one component of the
various training curricula, and because students generally
have limited access to learned journals and specialist
texts, our contributors to the series have restricted
their use of references, while at the same time providing
short lists of annotated readings. In addition, they have
provided review questions to help students organize their
learning and prepare for examinations. Further teaching
materials, in the form of additional references, projects,

exercises and class notes, are available in Tutor Manuals prepared for each book. A comprehensive tutorial text ('Psychology and People'), prepared by the Series Editors, combines in a single volume all the key topics, together with their associated teaching materials.

Antony J. Chapman
University of Leeds

Anthony Gale
University of Southampton

January 1986

Introduction
Martin Herbert

The central theme running through the many definitions of
the social work task, no matter what the school of
thought, is a statement about a genuine, humanely
motivated attempt to assist people to cope with the
troubles and crises of everyday life in a way which does
not diminish their worth or dignity as human beings.

Pincus and Minahan (1973), authors of a highly
influential textbook, list among the purposes of social
work: (i) enhancing the problem-solving and coping
capacities of people; (ii) linking people with systems and
providing them with resources, services and opportunities;
(iii) promoting the effective and humane operation of
these systems, and (iv) contributing to the development
and improvement of social policy. With a remit as broadly
conceived as this, it is not surprising that social
workers feel confused about the nature of their
contemporary social work task and the overinclusive
knowledge it seems to imply. The knowledge base of social
work, after all, has to encompass the facts and theories,
skills and attitudes necessary for effective and efficient
practice. That practice might have the social worker
acting variously (and at different times) as therapist,
mediator, resource-mobilizer, resource-generator, social
broker, advocate, co-ordinator, teacher and friend (see
Yelloly, 1980). All this calls for a remarkable
flexibility of response and conceptual sophistication.

The social worker's role involves even further diversi-
fication in that interventions are directed towards
individuals, groups, communities and organizations.
Whatever else is required, social work theory and practice
obviously call for a significant input on the
psychological principles affecting both individuals and
groups.

As knowledge in the psychological disciplines
increases, it is important that social work practitioners
are aware of new (as well as tried) theories and
technologies; they should be able to evaluate them in
terms of their usefulness in furthering social work goals.
A familiarity with (and ability to evaluate) new inputs of

psychological knowledge is not enough. Practitioners should be able to identify and clarify different ideological positions, so as to liberate themselves from undue reliance on any particular stance which could deflect them from evolving novel solutions or flexible ways of working in the light of specific demands of the tasks which face them.

Psychology is an inordinately untidy and many-sided subject. Psychologists themselves are likely to be wondering how it is possible to keep up to date with, let alone evaluate and integrate, the theoretical and factual out-pouring from the discipline. The knowledge is often fragmented and the psychologist is presented with the difficult task of achieving a 'working synthesis': a 'map' to chart thinking and actions. If psychologists have not done this for themselves then they cannot expect their students - adrift in a sea of strange and apparently disparate concepts - to 'get it together'. This in turn makes the task of connecting psychological theory and social work practice highly problematic.

And therein lies a painful dilemma for the inexperienced lecturer. I can only speak as a teacher of psychology, but I imagine that most social scientists who are serious about teaching social work students (a commitment requiring a serious study of the complexities of the social task) suffer from deja vu: a disconcerting sense of failure at the end of the umpteenth revision of their course. The hapless lecturer has probably tried the role of courier, the Grand Tour of Psychology approach. It parallels the 'Guided Tour of Europe' experience: 'I know this is Pisa because it's Wednesday'. Like those passengers 'doing' Europe in three weeks, his or her charges disembark feeling exhausted, amnesic and none the wiser. So the lecturer changes direction (and the metaphor) and tries the gourmet approach: customers are introduced to a few choice morsels, allowing them time to savour the rich fare; the lecturer tends (inductively) to educate their palates. But still the consumers complain; so many significant items are absent from the menu, and, in any event, what has such a seletive diet got to do with ordinary everyday eating? It is a Catch-22 situation!

After many false starts, I would see my task as a psychology teacher (and as editor of this revised volume) as providing a 'map' of psychology, and its possible application in social work assessment and intervention. It is impossible to teach everything, but I would hope, by way of my own introductory section, and the more elaborate and detailed specialist contributions, to introduce social workers to 'map-reading' skills: in other words, the symbols, language, and relevant principles of psychology. Such an approach also gives them personal access to the wide psychological literature. It is, in general, a relatively small-scale map that I give in Part I; a guide on which I draw fairly broad features to give a picture of that part of psychology which throws into relief the problems that social workers meet. In the specialist contributions written by professional psychologists (Part II), the authors have provided the sharper focus of an 'ordinance survey map', putting in finer and important points in detail.

My aim in planning this psychology volume for social workers is to provide them with the wherewithal to carry out 'psychologically informed' social work. I wish to encourage social work practitioners and students to identify and understand ('internalize') a relatively small number of general and operational psychological principles and skills which are necessary for effective practice in a variety of situations and changing circumstances. By internalization I mean the assimilation of psychological ideas into the 'organic' construing system of the practitioner, so that psychological thinking is not simply 'tacked on' as an afterthought. Such a desideratum poses a daunting problem in terms of methods and imaginative styles of teaching and learning. Psychology deserves to be part of the core curriculum of a social work course. Whether it attains this status or is pushed into an ancillary role chiefly depends on the skill and commitment with which it is taught.

Despite the plethora of social work tasks decribed above, the social worker is still viewed primarily as someone who works directly with individual clients. Rightly or wrongly, the modern social worker tends to view casework as a psycho-therapeutic treatment process, in which the major emphasis is on the casework relationship and direct counselling or therapeutic work with the client. It has been argued (Yelloly, 1980) that social work's commitment to a therapeutic person-orientated ideology, especially psycho-dynamic psychology, may have inhibited its study of, and involvement in, those social and situational factors which themselves create or contribute to personal distress.

In this new edition I have attempted to illustrate how the systems-based approach called behavioural casework gives proper weight to social and situational factors. I have chosen the conduct disorders of childhood and adolescence as the individual context for this discussion. The chapter on 'Institutional Climates' by Orford provides an analysis of these factors at a community level.

How is it possible to keep up to date with, let alone evaluate and integrate, the many available theories and facts? Lewis (1972) states that ultimately the test of the value of the knowledge used will be its effectiveness in practice: the results achieved in relation to the original goals as evaluated by the practitioner and client. He insists that if what we do is based on what we claim to know and value and is intended to achieve preferred ends,

then the results of our professional actions should test
our claims and show us how to improve our efforts. Sadly,
there has been only too often a cavalier attitude towards
(not to mention ignorance of) the evidence of competing
claims. The discussion of scientific method (chapter 1) is
a reminder of the need for empirical confirmation of
theories. Having said that, it is necessary to add that
competence involves not only the skilled use of particular
methods, but also the ability to employ theoretical
knowledge in various practical settings in an imaginative
fashion. I would link the word imaginative to the concept
of intuition.

The arts as well as the sciences are the progenitors
(in social work) of practice and theory. Some of the
students who come from an arts background feel themselves
to be at a disadvantage compared with those with a science
training. I would deny this! Henry Maas (1978) reminds us
that: 'In large measure, our Social Work practice -
whether policy development or direct work at the community
level - is a craft.' Each art has its technical side; the
most fruitful communication of those who work primarily
with symbols (the artists) and those who work primarily
with sense data (the scientists) occurs in some of the
crafts. I would deprecate the tendency of some social
workers and social work educators to argue as if the
values, language and perspectives of one part of social
work are so radically different from the other, so
mutually exclusive, that they must alienate the tender-
minded (the intuitive 'artists') from the tough-minded
(the 'scientists'). Both the arts and the sciences
'involve intellect, intense creativity and passionate
commitment to purpose and to the means for its attainment'
(Maas, 1978).

The eminent personality theorist, Gordon Allport,
insisted on a marriage of the 'nomothetic' and
'idiographic' approaches for a true understanding of the
person and his or her situation (Allport, 1937). The
nomothetic disciplines seek general laws and employ only
those procedures admitted by the exact sciences.
Scientists can be overbearing in their arrogant assumption
that the only path to truth lies through scientific
method. Notcutt (1953) railed against 'scientism', the
pharisaical insistence on the letter rather than the
spirit of scientific method. Although there are many
routes to truth, psychology has been very dependent on
scientific method (as we shall see) to lift it out of the
rather unprofitable realm of 'armchair philosophy'.

This volume ranges from the microlevel of analysis
(Herbert, chapter 2, on learning principles) to the
macrolevel (Frude, chapter 9, on the family); and from an
introduction to that most individually-orientated skill,
interviewing (Wicks in chapter 18), to those important
group and socially-related skills (Argyle in chapter 13).

Introduction

It is hoped that this coverage - emphasizing the links between theory and practice - will help social workers in their onerous but essential social work task.

References

Allport, G.W. (1937)
Personality: A psychological interpretation. New York: Holt, Rinehart & Winston.

Lewis, H. (1972)
Developing a programme responsive to new knowledge and values. In E.J. Mullen and J.R. Dumpson (eds), Evaluation of Social Intervention. San Francisco: Jossey-Bass.

Maas, H. (1980)
Research and the knowledge base. In, Discovery and Development in Social Work Education. Vienna: International Association of Schools of Social Work Publications.

Notcutt, B. (1953)
The Psychology of Personality. New York: Philosophical Library.

Pincus, A. and Minahan, A. (1973)
Social Work Practice: Model and method. Itasca, Ill.: Peacock Publications.

Yelloly, M.A. (1980)
Social Work Theory and Psychoanalysis. London: Van Nostrand Reinhold.

Annotated reading

The following books will provide the reader with useful supplementary knowledge of psychology, both theoretical and practical.

Gale, A. and Chapman, A.J. (eds) (1984) Psychology and Social Problems. Chichester: John Wiley & Sons Ltd.
Describes how applied psychology works in various settings and with different problems.

Herbert, M. (1985) Caring for Your Children. Oxford: Basil Blackwell.
This is a simply written (but not simplistic) book on psychology, child development and learning for parents and care staff. Social workers may find it a useful adjunct to their work with families, especially where there are worries about the 'normal' and 'not-so-normal' problems associated with rearing children.

Taylor, A., Sluckin, W. et al. (1983) Introducing Psychology. Harmondsworth: Penguin Books - second edition.
A popular academic text on general psychology, written by staff of the psychology department at the University of Leicester.

Warr, P.B. (ed.) (1978) Psychology at Work.
Harmondsworth: Penguin Books - second edition.
    Applications of psychology described by 16 authors.

Part one

Concepts and Concerns of Psychology

Martin Herbert

1

What is psychology?

'The age of anxiety' is an expression commonly applied to the turbulent times in which we live. This somewhat melodramatic label for our day and age does contain a grain of truth. In a period of rapid change and great technological sophistication, many people feel that they are not in control of their own lives, that they are not really in touch with other people. Somehow the person - the individual - has become lost in what seems to be a vast, impersonal and somewhat meaningless world. And here is the first attraction of the discipline of psychology: psychology is basically about the individual person!

Social workers know only too well how many people (especially women) are on tranquillizers or anti-depressant drugs in order simply 'to keep going', for twentieth-century men and women find themselves at the centre of a paradox. In a period when we know so much about the laws of the physical universe, we know relatively little about the workings of our mental world. There seems to be a frightening discrepancy between our understanding and mastery of our material environment and our knowledge and control of ourselves. Our psychological awareness is still rudimentary. Nevertheless, psychology, for all its limitations, has much to offer in the way of answers to serious human conflicts. More and more institutions (clinics, educational centres, industries and governmental agencies) are turning to psychology for solutions to problems that beset individuals in their home life, at school, at work, and in their social and political existence.

It has been said of psychology that it has a short history but a long past. What this means becomes clear when we look at one of the contemporary definitions of psychology: 'Psychology is the scientific study of mind and behaviour.' Two of these terms (study and mind) belong to psychology's ancient past; the other two (scientific and behaviour) are part of its recent history. We have to go back in time to find the origins of this discipline. The word 'psychology' is made up of two Greek words:

* 'psyche', which means soul or mind;
* 'logos', meaning word or study.

PSYCHE: from time immemorial human beings have been
preoccupied with the world of spirit and mind, fascinated
and frightened by nightmares, emotions, thoughts and
fantasies. In other words we have tried to understand, in
a personal and informal sense, those of our experiences
which can be properly categorized as 'psychological
events'. And for thousands of years scholars have been
asking and trying to answer questions - in a more formal
way, in treatises and books - about human and animal
nature. These can be described appropriately as 'psychological questions'.

LOGOS: it barely a century ago that psychology emerged
as a separate discipline: that is, as a distinct area of
study (logos), and the first real psychologists appeared
as a 'profession', separate from the many academics and
other groups who had speculated about things of the mind.
Philosophers ('lovers of wisdom'), theologians, writers
and artists have always sought to unravel human understanding and mastery of the material environment and the
person's knowledge and control of himself or herself. The
newenquirers were not simply interested in psychological
reflection from the vantage point of an armchair. Their
place was in the laboratory; their methods of study were
systematic and scientific.

Although psychology's graduation as a science is so
recent, its beginnings as a topic of serious study go
back, like so many other subjects (notably education,
philosophy, architecture, politics and history), to
Ancient Greece. Science itself started there. The Greeks
were fascinated by the problem of causation. The early
philosophers searched for a material or physical cause of
the world. The four elements, earth, air, fire and water -
separately or in combination - were given this honour. One
school of thought, the cosmologists, postulated an atomic
theory of the universe. They were reductionists in the
sense that they tried to reduce the physical universe into
the irreducible elements of which they believed it to be
made. Psychologists, many centuries later, were to apply
an atomistic reductionist analysis to behaviour as we see
later.

These early beginnings of the physical sciences were
the first steps in a triumphant journey towards the
present-day exploration of the physical universe in space
itself. Somehow the exploration of the mental world was
left far behind. Although the Ancient Greeks began the
process of asking psychological questions about the nature
of such things as knowledge, happiness and justice, during
the centuries which followed scholars did not evolve a
scientific way of looking at these problems as had been
the case for the physical universe.

The subject matter of psychology

This delay means that we are still asking the same sorts of questions as the ancients. A founder-figure of modern psychology - the American theorist Edward L. Thorndike (1911, 1932) - reduced psychological questions to four topics:

* the nature of the different kinds of thoughts and feelings;
* the purposes which they serve in life;
* the laws which govern their behaviour and that of the bodily states and acts connected with them;
* the ways in which they are related to the actions of the brain.

These questions contain certain assumptions about mental life and the mind and body.

The nature of mental life (mind and body)
In trying to understand themselves and others, human beings have evolved a psychological vocabulary which helps to make sense of the world, and one of the objectives of this introductory section is to provide the reader with the more important terms and concepts in that vocabulary. This is done by ordering and classifying our experiences. We experience, think, desire, regret and remember. These 'events' we classify as being of one kind (mental events). We feel pain, sensuous pleasure, cold and heat; we sometimes gets breathless, exhausted and ill. These 'events' are conceptualized as being of another kind (bodily events).

The point must be stressed that human behaviour is a complex combination of acts, feelings, thoughts and motives. The distinctions we make between body and mind and the further sub-divisions of mental life we make use of, such as emotion, intellect, drives (motives) and so on, are artificial and matters of convenience. These physical and mental processes are essentially indivisible, interacting and interdependent. We have to isolate them so as to study them and talk about them.

This point of view was not always accepted. There were endless, and somewhat futile, debates about the precise nature and relationship of body and mind. The extreme theory that mind and body are quite separate (called Cartesian dualism after the philosopher who formulated it: Rene Descartes, 1596-1650), is summed up in the jingle: 'What is mind? No matter. What is matter? Never mind.' Descartes gave the soul a place in the body - which was likened to a machine - but he did not think of it as a 'thing'. This notion of what might be called a 'ghost in the machine' led psychological inquiry up a long-lasting cul-de-sac of inconclusive speculation. Because the idea lingered on that the psyche (mind/soul) is a non-material substance, it was assumed that the methods of the natural sciences - observation and laboratory experimentation - could only be applied to our bodily processes, and were inappropriate for studying the mind.

Public versus private events
The distinction of body and mind has important implications. As we saw earlier on, contemporary psychology is committed today to the scientific approach to knowledge. And the knowledge of our bodily activities including speech is, so to speak, visible to others and therefore public. But knowledge of our mental functions, our plans, ideas, and wishes, is hidden from others. They remain invisible to others and private, unless we wish to tell others about them.

Introspection - looking inwards on one's own thoughts - was thought to be the proper method of studying these private events and came to be known as 'armchair psychology'. Although the method provided some useful information, and adaptations of the technique are still in use today as a major technique of a major school of psychology, it proved a blind alley. Such highly individual and subjective methods of study are unreliable and wide generalizations about human behaviour are not possible. Mental life, in any event, is incapable of analysis on such a restricted basis.

The really crucial milestone in the history of psychology came with the rejection of a clear-cut distinction between mental and bodily events. Psychologists began to focus the powerful spotlight of science on the bodily manifestations of our psychological existence. They adapted the general methods of science to investigate (in particular) our public psychological acts: that is, our behaviour. Behaviour is what a person does and says, and it can therefore be seen and heard. Contemporary psychology is, as we shall see, not only a social science, but also one of the biological sciences. Just as physiologists and zoologists study the form and function of all the members of the animal kingdom, psychologists investigate the behaviour of animals as well as humans. Men and women are regarded as social animals (see Argyle, chapter 13). There are many points in common between human and animal behaviour. Animals show, in elementary forms, some of the processes which make up human behaviour; however, it is misleading to extrapolate too much from animal to human behaviour. The point about our concentration on behaviour is that we can obtain appropriate conditions for the application of scientific methods.

The nature of science
What do we mean when we characterize a discipline as a science?

Science is empirical
This means that it is based upon observations rather than

on opinion, belief, prejudice or argument. Truth is a
relative concept and the 'facts' of today may be rejected
as ignominious myths tomorrow. It is important to be just
a little sceptical of received wisdom lest it be elevated
to the status of doctrine. The ideas about maternal
deprivation and maternal bonding (see Chapter 4) are good
illustrations of this. One should find out, and know how
one comes to know. It is not simply casual observations
which make a science empirical; observations must be
reliable, which means they must be repeatable and carried
out according to a strict set of rules (Popper, 1976).

The knowledge social workers use may derive from their
own personal experience. For example, they may find that a
particular intervention is successful with a particular
kind of social problem. Unfortunately, there are many
hazards in relying on personal experience. The observation
and recording of what is experienced may be unreliable.
Generalizations may be formed on the basis of inadequate
evidence. Evidence may be distorted by personal biases or
neglected because it does not accord with previous
experience. The salient features of a situation may not be
distinguished from those which are irrelevant. Causal
inferences may be incorrectly or prematurely drawn.

Empirical knowledge is the agreement in reports of
repeated observations made by two or more individuals
under rigorously specified (controlled) conditions.

Empirical knowledge about the world is regarded by
many as the most trustworthy form of knowledge. It may
arise in many ways but there are extreme and contrasting
possibilities. At one extreme is intuitive belief. This
will be asserted by an individual as his or her view about
an aspect of the world. It may be grounded on personal
experiences, it may be a belief based only on other
peoples' stories of their experiences, or, most likely,
some vague blend of both. Intuitive belief contributes to
our views about the world and is the basis of 'common
sense'. Indeed, you may affirm that as a social worker you
rely, in part, on common sense. Of course, common sense
'theories' must not be denigrated. A common sense view of
what the world is like, and how people are likely to react
to us, serves most of us fairly well in our day-to-day
life. But there are different levels of understanding (and
of explanation) when behaviour is investigated. Dr Harry
Kay, a psychologist and a previous Chairman of the Central
Council for Education and Training in Social Work, had
this to say:

> I am a great believer in common sense, in relying on
> the good sense of mankind to 'get it right'. It
> generally does in the end. But the fact that common
> sense may have had it wrong for a few preceding
> millenia does mean that we need to be on our guard and
> not be too hasty over the certainty of any answers.

For example, at one time everybody knew we lived on a flat world; it was self-evident until someone went to the edge and did not fall off. About the same time, everyone knew that the sun charioted around the earth each day, whilst the earth was the centre of the universe, and so on. As we have come to accept, blood has to be spilt before common sense accepts change, but eventually it does and yesterday's heresy becomes today's credo, whilst common sense forgets that it was ever otherwise.

Science emphasizes measurement
The history of every scientific discipline is signposted by its attempts to measure with ever greater precision.

Science is systematic
Although data (observations) are the lifeblood of a science, by themselves they are of little value. They have to be put into some order or 'system' so as to make sense of the world.

Can there be a science of mind?

Having described the essential criteria of the scientific approach, can they be applied to 'mind' as such? Can we observe mental processes or measure them?

The problem of mental life
I said earlier that knowledge of our mental functions - our experiences, thoughts, plans, ideas, and wishes - is hidden from others. They remain unknowable to others. Our 'minds' are not entities in the sense that they have a location, and identifiable boundaries. It is not even theoretically possible that with new techniques we shall one day be able to observe the mind. For this reason mind cannot be studied empirically. The same applies to 'mental processes' such as thoughts! Scientists are unable to investigate anything that is outside the range of their senses, or which cannot be brought within this range by means of instruments such as microscopes, cameras, amplifiers, and so on.

The American psychologist Donald Lewis (1960) predicts (probably quite accurately) that by this time you will be saying 'I think. And I have ideas too. And no psychologist is ever going to convince me of anything different.' Lewis replies, as would other psychologists: 'Of course you think. And so do your neighbours. But the point is that nobody else under any condition whatever, knows what you are thinking, or even if you are thinking, unless you tell him. And if you tell him, right away it is your verbal behavior that is being observed, not your ideas. Again, all we can ever observe directly is behavior.' All this is not to suggest that psychologists ignore what is known as conscious experiences (see Bannister, chapter 8). Private (subjective) processes, such as ideas, constructs, decisions and other aspects of thinking, can only be dealt with scientifically by trying to objectify them (i.e. by looking at their external public manifestations).

The nature of behaviour

Behaviour, as we saw earlier, is what a person does and says (verbal behaviour) and it can therefore be seen and heard, recorded and quantified. Behaviour is not just a series of unco-ordinated, discrete activities. It is a continuing process. Mental processes can only be inferred; they cannot be directly observed. Nevertheless, 'models' of mental processes can be deduced from their effects on behaviour. For example, the nature of intelligence - a highly mentalistic notion - has been deduced from the ways that thousands of individuals perform on tests which are assumed to measure ability. The same kind of analysis has been applied to the concept of personality. We now have, in the definition of behaviour given above, the appropriate conditions for the application of scientific methods.

Gordon Allport is clear that the objective of studying behaviour psychologically (that is to say, scientifically) is to produce 'understanding, prediction, and control above the levels achieved by unaided commonsense' (Allport, 1937).

Science is always in a state of flux; there are no ultimate answers. Principles are continually being defined, tested, reformulated, tested again, and so on. There is always a need for further investigations and extended principles and themes. In this painstaking manner, the frontiers of psychological knowedge are slowly pushed outwards. Although the scientific method is a very valuable way of acquiring new knowledge it does not yield absolute or eternal truth; rather, one can say that it reduces uncertainty.

References

Allport, G.W. (1937)
Personality: A psychological interpretation. New York: Holt, Rinehart & Winston.
Kay, H. (1978)
Preface. In J. Radford and D. Rose (eds), The Teaching of Psychology. Chichester: John Wiley & Sons Ltd.
Lewis, D. (1960)
Quantitative Methods in Psychology. New York: McGraw-Hill.
Popper, K. (1976)
Unended Quest: An intellectual autobiography. London: Fontana/Collins.
Thorndike, E.L. (1911)
Animal Intelligence. New York: Macmillan.

What is psychology?

Thorndike, E.L. (1932)
    The Fundamentals of Learning. Columbia University, New
    York: Teachers College.

2

Analysing behaviour: social learning principles

Before psychologists can apply themselves to any analysis
of behaviour, they need to know what to look for, and how
to look for it. This is the all-important matter of observation. The scientific way of looking at things is to
begin with the most basic units of phenomena. The 'atoms'
of the physical sciences have their equivalent in the so-
called S-R (stimulus-response) units; the atomic laws have
their figurative counterpart in the S-R laws.

Looking for lawfulness in human behaviour
Behaviour is lawful. If it were not so, society would collapse into anarchy. We can rely on most car drivers to
respond to the stimulus of a red traffic light by stopping. If we could not, chaos would ensue. We can depend on
the vast majority of parents to respond to the stimulus of
crying children by caring for their needs, otherwise children would not survive.

The words 'most' and 'majority' in these statements
about the lawfulness of human behaviour point to a problem
in the study of psychological causation which we shall
take up later.

In chapter 1, psychology was described as a science
that studies the causes of behaviour in order to achieve
understanding, prediction and control. This is the same
thing as saying that psychologists are trying to discover
laws of behaviour. Laws are statements about the regu-
larities, the order to be found in the world. As such, a
law is a statement which describes the relationship
between two or more events.

Basic components of behaviour
In all, there are four particularly vital components which
the social worker needs to identify in order to understand
and analyse behaviour. Any situation in which behaviour
occurs can be analysed fruitfully with the aid of these
components, which are in fact psychological concepts.
Psychological laws often take the form of statements about
the relationship between events called STIMULI (on the one
hand) and RESPONSES (on the other). These are called stim-

ulus (S)-response (R) laws: for example, 'Given stimulus Y one would expect response Z', or more economically: 'If Y, then Z.'

*   a STIMULUS (S) is anything (e.g. an event or happening, physical or psychological) that initiates or influences behaviour or arouses a state of conscious awareness; any event, in other words, that activates actions and/or thoughts and/or feelings.
*   a RESPONSE (R) is a reaction of (for example) a muscle or gland, or (on a larger scale) it may comprise a complex series of actions, elicited by stimulation. Some examples of stimulus-response (S-R) sequences are: (i) I click my fingers suddenly in front of your eyes (physical stimulus); you blink (physical response) and probably say: 'Why did you do that?' (verbal response); (ii) someone smiles (social stimulus) and says 'Hello' (verbal stimulus); you probably respond by smiling back (social response) and replying 'Hello' (verbal response).

There are two more important terms you need for a behaviour analysis:

*   thoughts (cognitions) and motives: anything within or outside the person that creates plans, desires or needs. O is the symbol for events such as 'drives' occurring within the organism.
*   reinforcement consequences: reinforcers (positive). When certain stimuli closely follow a particular behaviour they increase the probability of that behaviour occurring again in the future. Stimuli that serve this function are called 'positive reinforcers'.
        Reinforcers (negative). Other stimuli (aversive/punitive events) increase the probability of behaviour occurring again when their removal closely follows that behaviour. These stimuli are called 'negative reinforcers'.

If you wish to understand the behaviour of another person the first thing you should do is try to identify each of the four aspects of the behavioural situation described above.

Analysing responses
Overt behaviour can be studied in terms of responses to various stimuli. Nearly all psychological functions can be described as responses because they are involved in the business of adjusting (adapting) to the environment.
        Psychologists put the relationships between Ss, and Rs and Os as follows: $S \rightarrow O \rightarrow R$

$$R = f(O, S)$$

i.e. R is a function of O and S
or R depends on O and S

(Later we refer to these relationships more simply as the ABC of behaviour.) When we want to influence behaviour, we manipulate (vary) O or S or both.

Men and women are creatures of habit. This means that they rely on learning rather than instinct (complex, rigid and inborn patterns of behaviour universal to a species and not reliant for their appearance on experience).

The higher we go up the evolutionary scale, the less dependent are species on stereotyped inherited instinctive responses. At the summit are human beings, the most flexible of all creatures, who have reached this pinnacle because of their adjustive equipment, notably their possession of a highly developed brain. They have a tremendous capacity to learn and to change, and then to adapt to novel situations. Here is a crucial source of the great variety of men and women, their susceptibility to many different types of environment. (An environment is defined as all the forces, physical, social, psychological and so on, to which the individual is exposed.)

Flexible (adaptable) and healthy people are much better placed to cope with these changes because their ability to learn - their openness to new ideas, their acceptance of reality - is efficient and always in a state of readiness. Their first learning environment is likely to be provided by the family.

Parents as teachers
The birth of a first child to a couple makes parents of them and transforms their partnership into a family. Living together in small groups, or what might broadly be thought of as 'families', has been the universal pattern for homo sapiens and his forebears for some 500,000 years. It would seem reasonable to claim that an institution that has endured from the middle of the Pleistocene period to the present day must have significant survival value for its individual members, and their species.

However, the family, led by adults (parents), is not only crucial for the care and protection it offers the young during their relatively prolonged period of dependence; it plays a major role in the introduction of infants into the ways of their social environment - their culture. Our cultural heritage does not and cannot depend upon any biological device such as a genetic code as is the case with our physical equipment for living. The transmission of culture cannot be inflexible and yet it cannot be left to chance. As Lidz puts it:

The welfare of the individual and the continuity of the culture which is essential to man depend upon his having satisfactory means of indoctrinating the mem-

bers of the new generation into the mores, sentiments
and instrumentalities of the society, and to assure
that they, in turn, will become satisfactory carriers
of the culture. The major task of indoctrination
devolves upon the family, even though the members of
the family often do not know that they have the task
(Lidz, 1968, p.41).

A young child is open to learning in all its forms: the
development of habits and traits, and ways of perceiving
and dealing with the world, and the absorption of a vast
amount of knowlege and new material.

Learning can be one of the most rewarding and mind-
expanding experiences. Social workers can apply learning
theory to help people develop as individuals, become
better at managing their lives and getting on with their
fellow men and women. Erik Erikson (1965) claims that the
period of infancy is the time in which the baby learns
whether the world is a good and satisfying place to live
in or a source of pain, misery, frustration and
uncertainty. He called those contrasting points of view
'basic trust' and 'basic mistrust', and they are very like
our adult attitudes of optimism and pessimism. This is our
cue to look more closely at learning processes.

The nature of learning
Learning is a relatively permanent modification of behaviour resulting from experience. Memorizing a formula,
recognizing a face, reading music and becoming fearful of
doing maths or going to parties, are all examples of
learning

Observational learning
Social learning theory places great emphasis on the social
context and nature of learning. People learn much of their
social behaviour (and many other complex acts) by modelling themselves on their observations of the significant
people in their environment, imitating what they do and
say. This form of learning, which is based on cognitive
(intellectual) processes rather than training by means of
external reinforcement, is called 'observational learning'
by psychologists and is referred to more colloquially as
imitation.

The child's ability to imitate also has its negative
aspects. It plays an important role in the acquisition of
undesirable deviant behaviour. We often forget that children are just as influenced by their parents' behaviour
(what they do) as by what they actually say.

We have to distinguish between learning an action or
behaviour and actually performing it.

The ABC of learning
This is where the 'ABC' of behaviour (see chapter 11) will

prove useful. A stands for antecedents or what went before B, which stands for behaviour (or what the client actually does); C stands for consequences (or what occurred immediately after the behaviour).

We know that it can be very helpful to look at a client's problematic behaviour by analysing very precisely the behaviour itself, what led up to it and what happened immediately afterwards. Essentially, B depends upon C. That is to say, consequences are what shape behaviour. Parents and teachers (for example) shape behaviour by manipulating the consequences of the child's behaviour. The technical term for this learning principle is operant (or instrumental) conditioning. We shall return later to the A term.

First principle

If a consequence of a behaviour is rewarding (i.e. favourable) to the person, that behaviour is likely to increase in strength. For example, it may become more frequent! Put another way: if a client does something, and as a result of this action something pleasant happens, then he or she is more likely to do the same thing in similar circumstances in the future. Psychologists refer to this pleasant outcome as the 'positive reinforcement' of behaviour; they have in mind several kinds of reinforcers: tangible rewards (e.g. treats, privileges, money); social rewards (e.g. attention, a smile, a pat on the back, a word of encouragement); and self-reinforcers (e.g. the ones that come from within and which are nontangible - self-praise, self-approval, a sense of pleasure).

Second principle

Behaving in a manner that avoids an unpleasant outcome leads to the reinforcement of behaviour, thus making it more likely to recur in similar circumstances. If (say) children do something their mother doesn't like, such as losing their temper too easily, she may increase their ability to think first and keep their temper, by penalizing them consistently for failing to do so; in this way she is providing what is called 'negative reinforcement' for their efforts to 'keep their cool'.

Third principle

If a desired behaviour (and for that matter, an undesirable action) is not reinforced it is likely to reduce in frequency, and perhaps vanish altogether ('extinguish'). You will see how we make use of this principle for casework and training purposes later on.

Fourth principle

If a person does something and as a result of this action something unpleasant - a penalty, sanction or punishment -

follows, he or she is less likely to do the same thing in the future, i.e. the undesired behaviour may be decreased.

Failure to learn

Many problems are not due to the client learning inappropriate responses, but are the consequence of a failure to learn an appropriate behaviour or skill. Here is an important difference in the nature of behaviour disturbances in children and adults. Many behaviour problems in children (especially in the early years) are associated with inadequate skills or behaviour control. These deficiences are often connected with the activities of eating, sleeping, elimination, speaking and expressing aggression. In most instances the problem arises because the child has failed to develop an adequate way of responding - for example, in controlling anger (tantrums), in learning to control wetting (enuresis), and in learning to articulate speech smoothly (stammering). The over-aggressive child has failed to learn the socially desirable restraints over his or her hostile acts.

Most problems in adults seem to be concerned with what is called 'maladaptive' behaviour, and the purpose of casework or therapy is generally directed at eliminating the undesirable responses (e.g. phobias, anxiety states, depression, abusive behaviour and self-defeating thoughts). Most often, in adult therapy, the aim is to break down, alter or eliminate a behaviour pattern, whereas, in child therapy, the therapist usually has to build up or construct an adequate behaviour pattern to fill a gap in the child's adjustive skills.

The social worker will often be less concerned with the consequences of behaviour, but more interested in the antecedents of behaviour, i.e. what goes before, or leads up to, the particular action. This is our A term. For example, a child might learn vicariously to fear a teacher because she's observed him treating another child harshly. All of this is not to deny the importance of the C term (consequences) in this example of observational learning. A child's imitations of various socially-approved behaviours are given even greater impetus by praise and encouragement; in other words, they are reinforced by 'social' (or 'symbolic') rewards.

We elaborate these ideas in chapters 3 and 11.

References

Erikson, E.H. (1965)
  Childhood and Society (rev. edn). Harmondsworth: Penguin Books.
Lidz, T. (1968)
  The Person. London: Basic Books.

3

Analysing behaviour: developmental principles

It is time to introduce the reader to a branch of psychology called 'developmental psychology' (see chapter 5). The study of child development involves a special and crucial way of looking at the human changes, events, characteristics and behaviours studied by general psychology. The developmental theorist looks at these psychological happenings and events, which are separated in time, as being lawfully and meaningfully associated with each other in a process of progressive change over time; a movement called 'development'. Development thus refers to the multiple forces and processes which are responsible for shaping each individual's personality.

Integrated behaviour begins with the reception of information (stimuli) from both the external and internal environment. Information from the external environment is processed by the brain and translated into actions. After a discussion of some of these aspects of human psychology, we move from the so far rather abstract look at behaviour to the new human being - a human baby - as a means of illustrating some basic psychological principles.

Helpless (but not as helpless or as incompetent as people once thought), young babies lie in their mother's arms and explore their surroundings with their eyes. What do they make of their world; indeed, what can they make of it? If they seem totally dependent, capable of little save eating, sleeping and crying, then the casual eye is deceived. The infant is, in fact, a surprisingly well-equipped creature, more able than many developmental theorists ever suspected in their most speculative musings.

If the infant is to grow and flourish, then the priority of the day is simply to stay alive. The baby has several 'ready made' reflexes which serve this purpose. Reflex actions are controlled by the central nervous system - the brain and the spinal cord - and are inborn and automatic responses to an outside stimulus. A reflex action is a very simple form of behaviour and it is usually a protective device. If a finger accidentally comes into contact with a hot radiator, it is automati-

cally withdrawn before it gets burnt further. The action
is so quick that the rest of the body is not really aware
of what has happened.

New-born babies react to an ouside stimulus in the
same way; for instance if they are suddenly moved they are
likely to show the 'Moro', or startle, reflex. Their arms
suddenly lift themselves from the sides of their body,
their hands open, and then the arms come back to the
body.

**Perception:
how we know
our world**

It is fascinating to speculate about what goes on beyond the
reflex level in babies' minds. Can they (for example)
differentiate among distinctive forms or is their world
lacking in order; no more, as the eminent psychologist
William James expressed it at the turn of the century,
than a 'blooming, buzzing confusion'? Is this world
ordered in any way? The information or messages that we
receive and act on (in order to adapt to the environment)
begin at the level of sensation. All our knowledge of the
world comes through our senses initially. Information from
the external environment enters the body by the stimulation of receptor nerves; it is processed by the brain and
translated into actions via the effector nerves. The
messages we receive about our environment are integrated
and organized into perceptions. What we respond to are
changes in physical energy. A bell is rung; the energy of
the hammer hitting the bell is transformed into physical
energy. A light switch is clicked, and electricity is
changed into radiant energy. Certain nerve cells (the so-
called receptors) in the body are sensitive to various
kinds of energy changes.

The physical energy to which such a cell is sensitive
is called a stimulus. When a receptor detects the presence
of a stimulus, it is said to respond to the stimulus and
this causes an impulse (a message about the environment)
to travel along the nerve until it reaches the brain. The
nerve cells which make up the various parts of the brain
perform different functions; these differences are reflected to some extent in the anatomy of the brain. For
example, some parts of the brain are known to receive
impulses from particular sense organs; the visual area (in
the occipital lobe) receives those from the eyes through
the optic nerve. The auditory area is connected to the
ear, and so on. The basic elements of the system are many
millions of nerve cells (neurons) which sense, store and
transmit information. They function like minute live
relays for scores of years, day in and day out.

Nervous transmission
The activity of the brain is mainly electrical. The brain
performs its tasks by sending and receiving electrical
currents from its own nerve cells to and from other nerve

24

cells in various parts of the body. The nerve impulses which allow us to sense, perceive, think, feel and act, travel at speeds ranging from two to 200 miles an hour, and are transmitted from nerve cell to nerve cell (some having fibres several feet long). They have to cross over a gap, the 'synapse', of about one-millionth of an inch wide. They do this by means of chemicals released to the cell endings.

The body contains millions of neurons which penetrate every corner of the body and are connected into a huge network like a giant telephone system (to use a favourite metaphor). The spinal cord is the main cable which carries the bulk of the messages to and from the brain. Every neuron in the body has a minute electrical charge associated with it, even when it is not being stimulated. The charge is produced by the chemical difference between the inside of the nerve cell and the tissue which surrounds it. The cells themselves consist of chemical compounds. The nerve impulses are essentially electro-chemical events.

All this means that a study of the biochemistry of the brain (as well as its anatomy and physiology) is crucial for understanding mental functions like learning. Neurologists have pointed out that the brain of the infant is different from the adult's; the cells are smaller and the connections between them poorly insulated. Although immature, the baby's brain (as we shall see) functions efficiently enough to serve some remarkable perceptual abilities.

The brain must always be on the alert. Each and every second of waking life more than 100 million electrical impulses flow into the brain. Even when asleep more than 50 million neuronal 'messages' are being related every second to and from the brain and different parts of the body. Every neuron is 'all-or-none' in its action; just as an electric light is 'on' or 'off', a neuron either generates an impulse or it remains inactive.

Coding information

A single impulse arriving at the brain, say, a neuron in the retina of the eye, is indistinguishable from an impulse generated by a pain receptor in the sole of the foot. Yet a complex pattern of 'on' and 'off' retinal messages will enable the brain to perceive a face, and a comparable series from the foot will produce the feeling of pain. The 'on' and 'off' messages which the brain receives every second are like a code. How the brain decodes a message into meaningful terms or how it makes decisions has yet to be fathomed.

All in all, the brain carries out simultaneously a staggering array of tasks which control the machinery of the body and mind:

* it exercises choice over how and when to react to particular situations;
* it integrates and organizes information from the senses into perceptions;
* it regulates countless adjustments - physical and psychological - required by the person in interaction with the environment;
* it stores and integrates vast amounts of information;
* it attends selectively to what is crucial in the individual's ever-changing environment.

The senses
With regard to the last point, adults can locate sounds to right and left with great precision, although there is no right and left within the auditory system. Perception of position of a sound source is elaborated from differences in the time of arrival and in intensity between the two ears, as well as patterns of vibration set up in the outer ear. It has been demonstrated that within seconds of birth infants can use this information, turning their eyes correctly towards a sound source. This shows not only auditory localization but also a simple form of intersensory (auditory-visual) co-ordination, an expectation that there will be something to be looked at: a source for the sound.

Vision itself has attracted rather more attention than the other senses, reflecting its greater importance in human functioning. Sustained visual fixation appears in rudimentary form within a few hours after birth. The smooth tracking of a moving object develops more slowly and can be seen at about five weeks, though rather unco-ordinated eye movements are present much before this. Tom Bower (1975) cites evidence to suggest that new-born babies can perceive distance even if they cannot do it quite as well as adults.

An American psychologist, Robert Fantz (1963), reasons that if babies can discriminate between different patterns and prefer certain patterns to others, then they will look more often at these. For an infant, people (and particularly the mother) are of great importance. He or she must learn to identify members of the species and, beyond that, discriminate between them. The pattern of the face is the most distinctive feature of a person and it is the most reliable way of distinguishing and identifying people. The human face may therefore be a specially powerful kind of stimulus for babies and one to which they might be expected to give special attention. In some experiments babies have been shown to select it above all other patterns.

Bower describes how observations made of mothers feeding their young babies reveal something of the way in which infants use their eyes during the first few months of life. For the first few days babies have their eyes

shut for most of the time. If their eyes are open they
tend to shut them when given the bottle or breast. Towards
the end of the second week a change occurs. Babies tend to
have their eyes open when given the bottle or breast, and
to close them only when they are coming to the end of the
feed. At the same time they tend to fix their eyes in the
direction of the mother's face for a large part of the
feeding period. By three or four weeks most infants have
their eyes open for most of the feeding time and they tend
to direct their gaze directly at the mother's face. Not
all infants display this pattern, but most do.

This behaviour may have several purposes. It ensures
that the infant has experience of a complex visual stimulus, and it may well help the development of the visual
system and of those parts of the nervous system concerned
with processing visual information. In addition, this
'looking at mother' may be one important aspect of the
infant's first social relationship. Although it is not
strictly possible to compare their vision with an adult's,
young infants have vision as good as adults.

I have dealt with only a few findings with regard to
infantile perception. Bower makes the interesting observation that we could not make many inferences about the
newborn's knowledge of the world from watching the spontaneous behaviour of babies in western culture. They have
very few behaviours, and those that they have are not
given much chance to appear in standard western baby-care
conditions. He explains that although newborns have some
quite precise head and eye movements and hand and arm
movements in their repertoire, when babies are laid on
their back (a standard examination position) these behaviours virtually disappear. They disappear because
babies, in this position, must use the head and arms to
hold themselves in a stable position. If they pick up one
arm to reach for something, they will roll in that direction. Even a head movement can result in a loss of pos-
tural equilibrium. Bower comments that the problem is
compounded if the baby is wearing a large wad of nappies
which tilt weight up towards the head. It follows that if
scientists wish to utilize these head and eye and arm and
hand behaviours to measure the baby's knowledge of the
world, the baby must be propped up in a position that
permits free head and arm movement.

**The stimulus
control of
behaviour**

Having looked briefly at the way in which the infant receives stimulus information, it is important to recognize
that stimuli are vital simply as stimuli and also because
they direct our behaviour. Put another way, stimulation is
a vital component of our psychological existence because
it is a 'basic raw material' that we need in various
forms, and because it has a controlling function over our
behaviour.

27

There is evidence that all individuals need a certain minimum level of stimulation. We all indulge in a certain amount of self-stimulation when the environment is monotonous; we hum or whistle, tap our fingers, touch our hair, and so on. Just as muscles thrive on exercise, so human brains thrive on a steady diet of varied and meaningful stimulation. There is also (incidentally) evidence that those who use their intellects (i.e. stimulate them) are the ones who tend to remain alert and intellectually undiminished in old age. Why these things should be so is not yet understood. But it does seem as though messages from the outside world act like a fuel for the brain. When they are not present in sufficient quantity, the brain no longer functions normally.

Deprivation of stimulation (sensory isolation)

At Princeton University, psychologists devised an apparatus called the 'Black Room' which is a small cubicle suspended inside a lightproof, soundproof room. Paid volunteers were asked to lie on a bed within the cubicle without moving or making a noise. This sort of isolation – the deprivation of normal levels of stimulation – resulted in the experimental subjects seeing things that were not there.

In a similar sort of experiment carried out at McGill University, 86 per cent of the student volunteers experienced vivid and sometimes alarming hallucinations. These occurred anywhere after between 20 minutes to 70 hours of confinement. Typically the hallucinations progressed from simple flashes of light to complex moving pictures. One person saw rabbits with knapsacks on their backs marching across a field. Another saw a tiny space ship firing pellets and felt them strike his arm. Many people experienced peculiar visual disturbances after leaving the isolation experiment. Walls appeared to move in and out. Objects changed their size and shape. Lights seemed brighter, and colours more intense. Some subjects left the laboratories in a state of panic saying that nothing would get them back there again.

Of course, we can never be totally deprived of sensation. But then we do not need to be for the effects of isolation to be felt. Simply a lack of sensory variety is sufficient to produce dramatic disturbances in the way you think, feel and see things. The reports of explorers, shipwrecked sailors, and prisoners in solitary confinement confirm this.

There is evidence that infants who are deprived of a continuing and varied supply of visual, auditory and social stimulation (particularly in the first year of life) fail to acquire certain crucial adaptive behaviours. Their ability to learn, to make emotional relationships, and to perform certain skills can all be adversely affected. Why the exposure to appropriate stimulation is

28

so vital is our next topic.

The development of stimulus functions

To understand the development of stimulus control we must start with the new-born child. Large aspects of the environment are essentially neutral in their effect; that is, they exert no influence on the child's behaviour.

As infants grow older they acquire behaviour. They learn to crawl, walk, talk, sit at table, co-operate, read, and so on. Aspects of the environment begin to assume special properties for children as a result of the quality of their experience of them. Some of them have pleasurable consequences, others have painful ones. They come to associate their mother with warmth, comfort, stimulation and many other pleasant feelings. They try to approach her or in some way ensure her proximity.

Some avoidance reactions to stimuli occur at an automatic level. If a child touches a hot stove the pain will cause him or her to withdraw their hand quickly. It will not take the child long to learn to associate pain and stoves and to avoid touching them.

Theorists state that the child's behaviour has come to be regulated by 'antecedent stimulus events'; and they call such learning the acquisition of 'stimulus functions'. In other words, the child has learned to respond appropriately to particular situations. Survival would soon be in jeopardy if these functions were not acquired.

Over time the person builds up habits of behaving and thinking. Some responses become functionally attached to stimuli by a process of association (or contiguity). This process, called 'classical conditioning', provides one explanation of how our behaviours come to be elicited by such a wide variety of stimuli. Some of them do not always have an obvious connection with the stimulus situation, nor do they always serve a useful purpose.

Let us illustrate human conditioning with an example known to all who have had the nerve-racking chore of taking a small child to the dentist. Over a number of such visits the child's behaviour and response to the situation change very markedly. On the first visit the youngster (if not already indoctrinated by an anxious parent or a worldly-wise brother) may sit quite calmly in the waiting-room and smile when introduced to the dentist. However, he or she cries when the first painful drilling takes place. On succeeding visits the child does not wait until the drill is presented before beginning to howl. On the second visit the child may yell the moment the dentist is seen, and on successive occasions it may be enough just to see the building containing the consulting room for the tears and screams to begin.

At first, the sight of the dentist (visual stimulation) was more or less neutral in its effect on the child. The painful (aversive) stimulus provided by the drill, on the other hand, elicited crying. After the sight of the dentist has been followed by the painful drill stimulus one or more times, the formerly innocuous visual stimulus (the dentist) acquires the characteristics of the painful stimulus, and the sight of the dentist is enough to provoke tears.

Adults are not immune to the influences of conditioning. The person who tends to munch sweets and biscuits while watching television is likely to find, after a few weeks, that a craving for food develops within minutes of switching the set on, no matter how recent the last meal. In other words a minor compulsion, or, if you like, a thoroughly 'bad habit', has been nurtured.

Instrumental conditioning

The phenomenon called operant or instrumental conditioning can be illustrated by an experiment which is the basis for educational and therapeutic work. The principle has been used, in fact, to aid the training of all sorts of humans and animals. Let us take a human experiment which illustrates the principle.

Yvonne Brackbill (1958) conducted an experiment on smiling in eight normal infants ranging in age from $3\frac{1}{2}$–$4\frac{1}{2}$ months. She studied her experimental subjects for two or three sessions a day for several days. After securing a base level of smiling in her infant subjects, that is, after she had measured the amount of smiling normally shown by the infants, she carried out the conditioning sessions. During these sessions she stood motionless and expressionless 15 inches above the subject. As soon as the baby (S) smiled, the experimenter (E) smiled in return, began to speak softly and picked it up. After holding, jiggling, patting, and talking to S for 30 seconds, E put it back in its crib. Brackbill put one group of four subjects on a schedule of regular reinforcement and the other group of four on intermittent reinforcement. Then she stopped the reinforcement altogether to extinguish the smiling response. The so-called extinction 'phase' was conducted in the same manner as the baseline period.

Brackbill measured the frequency of smiling through out, plotting on a graph the child's acquisition of smiling responses. The resultant cumulative curve showed a steep rate of acquisition for the infants subjected to conditioning. By contrast, a 'cumulative' curve plotted for a control subject, which was run, but without reinforcement, for 19 conditioning periods or three times longer than the experimental subjects, showed no acquisition. In other words, the smiling response of eight normal infants between $3\frac{1}{2}$ and $4\frac{1}{2}$ months was brought under control. Infants 'can be taught' to increase the frequency of their smiling.

In the experiment just described, what we notice about instrumental conditioning is that the individual CHANGES the environment in some way to produce a reward instead of merely anticipating events in the environment as in classical conditioning. It has been found that there is a positive relationship between the number of reinforced (rewarded) trials an animal (or human) has had during the 'acquisition phase' of the experiment and the number of responses made during the 'extinction phase' when one is trying to extinguish the response. The greater the number of reinforcements during acquisition the greater the number of responses made during the extinction phase. Let us translate this situation into 'down-to-earth' terms.

A down-to-earth example

Suppose a little boy cries when made to go to bed and that the mother, who cannot bear to see her child's tears, gives in and lets the child stay up late. After several similar scenes with the same outcome - mum giving in - she finally appreciates that she has been encouraging or reinforcing an undesirable habit. She decides to stand firm and be impervious to tears. So she makes the child go upstairs to bed no matter how long or heart-rendingly he cries. How long will it take to extinguish the crying habit? The child has discovered, of course, that crying is instrumental in obtaining the reward: that is, staying up late. The difficulty the mother will have in extinguishing the crying tantrum will depend in large part on how often she has previously let the child have his own way. We can see from this example how 'bad habits' may be reinforced.

Reinforcement consequences

Certain of a person's responses (behaviours) are strengthened when they occur in particular environmental situations; by making the appropriate responses to certain stimuli the person's actions are generally 'reinforced' by positive (rewarding) consequences. They can also be strengthened by the avoidance/removal of punishing consequences. The child's resolve to do homework is strengthened by the thought of the teacher's punishment if is not done.

Responses can also be weakened in the context of particular situations. Inappropriate responses usually result in negative (painful, punishing) consequences. They can also be weakened by the removal of rewarding consequences.

Imitation

Observational learning (as we saw earlier) takes place through children's imitation of the people, real and imagined, whom they observe and hear about. Imitated behaviour is often rewarded by praise and encouragement and approval - in other words social rewards - from the 'model'. Such modelling, particularly on the parents, is important for the development of conforming patterns of social behaviour.

31

Modelling effects have been demonstrated in a series of experiments by Bandura (1977) and his associates. They exposed one group of nursery-school children to aggressive adult models and a second group to models who displayed inhibited and non-aggressive behaviour. For the aggressive-model group the model exhibited unusual forms of physical and verbal aggression towards a large inflated plastic doll. In contrast, the non-aggressive-model group observed an adult who sat very quietly, totally ignoring the doll and the instruments of aggression that had been placed in the room. The children who observed aggressive models manifested similar patterns of behaviour, while those who were exposed to models who were not aggressive failed to show aggressive behaviour.

Cognitive learning
It will be apparent from the description of learning principles given so far that they seem to depend upon a rather mechanistic conception of learning. Insight, explanation, logic and other ways in which we come to modify or correct our view of things appear to count for nothing: the charge often levelled at the behavioural approach is that it ignores the conceptual thinking that is so peculiarly and importantly human. This charge can no longer be made with any validity. Cognitive behaviour therapy is a thriving treatment approach.

The family environment

The role of the family
The family is particularly significant in the moulding of the child because it is the first and most frequent agent determining which social stimuli will be presented to the child, what will be taught, which behaviour patterns will be rewarded and consolidated and which will be punished and inhibited.

So much is determined by the intimate contacts, the complex learning and the emotional attachments of the formative years within the family, that psychiatrists and social workers trying to unravel the causes of mental and social breakdown in adult life try to obtain a 'case history' of the patient's early years of development. They hope to find in the story of childhood and family upbringing clues to the patient's present difficulties.

Differential reinforcement
Experiences tend to reinforce particular personality traits, and the more often these experiences are repeated the more enduring the traits become. Through a system of reward and punishment, patterns of behaviour are often effectively formed. A child subjected to repeated and violent beatings early in life may learn that, by complete submission, the painful experience may be avoided. Subsequently, he or she may develop a generally submissive

manner in dealing with all other people. As a result of
similar experiences an individual with a different combination of environmental influences and genetic consti-
tution may believe that beating is the only way to produce
a desired behaviour in others, and so may become a strongly aggressive character.

The initial stage of learning patterns of behaviour
and of developing personality characteristics is followed
by a second period of development, the primary school
years, in which previous learning and experience is
consolidated. In the third phase, adolescence, as the
secondary sex characteristics begin to develop, there is
an advance in learning and in processing emotional
experience. This moulds the basic aspects of personality
into the more permanent form they will assume in adult
years. During adolescence there can be dramatic changes in
behaviour (Herbert, 1986).

References

Bandura, A. (1977)
Social Learning Theory. Englewood Cliffs, NJ: Prentice-
Hall.

Bower, T. (1975)
Competent newborns. In R. Lewin (ed.), Child Alive.
London: Temple Smith.

Brackbill, Y. (1958)
Extinction of the smiling response in infants as a
function of reinforcement. Child Development, 29, 115-
124.

Fantz, R. L. (1963)
Pattern vision in newborn infants. Science, 140, 296-
297.

Herbert, M. (1986)
Living with Your Teenagers: A practical guide. Oxford:
Basil Blackwell.

4

The child and the family

Introduction This chapter introduces the reader to some of the psychological information available for a psycho-social life
span study: a matter of concern to the social worker who
finds clients in all age groups, and is required to know
about the life-tasks (developmental tasks) and the potential crises associated with childhood, adolescence, maturity and old age. These so-called 'developmental crises'
are described in chapters 10 and 15. The purpose of the
present chapter is to introduce you to an area of study on
which social work places considerable emphasis, viz. 'The
child and the family'. When social workers arrange substitute care (foster home, day nursery, child minding)
there is concern for the quality of such provision. However, this concern may be undermined by vaguely conceived
(and even less rigorously assessed) parent-child attitudes
and relationships. A critical examination of the literature (Herbert, 1974) indicates how many inconsistencies,
even contradictions, there are.

  The promise of effective preventive work by social
workers, or better mental health through more lightened
psychological child care, remains a fond hope in professional circles, though still unfulfilled. Marian Radke
Yarrow and her co-authors of the book 'Child Rearing'
(1968) reflect sadly, from their own investigations and
their extensive review of available evidence, that we are
still searching for the specific conditions in children's
cumulative experience with parents that evoke, strengthen, or modify behaviour. Yet parent 'therapy' and education are still based on an assumption that there is a body
of knowledge about the best techniques of child care. It
follows that these can be taught to parents, foster
parents and residential care staff. Much has been made
(particularly in the psychoanalytic literature) of the
allegedly disruptive effects on infant adjustment of
different child-care practices, notably feeding, weaning
and toilet-training procedures. The social worker should
be familiar with the evidence (see chapter 9). We look at
four areas in this volume:

* the family heritage: some sources of individual
  differences are described;
* the child as a developing organism: this concerns the
  foundational influences of early experience; reference
  is made to the range, direction and potency of
  subsequent development;
* the family as a social system: this subsection is
  concerned with the dynamic inter-relatedness of a
  child's earliest encounter between self and others;
* the interior of the family: here we consider the unique
  experience of each family as a complex and dynamic
  psycho-social system.

It is a mind-boggling thought that, in a world containing
some four million million inhabitants, each one of us is
quite unique. Nowhere could we find an exact replica of
ourselves; no, not even when we have a so-called 'identical twin'. Mind you, this is the closest we get to a
perfect likeness. This is because our individuality begins
with the 'lottery' in which we received those units of
life called genes. These ultra-microscopic bits of matter
translate our family heritage into action. Identical twins
inherit the same set of genes. What makes them different
as persons is the unique effect the environment has in
moulding each one of us as a personality.

Genetics, the science of heredity, is devoted to
finding out about the way in which the hereditary factors
are handed down from parents to their children by literally reproducing themselves. Every time someone assures a
mother that her infant has his father's eyes or his
granny's mouth, they are stating a fact of human heredity.
All sorts of characteristics run in families. A tendency
to freckles, for example, is hereditary; so are hair, skin
and eye colour and the shape of face and features. There
are hereditary diseases like haemophilia and inherited
conditions such as colour blindness. Then again, important
psychological attributes like intelligence and personality
have a major genetic ingredient. Genetics as a science is
concerned with the way in which the genes make their presence felt during a child's growth and development by
producing the substances which influence the behaviour and
development of the entire cell: the unit of living matter.
It is also concerned with the way in which the action of
genes is modified by the environment.

The environment
Environmental influences determine whether individuals
achieve all their genetic potential. A youngster who is
well endowed genetically with intellectual potential will
fail to achieve it if deprived of opportunities to learn.

Height is another example of how heredity and environment can interact. Let us take two children who are unusually small. One is short because he has inherited a

gene by which a body chemical essential to growth is absent. (The internal environment of his body can be changed by supplying him with the missing chemical, and he will grow.) Another child possesses the genes which would allow her to reach average height, but she is shorter than normal because she is under-nourished. (Increasing this child's daily intake of food will change the way in which her genes are expressed. This, too, is a change of environment.)

The differences in the hereditary contents of the germ cells - the ones we transmit to our offspring - are not produced by any physical, spiritual or moral improvements we bring about in ourselves as would-be parents. No amount of body-building, yoga, spiritual commitment or leading the good life in the father or mother will make any difference to the genes transmitted to the new being. The child will have to spend years acquiring and developing his or her own intellectual, physical, spiritual and moral 'muscle'.

Mechanisms of heredity

All the genetic material a human child inherits comes from its parents and is housed in two cells, the sperm and the ovum (egg), which fuse when the sperm from the father enters the egg produced by the mother. The resulting cell - a barely visible particle of matter - is called a zygote. Each and every individual sets out in life in this way. The genes in this original cell turn up in all the estimated ten million million cells that eventually constitute the adult human person. From the moment of conception, every individual carries in these cells the information which determines the genetic aspects of development. This information is borne by the genes, which are made of DNA, a chemical with a regular structure which enables the genes to be accurately interpreted and reproduced. The genes are strung together on compact microscopic structures called chromosomes, themselves small bodies within the nucleus of every cell of the body.

Environment and heredity interact

From the moment of fertilization, the environment (including the womb or uterus) in which he or she lives and all the genetic capacities he or she possesses interact to produce a complete and unique human being. Although born with inbuilt characteristics that shape them, at the same time human beings' society, parents, brothers and sisters and other people in their world, influence them. Humans are creatures of habit. They learn about life and acquire modes of behaviour and strategies of adjusting to its difficulties. They are not dependent like other animals on stereotyped, inbuilt (instinctive) patterns of responding.

The child as a developing organism

Environmental influences can determine, as we have seen, whether an individual achieves full genetic potential. Thus a child who is well endowed genetically with intellectual potential will fail to achieve it if deprived of opportunities to learn. The opposite is true too: an unusually strong environment may lend assistance to limited genetic potential. A normal set of genes and an appropriate environment are each needed for satisfactory development and behaviour.

Characteristics influenced by environment

The vast majority of characteristics are influenced to a greater or lesser degree by the environment; for example

* height
* weight
* intelligence
* personality
* various physical illnesses
* mental illness.

When development goes wrong

Sadly, not all babies are born perfect. One in a hundred is born with an abnormality: perhaps a minor defect like a birthmark or hare lip, or a major abnormality such as spina bifida, that can cause death or tragic disability. Such conditions, present at birth, are known as congenital abnormalities; they occur because the orderly development of the unborn child breaks down. The blue-prints a child inherits may be faulty or the defences provided by the womb can fail. In either case it is quite likely that the resultant defective embryo will not go on to full development; there may be a spontaneous abortion or miscarriage.

Pre-natal influences

The nine months between conception and birth present more risks to the developing individual than any similar span up to the ninth decade. It is, of course, a period of rapid growth and development. For example, three weeks after fertilization, the whole sac containing the unborn child (the embryo) is only the size of a cherry, and the baby itself is about one-fifth of an inch long. Two weeks later, however, the embryo has DOUBLED in size. This is a quite fantastic achievement which will never be repeated in its life. The child-to-be faces trials which begin with fertilization and implantation; they continue with the development of the organs of the body and the establishment of the mechanisms required for the regulation of the internal environment; they come to an end with the birth process. The time scale for each physiological transition is finely prescribed, and failure to make the change at the correct time and in the correct manner is dangerous and can result in death or permanent damage to the organism. The concept of a 'critical period', so popular in social work accounts of early infant-mother attachment, comes from the study of embryology.

The first trimester of pregnancy is the most crucial in the child's development. The major organs and basic tissues are being laid down and developed during the first eight weeks after conception and these are therefore the ones during which disturbances in the child's first environment - the uterus - can produce major effects on growth. After this phase it is difficult, if not impossible, to affect the morphology of the organism in any fundamental manner; the embryo has all the important external and internal features of a human being.

It is apparent that children do not start life as psychological nonentities. From the beginning they already have an individuality that influences the adults around them. Thus a mother's initial task is not to create something out of nothing; it is rather to dovetail her behaviour to that of the child.

Temperamental individuality

Any nurse who has had the care of a nursery of newly born babies, or any mother who has had several children so as to be able to compare her babies, knows that they differ markedly in temperament right from the word 'go'. A group of research workers and clinicians, Stella Chess, Alexander Thomas and Herbert Birch (1968), have demonstrated just how important these inborn or constitutional aspects of personality - the temperamental qualities of the child - can be in the development of normal behaviour and emotional problems (see chapter 6).

Family inheritance is one source of this temperamental variety. The fertilized zygote brings together various combinations and permutations of parental chromosomes and in this way different genes are given to each child of the same parents. Ashley Montagu, in his book 'Human Heredity', estimates that in a single mating the possible combinations between the 23 chromosomes of the female and those of the male are 8,388,608 and the chance of any one such combination being repeated more than once is 1 in approximately 70 trillion. There can be wide variations within a family group, but nevertheless a child is somewhat more similar to his blood relations than to anyone else.

Implications for the development of individuality

In the wake of thinkers like Freud, Pavlov and Watson, almost exclusive emphasis was placed on environmental influences in the development of behaviour. And parents being the major feature of the child's early environment received all the blame when things went wrong. The possession of certain combinations of the temperamental qualities mentioned above can make a child exceedingly

'difficult' no matter how skilled the parents are. John B.
Watson, a psychologist at Johns Hopkins University during
the first decades of the century, believed that planned
habit training could mould the child in any desired direction. This is how he expressed it:

> Give me a dozen healthy infants, well formed, and my
> own specified world to bring them up in, and I'll
> guarantee to take any one at random and train him to
> become any type of specialist I might select - doctor,
> lawyer, artist, merchant chief, and yes, even beggar-
> man and thief, regardless of his talents, penchants,
> tendencies, abilities, vocations and race of his
> ancestors (1928).

He failed to take into account the potent proactive
influence of differences in children's individual capacities, and their often unpredictable interpretations of,
and reactions to, their environment. Environment (as we
shall see) is vital in determining individual differences,
but it is not the 'whole story', as some people assume.

The family as a social system

The family is a basic unit in a variety of societies,
ranging from the most 'primitive' to the most 'sophisticated'; indeed, it is a universal institution but one
which varies in the precise pattern or form with which it
manifests itself. For example, the father may take little
part in the upbringing of the children, some other member
of the extended family (such as the maternal uncle) being
the dominant male influence. Children may not be the
special responsibility of their parents at all in some
societies; they may be reared by all the members of a
group living together under one roof or in a small compact
housing unit. The family name, wealth and land may be
handed down from generation to generation through the
mother's side and not the father's. After marriage the man
may go to live with his wife's kin in their family residence. Or it may be the other way around.

The contemporary western nuclear family (as part of a
larger kinship network which, in turn, is a component of
the larger social structure) introduces children first of
all to their kin and then to the wider community and
society. In the family the child, as a member, has a role
to play, responsibilities to assume and is called upon to
give and receive attention. The family provides the individual with a sense of identity in terms of family name
and a feeling of belonging and being loved and needed.
This is a significant achievement (if successful) given
the tendency of our complex modern society - vast in scale
and impersonal in attitude - to subvert the citizen's
sense of importance, worth and meaning. At least the
family does not make the child feel like a small (and

replaceable) cog in a massive machine. (And this sense of
'special-ness' is what the child without a family feels in
all but the best-run and more intimate family-model care
institutions.)

This most enduring of human institutions has long
engaged the attention of social psychologists. After all,
if 'the proper study of mankind is man', then a key to the
understanding of human beings' ways must lie in the social
grouping - the family - that they have evolved, no matter
what part of the world or in what circumstances they have
found themselves.

Marriage is an important institution in the history of
the family. The reason why there are rules, regulations
and laws in all societies to institutionalize marriage is
that they provide a reasonably secure framework within
which to nurture and socialize children. They also define
who has rights and duties towards the child, and responsibilities for the child's care.

Parental functions
Specific family functions are usually divided between survival functions such as provision of shelter, space, food,
income, physical care, health and safety; and psycho-
social functions such as:

SOCIALIZATION: ENCOURAGING, GUIDING, SUPPORTING
AND REWARDING
Parents endeavour within the family setting to transform a
broadly asocial, biological organism into a social being
by the process called 'socialization'. Notions of right
and wrong, a code of behaviour, a set of attitudes and
values, the ability to see the other person's point of
view - all of these basic qualities which made an individual a socialized being - are nurtured in the first
instance by parents. They induct the infant into the
culture by determining which physical and social stimuli
will mainly be presented to the infant, what the infant
will be taught, which opinions and behaviours will be
reinforced and consolidated, and which will be discouraged
by various means.

THE PROVISION OF A SUPPORT SYSTEM FOR PARENTS
THEIR AND OFFSPRING
The family is part of a social network which is linked
with outside social institutions. One of its functions is
to provide parents with a variety of social, emotional and
economic support systems, (e.g. extended family, community, work). There have been several investigations showing that parents who abuse their children have fewer associations outside the home, receive less help in caring for
their offspring, and perceive their neighbours more negatively, than other parents (Orford, 1980). This emphasis
on parents' needs is a useful corrective to the emphasis

later in this chapter on the effects on offspring of specific parental and other interpersonal behaviours.

Parental influence

Parents, as 'agents' of society, exerting social influence and control on an impressionable, malleable child bear an awesome responsibility. It has fallen to the woman in most societies to carry the main responsibility for rearing the offspring. In less advanced but more close-knit societies than our own, child care is often a group effort which reinforces a child's sense of community. Life is obviously more fragmented in an urban environment. A youngster is given specialist care by a bewildering variety of experts: doctors, dentists, teachers, psychologists and social workers. Modern women are frequently inexperienced at child care. They may be unaccustomed to small children because they have been brought up in small families and have not been given responsibilities for caring for the young ones as older sisters of yesteryear (or in contemporary primitive societies) had to do. This is only remedied when they have children themselves. They need to learn mothering skills very quickly since they have not, unlike mothers of earlier generations, acquired these in the normal course of their own childhood. Social workers know well the potentially explosive situation of a socially isolated, inexperienced single parent, and a persistently difficult, screaming baby.

The very processes which help the child adapt to social life can, under certain circumstances, contribute to deviant, dysfunctional modes of behaviour. An immature child who learns by imitating an adult is not necessarily to comprehend when it is undesirable behaviour that is being modelled. Parents who teach their child (adaptively) on the basis of classical conditioning and instrumental learning processes to avoid dangerous situations can also, by mismanagement, condition the child (maladaptively) to avoid school or social gatherings.

The family can be conceptualized as a 'system' with its individual members as elements or sub-units within it. Whatever happens to one or more of its elements - say, mental illness in the mother or father, or serious marital disharmony - can affect the entire system. The privatization of the family - the heightened emotional intimacy and interdependence of the members - is thought to place a great burden on parents, most particularly the mother, and also the children. Parents are the crucial and therefore (potentially) the weak link in the chain of socialization. Taking care of young children is likely to be more stressful for some parents than others, especially in unfavourable circumstances (e.g. poverty, poor housing). The identification and specification of 'pathological' parenting should, in theory, lead to the remediation and better still, prevention of problems. Or, rather, this is the hope. Indeed, a popular aphorism of the 1950s (and the ideology underlying it persists today) stated that 'there are no problem children, only problem parents'.

When one considers the intimate, protracted and highly influential nature of parents' relationships with their children, it seems self-evident that the quality of such relationships must have a vital bearing on the development of the child's personality and general adaptation.

Many anthropologists and social psychologists claim that the family functions to satisfy certain universal needs which persist among all persons in all times. It is stated that the family is a universal phenomenon because it so accurately reflects and accommodates human beings' bio-logical and psychological make-up; it permits their survival by enhancing their inborn capacities for adaptation. It fulfils their need to establish a socially approved structure for gratifying the sexual drive, the need to reproduce and the necessity to provide a stable environment in which to raise children. It provides a shelter for its members within the society and against the remainder of society. It satisfies the child's biological and psychological needs, but at the same time restrains early antisocial tendencies and prepares the child for social living. The fact is that no completely workable substitute for the family has been discovered, although some compromises (e.g. the kibbutz) have been tried.

What the family does achieve is nothing less than the transformation of a biological organism into a social creature. Nothing could be more basic than this to social life. This transformation process is usually called 'socialization'. From birth, a child is protected and trained by the family. This training includes not only physical skills, among them walking and feeding, but cultural skills, too, from good manners to a love of music. It encourages the need to achieve. One of the most important cultural skills a child learns is language, the tool which is central to all further learning processes. Language enables humans to develop and transmit values, norms and moral judgements.

The patterns of co-operation and conflict which children learn through family relationships teach them how to relate to groups outside the family; initially neighbours and school friends, but later to wider groups. From their earliest years in the family children shown what is right, praiseworthy and acceptable, and what is wrong, ridiculed, punished. The family, then, is the primary transmitter of social skills and values; it acts as a mediator between the individual and society.

Another family function is that of social control. There are many agents of social control in society, but none has the continuous power of the family over its members. This is why the breakdown in family life is so often blamed for the dramatic rise in juvenile crime and violence. The family is in the best position to influence, cajole, threaten, and use all the positive and negative sanctions that come from intimacy, to get the individual to conform to family norms. Social control is reinforced by the related family function whereby the child receives a status in society and a set of social roles from the family at birth. The child may sometimes alter this 'ascribed' placement by personal achievements, but it often remains the basis of other people's view of the individual's social standing.

This point leads us on to a further family function, its role as an economic unit. Even in industrial societies, although the family does not work as a team, as does the peasant farmer's family, the household is still an economic unit which does much of its budgeting collectively. A significant degree of family continuity in certain employments persists among doctors, printers and dockers in Britain, for instance.

In all societies there are specialized roles within the family. The child learns these in the home. As well as the division by sex there is a specialization of function according to one's role and status within the family; the expected behaviour of 'mother', 'father', 'grandfather', 'paternal uncle', 'elder son', etc., is defined more or less closely by all societies. There is an immense variety of definitions of roles, however, and it would be unwise to assume that current western ones are valid elsewhere. This is crucial for social workers to remember as they come into contact with different ethnic groups. The ethnocentric social worker is likely to be a menace!

The interior of the family

The family as an institution is not a static entity, stereotyped in its forms, or unchanging in its functions. It is a dynamic system, susceptible to change; its influenced, in the short term, by the personally, development and relationships of its members, and in the longer term by the pressures of economic events and historical processes. The family adapts itself to changing conditions. The nuclear family which, as we observed, is the most common unit to be found in western nations is, in large part, the product of industrialization. Before the age of technology the family was frequently a working unit and children were important not for their own sake but for their potential as workers. Today, among the lower-income groups in our society, the children are still looked on as having an essential role in financing the household. But this tendency is disappearing with the increase in affluence; the children are valued for their own sake and not as economic providers.

The role of husband and wife within the family has also changed in the last two or three decades. Increasing educational opportunities for women and better career prospects have given them a higher status in the home; the nuclear family with both husband and wife in professional jobs is no longer the exception. Coupled with this is the growing authority of the mother and the lessening of the father's authority within the home, particularly in decisions on education and discipline of the children. The child experiences difficulty when parents do not provide a united front so as to provide an emotionally secure and consistent learning environment (Herbert, 1980a).

The duties and responsibilities of the nuclear family have been lessened by the taking over by the state of many functions, education being an obvious example. In the past the family has always had a responsibility for the care of its elderly members, but this too is sometimes being abrogated to the state as mobility increases and the nuclear family becomes more isolated. The elderly have become the major clients of the health and social services, an issue elaborated by Coleman in chapter 15. For all these changes, there is little evidence that the family as an institution is seriously threatened. Persistent notices of its demise are premature.

Parental choice
Biological evolution in human beings has resulted in a degree of choice and a variety of motives in the assumptions of parenthood which is absent in lower species. Different motives lead to a variety of parental attitudes toward the parental role and, indeed, to different ways in which parents formulate goals for their children's future. In the past (and even today, in societies remote from industrialization) the child was likely to be groomed along very rigid lines for a predetermined role in the kinship system. Unlike modern industrial society, the subsistence economies could not afford the luxury of choice for their offspring.

The contemporary family can branch out individualistically, as can its members. The idea of privacy in the family household is a relatively modern conception. Such privacy dilutes somewhat the pressures on parents to conform; and this degree of flexibility results in a greater range of individualism in the children produced by the society. In addition, there is a greater risk that many parents and their children will be out of step with their society.

The parental role: mothering
'Mothering' is regarded in our society as the most appropriate term to describe the tender loving care of children. Significantly it is a feminine word and reflects the matricentric nature and connotation of child care. This connotation - mother - implies, in turn, that the woman is a housewife and that her role is minding home, husband and children. Biology and social convention have foisted these

duties on her. For many women these roles are joy and are
sufficient to fulfil her; for others they are not enough.
Social workers need to be alerted to some of the facile
rhetoric in the literature about motherhood. Myths and
erroneous beliefs which have attained wide acceptance due
to misunderstandings and publicity surrounding and following the work of Bowlby and others (and it must be emphasized that a lot of good was achieved for social work
theory and practice with regard to child care) have done a
great disservice to the confidence and spontaneity of
women. Among them is a concept of 'motherhood' which has
raised it to a position of unprecedented importance. Many
would say that an intolerable burden of anxiety and guilt
was placed on parents; the idea of a critical period
implies that parents are all-powerful, all-responsible
'and must assume the role of playing preventive Fate for
their children' (Bruch, 1954). The clinical and social
work literature on child and adult psychopathology over
many years was replete with 'bad mothers': schizophreno-
genic mothers, asthmagenic mothers, mothers accused of
suffocating their offspring with 'smother' love, or in
some other way overprotecting, rejecting or double-binding
them into abnormality. Chess (1964) refers to this phenomenon as 'mal de mere'.

Maternal behaviour in animals is more closely governed
by basic instincts than is the case in humans. Nevertheless, there are 'bad' mothers in the animal world as there
are among humans. Harry Harlow (1960) demonstrated how
rhesus monkeys, deprived during infancy of their mother or
of social contact, grow up to be incompetent, rejecting
and even vicious mothers. The human species would soon be
extinct if people carried on with the same carelessness as
fish, which spawn eggs and then pass on, or turtles, which
come together at random and abandon their fertilized eggs
to the tender mercies of the environment.

Marriage and parenthood are the two central institutional elements of the family. Marriage, as we saw, is a
formalized way of regulating parenthood. By trying to
insist that parenthood be confined within the family,
society provides attention and care for both mother and
child. There is usually a differentiation of role between
the sexes, certain tasks and privileges being regarded as
feminine and others as masculine.

The mother, in our society - despite the feminist
movement - bears a special responsibility for the care of
the children. Whatever the lip-service paid to changes of
attitude by men, this is still the reality. Our society is
markedly matricentric in this aspect of life. When there
is a showdown it is the mother who is expected to stay
(and usually does) with the children. She is made aware by
the mass media, the books she reads and the experts she
consults, that the child's growth, contentment, and even
survival depends to a significant extent on her skill at

being a stimulating and tender parent. The father is often
out at work so that a child in western society may spend
the first crucial years of life in the almost exclusive
company of the mother. From a historical and cross-
cultural perspective, this is a unique situation. It is
only since approximately the beginning of this century
that western society has seen such an intense preoccupation with the needs of children. This concern has done a
lot to enlarge the mother's duties towards the child.

Motherhood may mean many sacrifices, hard work and
pain to women, but it is still rare (although not as rare
as it used to be) to hear women say that they do not enjoy
their role, for all its irritations and frustrations, or
to find others who repudiate the role of mother. In part
this is due to a deep-seated biological awareness of their
capacity to create new life, and in the younger woman, the
reminder - in the form of menstruation - of the ovum. The
potentiality for life which might have been fertilized is
shed each month. But much of the undoubted need of women
to have children is built in to their expectations by the
manner in which little girls are encouraged to play with
dolls, and to take the part of the 'little mother'. All in
all, today's mothers bear much more responsibility in the
child's early years than their predecessors and their
counterparts in earlier societies.

Being a mother in western society requires considerable adjustments. The modern mother is quite likely to be
a woman who is educated, and perhaps highly trained in
some skill. She has usually been employed for a number of
years. Marrying in her twenties she will have her children
before she is 30, and during this time usually remains at
home with them. Many young women making the first adjustment to motherhood find their economic dependence on their
husband frustrating. They may also find that one important
loss, due to the initial move from a working environment
to full-time housework at home, is the loss of the social
contacts which were enjoyed at work. Similarly, a woman in
her forties making the adjustment back again to the world
outside the home may find her capacity for forming new
social relationships inhibited by the years of full-time
domesticity. The most demanding change in the life of
today's mother has been introduced by the appearance of
the nuclear family unit. New opportunities take families
away from their familiar surroundings and set them down
among strangers in a strange town. This is an inevitable
result of the increasing 'upward social mobility' that is
disrupting traditional working-class social structures by
providing individuals with the opportunity to improve
their standard of living but often at the cost of resettle-
ment. Environmentally the modern western family tends to
be very much an isolated unit: the husband and wife in
their own home, living perhaps miles away from even their
closest relations.

Housewives used to experience a sense of community in living amongst parents, brothers, sisters, cousins, all setting up home within reach of one another. The housewife in such a community did not suffer the problem of loneliness. She had a firmly established background that provided a reassuring certainty to everyday life. It might be said that the malaise of today's housewives is loneliness; a new condition with the attendant symptoms of nagging boredom and an acute sense of wasting oneself, of unfulfilment. The woman who is today's housewife may find herself on her own for hours on end, day after day, month after month, especially as one or more of her children reach the age when they go away to school. Lack of a feeling of belonging and community can do great harm to mothers' sense of purpose or well-being. Depression, a sense of being trapped and helpless, are the 'symptoms' with which such women fill social workers' case-notes; also other ill-defined feelings of anxiety and discontent. Without suitable outlets, these vague feelings can build up into a strong sense of alienation and of not being in charge of their own lives and destinies.

The consequence of our modern definition of the mother's role is that children receive much better care physically and emotionally than they did a century ago, or than they do in 'primitive' societies today. But at another level this highly focused relationship has allowed children to become much more vulnerable. The strains and tensions in modern family life come not so much from its economic or socializing functions but rather from the fact that it is to such an extent the source of emotional support in the contemporary world. Where marriage is contracted, not by arrangement, but in romantic love, and where many of modern people's social relationships are fleeting and superficial, they rely more and more on the family for their deepest emotional satisfactions. In fact, with the decline in its other functions, rather too much emphasis is placed on the emotional rewards provided by the family and inevitably in some cases disappointments and a certain amount of disillusionment result. It is a heavy burden for the family to carry. Margaret Mead (1935), the eminent anthropologist, has observed that Samoan children, brought up a household of between 10 and 20 people, are much less likely to be hurt by the death of the parents, or by a poor relationship with either of them, than children reared exclusively by the mother in a nuclear family setting. In the intimacy of the modern mother-child relationship a child can prosper, but can also suffer. The mother too is much more vnerable. She has been made to feel even more vulnerable by the long-standing debate on maternal deprivation.

Maternal deprivation
The debate over the 'maternal deprivation' theory, gener-

ated by Bowlby's (1951) report to the World Health Organization, focused attention on the possible importance for
future development of the child's first interpersonal
relationships. Research relevant to this debate suggested
that lack of opportunity for the child to form, in the
first years of life, a specific relationship with the
caretaker or other adult may have been responsible for the
later difficulties in personal relationships experienced
by children who had spent their early years in the older
type of institutional care.

This lack of a specific tie may - in addition to the
deficiency of environmental stimulation - contribute to
the retarded intellectual and educational development
found in many of these children. Controversy over the so
called critical or sensitive period in childhood is described in the excellent text by Michael Rutter, 'Maternal
Deprivation Reassessed' (1972).

Freud put forward a somewhat similar 'sensitive
period' theory regarding the early and long-term antecedents of attributes such as optimism, pessimism and
narcissism. He described certain character traits which
are thought to be associated with either too great frustration or overly indulged gratification at each of three
psychosexual stages of development: the oral, anal and
phallic stages. (We look at these in the following
chapter.) Sadly, the concept of maternal separation (or
maternal deprivation) has been a great 'thought-stopper'
for some practitioners. So, in more recent times, has been
the concept of emotional bonding.

There is the other side of bonding: the parents'
commitment to their offspring. When all goes well - and it
usually does - an attachment is cemented between a mother
(say) and her baby, a relationship implying unconditional
love, self-sacrifice and nurtural attitudes which, for the
mother's part, are quite likely to last a life time.
Obviously, a great deal is at stake in the attachment process: child-to-parent and parent-to-child! if they haven't
enough to worry about - what with the real dangers of
smoking and drinking and scare stories about various kinds
of medication - pregnant women are now warned of the
adverse consequences of being separated from their newborn
babies. This fear arises out of a widespread belief in the
theory of maternal bonding.

This is the view that mothers become bonded to their
infants through close skin-to-skin contact during the
'critical' hours and days following birth. To bond or not
to bond became, from the early seventies to the present
time, a matter of great concern. What will happen if the
newborn infant is ill, or hospital arrangements are inflexible, so that the baby is separated from its mother during
this critical period? Could a fortuitous separation from
her baby really put a blight on a mother's love? Could the
baby's development be adversely affected?

Sadly, this belief about the ties of affection is also
quite likely to engender apprehension and pessimism in
would-be adoptive parents. Just as an infant becomes attached to its mother, so also a mother can be attached to
her infant or infant-surrogate. This kind of attachment is
known as maternal attachment. The social work and pae-
diatric literature is full of dire warnings about the consequences of failures or distortions of mother-to-child
bonding. These have been blamed for a variety of problems
including children's failure to thrive, infantile autism
unsuccessful adoptions, and, notably, child abuse. Thus,
it is not only parents, but people in the medical and
helping professions - paediatricians, obstetric nurses,
midwives, health visitors and social workers - who are
concerned about the implications of the bonding theory for
the care of premature or disabled infants.

The eminently sensible and humane idea of allowing a
mother and her new baby to get to know one another by
early and frequent interaction, becomes oppressive when
the permissive 'ought' is replaced by the dogmatic 'must'.
It is well to remember that the bonding precept is only
one of the most recent milestones in the long history of
child care practices. Ideas and prescriptions for the
early management of children are like fashions, or even
fads. They wax and wane. So let us look for some hard
evidence to help us make up our minds about these issues.

Maternal bonding

The notion that this special tie, the loving, caring
attachment of mother to child, develops rapidly during a
relatively short sensitive period, is similar to the
phenomenon of imprinting mentioned earlier in this chapter; the idea that human mother love depends on an
imprinting-like process is derived from some early
experiments with female sheep and goats. These animals
appeared to learn the smell of their babies in a rapid
manner immediately after birth (a phenomenon called
'olfactory imprinting') and thereafter would reject, by
butting away any lamb or kid other than their own. Additional support seemed to come from comparisons of human
mothers who had little or no direct contact with their
newborn infants with those who had extended contact. The
results suggested that the former were less attached to
their babies.

Mother-to-infant attachment is typically inferred from
the manifestation by the mother of specific behaviours in
the presence of her baby, such as gazing, fondling, vocal-
izing, smiling, touching, putting her face close up and
the like. We have to be careful about such inferences.
Research findings in the USA indicate that such forms of
behaviour are more often observed among English speaking
mothers and are less evident (although not entirely
absent) among Spanish-speaking mothers. In some cultures,

girls get customarily much less attention than boys. In attempting to define precisely what bonding is, can we rely on the mother's own report of her attitudes and feelings towards the infant? She might be thought of as 'attached' to her infant if she consistently, over an extended period of time, reports that she loves and feels responsible for her child, and has a sense of their mutual belonging. This is all very well, but actions are more eloquent than words. By this token mothers are bonded to their babies - demonstrate their love for them - if they look after them well (being aware of and responding to their needs), and give them considerable and considerate attention. These and similar points suggest that a great deal of caution must be exercised in assessing matters such as the degree of maternal attachment, let alone in judging whether the particular mother is or is not bonded to her child.

The evidence
In 'Maternal Bonding', the present writer and his co-authors reviewed the arguments and evidence for the maternal bonding doctrine.

Carefully controlled scientific work from the United States and Sweden on mother-to-infant attachment, relies on what mothers say and on what they do. And it does not support the far-reaching claims for the bonding theory! There really is no need for mothers to feel anxious less this or that practice will have dire psychological effects for years to come. Contrary to a variety of strongly held beliefs, there is no clear-cut evidence that events around and soon after the time of birth can readily or seriously distort either the development of the infant's personality or interfere with the growth of maternal love and attachment.

If there are any initial differences in attachment behaviour between mothers who have extended contact with their babies and those who have no contact, they soon disappear with time. Even the animal studies (and it is always foolhardy to draw close parallels between animals and human behaviour) fail to support the theory of bonding. It would be interesting if the rapid kind of bonding which is said to occur in human mothers could be observed in our nearest mammalian relatives, the various infra-human primates. No such thing, in fact, has been reported and not for any species of mammal. Well then, what about the sheep and goats so often quoted in the bonding literature? Recent studies in the USA have shown more clearly how the she-goat functions after birth. What happens is that female goats butt away any incorrectly 'labelled' young, that is all those that are contaminated with alien smells. Any young, on the other hand, that are free from the 'wrong' smells, or those that by some means have been freed from them, are accepted and allowed to nurse at any

time. It cannot therefore be argued that in these particular animals maternal attachment is brought about by
contact occurring immediately after birth.

Fostering and adoption

Foster mothering does sometimes succeed in animals; and
the use of adoption and fostering for the substitute care
of human children has been a spectacular success. Acceptance and adoption of the young do not necessarily occur
immediately or even soon after birth. A foster or adoptive
home is a child's substitute family. If the bonding view
were correct, it would hardly be possible for foster or
adoptive parents to form attachments to their charges. It
may well be that it is possible to look after children
satisfactorily without ever becoming attached to them. But
as children may need both care and affection if they are
to thrive, then it is clearly better for them to be looked
after by people who show affection and whose affection
stems from attachment. Tragic 'tug-of-love' cases have
occurred because of foster parents who have grown to love
their charges.

What about fathers?

Paternal love and attachment likewise put a large question
mark over the pessimistic implications of the bonding doctrine. For the doctrine would seem to imply that paternal
love is of a different order and quality from maternal
love. The fact that a female gives birth does not necessarily mean that she invariably cares for the baby. This is
so even in some animal species; male marmosets, to take
one example, carry the infant at all times except when the
infant is feeding.

There have been variations among human groups. Anthropologists tell us that children may not be the special responsibility of their parent at all in some societies; they
may be reared by all the members of a group living together under one roof or in a small compact housing unit. Contemporary western society is witnessing a massive increase
in the number of single-parent families, in some of which
the father is the care-giver.

Assuming that one can identify a failure of bonding,
for instance of mother-child attachment, with the appropriate degree of reliability and validity, how much would
it contribute to making a diagnosis? The value of a diagnostic term lies in its descriptive functions, and its
implications for aetiology, treatment and prognosis. A
label without implication would be pointless. How appropriate then is the concept of a maternal bonding as a
descriptive term for maternal behaviour? There is no general agreement about what are the most desirable attributes of maternal behaviour, and there is little available
information (Herbert, 1980b) to indicate which aspects of
parental behaviour foster particular traits - good or bad -

in their offspring, or which make for optimal conditions in mother-child interactions. Nevertheless, bonding is generally valued as a necessary and desirable condition, and its absence as putting the child at risk. But does it describe a consistent set of attitudes or actions? The fact is that we cannot assume the simplicity or the unidimensionality of mother-infant attachment behaviour. Whiten (1977) has demonstrated, in his study of the effects of perinatal event that it is extremely difficult to arrive at a sensitive and objective description of those features of mother-infant interaction which are important in terms of their developmental significance or prominence in the everyday life of the mother and baby.

It is the present author's experience that particular weight is given to the influence of these periods of separation while the consideration of the influence of other potentially important variables, such as the parity of the mother, the sex and temperament of the infant, state variables in the mother and family social class are neglected (see Sluckin, Herbert and Sluckin, 1983, for a full review of the evidence).

Like so many other would-be explanatory concepts in social work, 'maternal deprivation' and 'bonding' are over-inclusive and too imprecise to be of any predictive value. They have been used as if they described unitary phenomena. In fact, as the evidence suggests, there are many moderating influences which determine the seriousness of the consequences for the child (Rutter, 1972).

Should she go out to work?

Sadly, there have been some doom-laden speculations and peculiar interpretations of the research literature, which have caused needless worry to mothers about the day-to-day separation forced on them by the fact of working in a society that does not provide proper facilities for working mothers. As Michael Rutter expresses it:

> Bowlby's writings have often been misinterpreted and wrongly used to support the notion that only twenty-four hours' care day in and day out, by the same person, is good enough. Thus it has been claimed that proper mothering is only possible if the mother does not go out to work and that the use of day nurseries and creches has a particularly serious and permanent deleterious effect (Rutter, 1972).

Mothers often feel guilty at handing over their child to someone else for a large part of the day. They feel that, somehow, the daily separation may be doing them harm. It is reassuring, then, to know that there is no evidence that children whose mothers work suffer adverse effects. But there is a most important proviso: finding good substitute care for the child. On the whole, children

who go (say) to a high quality nursery may stand to gain
socially and intellectually by becoming more independent
and by coming into contact with other children in day
care. Mixing with other children broadens the range of a
child's social behaviour. The more children have to adapt
to a variety of other individuals, the more their repertoire of social skills will grow. They learn how to give
and take, solve conflicts and to cooperate to make play
more fun. The extra stimulus of other developing minds
gives an intellectual boost and, at any good nursery, they
will find all sorts of play materials which help to bring
out creative abilities (see Herbert, 1985).

What is critical is that a mother feels confident
about her motives for working, and is not crippled by nagging doubts. Parents should also be painstaking in their
provision of substitute care. The evidence suggests that
children of working mothers do not suffer proved that
stable relationships and good care are provided by the
caregivers. However, for parents who retain serious doubts
about the wisdom of working, it is probably best (where
they have a choice) to err on the side of caution, least
while the child is very young.

Michael Rutter is critical of the blanket condemnation
of day nurseries and creches - the popular forms of care
used by working mothers. These substitutes for maternal
care, like maternal care itself, vary in quality. Dogmatic
generalizations, as is usually the case in psychology,
prove misleading, because of their over-simplifying complicated and many-sided issues. Good day care need not interfere with normal mother-child bonding. The use of day nurseries does not appear to have any long-term adverse psychological or physical effects. Children of working parents are no more likely to develop emotional problems or
turn into delinquents than children whose mothers stay at
home. An investigation of working mothers showed that the
only children to suffer were those who were sent from
'pillar to post' in a succession of unsatisfactory and
unstable child-minding arrangements. They tended to be
attention-seeking and clinging.

The important thing to remember is that a good mother-
child relationship does not depend on mother and child
being together every minute, day in, day out. It depends
on what happens between them when they are together and
the quality of care given. A loving mother who can manage
to save enough energy to enjoy the company of her child
after her day's work can have a far better relationship
with him than a mother who is lonely and resentful about
being imprisoned at home all day.

Fathering
The contemporary young middle-class husband, as he fulfils
his paternal role, is quite likely to assist with the feeding or bathing of the baby for his working ife. Such no-

tions of fathering are alien to earlier times and other species. Throughout the animal kingdom, males play little or no part in the care and nurture of their offspring. Students of human societies believe that men learnt to develop a relationship with their children as a result of setting up long-term living arrangements with one or more women. The human male established a family unit whereas most male and female animals come together for mating purposes and then part. In fact, humanity took a long time to discover what fatherhood was. The 40 weeks of pregnancy dividing the moment of conception from the birth of a baby prevented our ancestors from connecting the two events.

Henry Biller (1971) has examined the father's contribution to family life and concludes that any new father should be encouraged to spend as much time as possible with his wife and child. The earlier he can feel involved with the child, the more likely is a strong relationship to develop between them. He believes that having a child should be a careful decision for both father and mother, and before the child is conceived the prospective parents ought to feel a joint commitment to their future family. This mutual interest should carry on through pregnancy, though it is easy for the father to begin feeling left out at this stage. Too often all the attention is focused on the expectant mother and the expectant father is left out in the cold. Biller found that it helped for husbands to be involved in pre-natal visits to the doctor and then, if the hospital allows it, they can be with their wives during labour and in the delivery room, where they can be of enormous support. A father can be very important to his child's development even in the first year of life.

Western society is becoming increasingly compartmentalized as specialized social groups become larger and people's social contacts increase. For instance, a man's role in the work situation may have nothing to do with his role as a father and husband, or as a member of the local sports club or political party. The most frequent barrier between father and child is the father's work schedule. Many fathers, because of long-term goals, sacrifice time with their families only to find that they have lost their children, at least psychologically, in the process. They may end up with financial security but a very empty family. In some cases, modifications in the daily work routine may be possible to ensure his fuller participation in family life, but all too often work is used as an excuse for avoiding family responsibilities. Many fathers who are competent and active at work feel totally inexperienced and ineffectual when at home with their children.

Where previously mothers were inculpated in the psychopathology of childhood, almost to the exclusion of fathers, we now see the return of the father to share the 'blame' as well as the glory. There are not many references to 'paternal rejection' per se, in the literature, which is surprising as fathers are much more likely to abandon their families than mothers. However, much of the present interest in discovering how fathers contribute to children's development was stimulated by studies of what occurred in children's development when the father was absent from the home environment. This deficit model of development is similar to the approach used when research- ers first became interested in the effects of maternal deprivation. Studies of children who lack the fathering experience indicate that their adjustment is difficult in various areas of personality and social development (see Sluckin and Herbert, in press).

The child is father to the man

It is probably true to say that among the many factors that determine what an individual becomes - of the forces that shape abilities, interests, motives, goals, desires, personality characteristics and social attitudes - none will be as influential as the family into which he or she is born. It is a popular saying that 'the child is father to the man'; those who make a scientific study of beha- viour agree that the early experiences of infancy and childhood have a profound influence on adult behaviour. For example, despite the fact that fathers spend most of their time away from their families, they are expected in today's climate of opinion to participate in child-rearing responsibilites as much as possible. The control function of fathering has received more attention from researchers than the nurturant function because social control is con- sidered to be an integral by-product of the power and authority associated with fatherhood. Research generally indicates that the father rather than the mother is respon- sible for reinforcing the dependent nature of the child's behaviour. This effect may be more visible in a girl than in a boy. A number of dependent-type behaviours are shown by children whose fathers place intense pressures on them to be neat and orderly, punish or fail to reward indepen- dent behaviour, reward traditional sex-typed behaviours of both boys and girls, and discourage children from express- ing their affection for them physically. Many studies indi- cate that fathers, as opposed to mothers, rely on power- assertive techniques to control children's behaviour. One of the more consistent findings about extreme power asser- tion by a father is that their children tend to show a high level of aggression toward others. Aggression towards the child by the parent is thought to breed aggression in the child. The parent may act as a model of aggression for the child, who, in seeing the father behave in this man- ner, transfers the aggression to his or her relationships with siblings and peers.

Family cohesion

Evidence reviewed by Orford (1980) indicates that family

cohesion is a key factor linking work in otherwise separated problem areas.

Table 1

The syndrome of cohesion in families hypothesized to be associated with the psychological well-being of group members

1. More time spent in shared activity.

2. Less withdrawal, avoidance and segregated activity.

3. A higher rate of warm interactions, and a lower rate of critical or hostile interactions amongst members.

4. Fuller and more accurate communication between members.

5. A more favourable evaluation of other members: a lower level of criticalness of other members.

6. More favourable meta-perceptions: i.e. members more likely to assume that other members have a favourable view of them.

7. A higher level of perceived affection between members.

8. A higher level of satisfaction and morale, and greater optimism about the future stability of the family group.

Families which lack the characteristics listed above make their members vulnerable to experiencing psychological distress. Particularly at risk are those family members who are already vulnerable for other reasons - the young, the elderly, those suffering from other types of stress (e.g. hospitalization, alcohol dependence, coping with a large number of children).

Lidz (1968) maintains that a coalition between the parents is necessary not only to give unity of direction to the children but also to provide each parent with the emotional support essential for carrying out his or her cardinal functions. In one type of family situation which is frequently found as a background to the development of schizophrenic withdrawal in children, the members are torn by a 'schismatic conflict' between husband and wife, so that the family is divided into two hostile factions. The children become involved in an emotional tug-of-war. This destructive situation - a complete negation of a parental coalition - may go on and on. Although a divorce would probably end everybody's misery, it does not occur, and a state of what is called 'emotional divorce' persists - a corrosive situation pervaded by continual bickering, mutual recriminations and venomous hatred. If the child shows affection to one parent, this is regarded as betrayal by the other.

In another disturbed familial pattern, called 'marital skew', one parent dominates the roost, and his (or her) psychopathology - abnormal thinking, bizarre style of living and abnormal manner of child-rearing - is passively accepted by the spouse. Suspiciousness and distrust of outsiders amounting to paranoia may prevail, and these deluded attitudes, together with other irrational interpretations of life, may be conveyed to the children. Such parents provide faulty models for their offspring to emulate; they transmit faulty modes of thinking to their children. Both these types of environment immerse the child in an irrational family atmosphere which is thought to negate the development of a healthy ego.

Divorce

If all divorces, all broken homes, led to serious psychological difficulties, society would have an appalling problem on its hands. You have only to look at the statistics. About one quarter of the babies born in the United Kingdom today are likely to experience a separation of their parents before they reach school-leaving age. The highest risk or likelihood of a divorce (at present) occurs in the fourth year of marriage. In other words, it is very likely to be young children who are caught up in the lead-up to, and aftermath of, a divorce. Separation - the event that really hits children - is likely to precede divorce by several years. The most common reaction on the part of children is anger towards the parents for separating. Children of all ages frequently express the wish that their parents be reunited and they blame either, or both of them, for the split; most children do not want their parents to separate and they may feel that their father and mother have not taken their interests into account.

A marital separation may result in children reappraising their own relationships with their parents and, indeed questioning the nature of all social relationships. For younger children in particular, there is the painful realization that not all social relationships last forever. If mum and dad can end their marriage, what is safe? Couldn't the same thing happen to their own relationship with either parent? Many childish reactions at such a time are expressions of their fear of being abandoned by one or both parents. These fears are likely to be most acute if contact has been lost with a parent. If only relationships between parents and child can remain intact and supportive, these fears will usually be short-lived. (We look at these and other issues concerning family life, in more detail, in chapter 9.)

The psychologist Erik Erikson proposes that the essen-

tial task of infancy is the development of a basic trust
in others. Because human infants are so totally dependent
for so long, they need to know that they can depend on the
outside world. If their basic needs are met by the world
they inhabit, they are thought to develop a 'basic trust'
in the world, and thus to evolve a nucleus of self-trust,
which is indispensible to later development.

But how profound and irreversible are these early
influences? It is assumed that the child's personality
traits are 'fixed' in the family mould during earliest
childhood and that all that happens subsequently is that
they continue to grow, emerging in recognizable but more
elaborate form (i.e. in full bloom) at maturity. Some do.
But there are difficulties in predicting adult personality
from traits observed in early childhood.

Studies that follow up children over long periods of
time show that there is only a modest correspondence
between many specific traits seen during earliest childhood and adult life, although overall trends enable one to
identify some fairly gross stabilities or continuities in
personality. The characteristic which is most stable (that
is to say, unchanging) is achievement-orientation. Most
other traits are very poor predictors of adult personality
development. These findings are somewhat out of keeping
with the ideas held by many theologians, philosophers and
psychoanalysts, that the learning experiences of the first
five to seven years of a child's life are all-important in
determining the sort of person the individual is to be;
that what happens to an individual after that is merely a
ripple on the surface of an already 'set' character
structure!

Early learning
What is the evidence - rather than the folklore - about
these issues of early learning and their consequences?
Clarke and Clarke (1976), British psychologists, have pain-
stakingly reviewed the available evidence. Their conclusions are as follows:

*   At the moment valid scientific knowledge is sadly lack-
    ing. Indeed, dogmatism about either the long-term
    effects or non-effects of early experience is at the
    present time entirely misplaced. Nevertheless, it is
    possible to identify certain consistencies in the
    data.
*   There is little reason to suppose that infant learning
    is acquired more easily than later learning. Nor is
    there any indication that it is better retained or
    more resistant to extinction. Experiments in fact
    suggest that infants and young children are strikingly
    inferior to adults in many dimensions of learning.
*   The long-term effects of short-traumatic incidents seem
    to be negligible both in animals and young human

beings. Only when early learning is continually reinforced do long-term effects appear, and these may well
be the result of the later reinforcement rather than
of the original learning as such.
* With human infants the specific effects of experiences
before seven months of age appear to be of very short
duration. Indeed, it is experiences after the first
year of life which appear to have a longer-term
effect, and even so, extinction occurs unless there is
reinforcement.
* It is unwarranted to assume that all psychological
processes are affected to an equal extent by early
experiences. Different functions appear to show different degrees of recovery following early adversity
with the motor processes being the most resilient and
emotional functions least so.
* There seem to be large individual differences in
vulnerability to early adverse experiences, and in
resilience thereafter. This may be due to genetic
factors, or to minimal brain injury which could be
very common.
* The rigidity of personality structuring during infancy
appears to have been exaggerated by some authorities
and early learning experiences appear not to set for
the child a necessarily fixed and invariable path.
After all, the newly born and young infant is an immature creature who can be said to be culturally neutral
and psychologically uncommitted. It can only slowly,
and with much parental effort and the gradual maturation of its faculties, be socialized.
* The view commonly held by workers in the field of mental
health that early characteristics remain relatively unchanged seems to be true only of a specially vulnerable section of the population.
* Evidence suggests that early learning is of importance
mainly for its foundational character. Development
proceeds at different rates through a sequence of well-
marked stages. Each stage depends on the integrity of
previous stages. It seems appropriate to talk of optimal periods of learning in human beings. Deficits
arising from early environmental handicaps can, to
varying extents, be made good.

The Clarkes emphasize the point that children should not
be viewed as passive organisms whose characters are
moulded solely by the impact of environment upon genetic
predispositions. Children themselves act indirectly as
reinforcers of their own behaviour. For example, the
mother-child pair (dyad) is a feedback system (see Lee,
Wright and Herbert, 1972), and the degree to which the
child's actions have the power to change the mother's
behaviour increases with development. The child is not a
passive reactor to events, as has often been assumed to be

the case. This notion of an essentially passive and reactive infant on whom the environment made its mark led to the corollary that the early environment should receive all the 'blame' when things went wrong. Children labelled 'at risk' have often been regarded in the social work literature as passive victims of external forces. The victims have often been deliberately excluded from study because their roles have been presumed to be irrelevant. Because much of the research on child neglect and abuse has been prompted by concerns with prevention and remediation, attention has been focused on those aspects of the problem which have been thought to be more easily changed. The parents and their child-rearing practices (again), rather than the children themselves, have been most frequently nominated for this role. For a long time in chology the infant was misleadingly viewed as a 'tabula rasa' - a blank sheet - passively reacting to the environment, and thus the research literature on such fraught problems as the battered child or the child who fails to thrive has generally adopted the 'mal de mere' approach to the study of developmental failures.

Theorists failed to take into account the influence of childrens' individual capacities and active manipulations of, as well as reactions to, their environment. They 'reach out', using their magnificent repertoire of grasping, smiles, cries, baby talk and the like, to shape their parents' behaviour. They are themselves agents of socialization and in Rheingold's telling phrase: 'of men and women he (the baby) makes fathers and mothers' (1963). Th child's temperament, age, sex and state, cuddliness and individual demandingness all influence the mother. The possession of certain combinations of temperamental qualities can make a child exceedingly 'difficult', no matter how skilled the parents are. It is just such idiosyncratic features which cause the mother to change her methods from one of her babies to the next, or to adapt her style of mothering away from preconceived plans and theories she might have had about child-rearing. For, despite their apparent helplessness, even new-born infants (as we saw earlier) have considerable physical powers.

The emotional 'bond'
In any discussion of the development and rearing of infants, with social workers and social work students, the child's attachment to parents and others (and how it comes about) constitutes a major theme. There is a strange paradox, in a sense, about a child becoming a person in his or her own right. In order first of all to become a person the child must become attached to the mother by that all-important bond of love, as she will shape her child's early encounters with the 'world' which give the child social awareness. For it would only be correct to speak of a child as a person when he or she becomes aware of other

persons and of himself or herself as a separate individual: in other words, a social being. Then, in order to
become a person in his or her own right, the child must
later detach himself or herself, at least partially, from
the mother's protective cocoon, and develop an independent
a point of view. The child must move out of safe orbit
around mother and strike out to find his or her own place
in the world.

It is the child's early yearnings for love and related-
ness which are among the most important driving forces in
the shaping of the personality. There is fairly general
agreement among experts that the infant's first human relationship is the foundation stone of personality, and as
the child's first tie of love is usually to the mother, a
great deal of research effort has been put into studying
this 'attachment' between children and mothers.

**Loss and
bereavement
in the
family**

The spectre of the death of a loved person - someone in
the family - plays a central role in the life of every
individual. We have all known, or will come to know,
death, grief and mourning. A continuing challenge for the
social worker is meeting the needs of clients who are
bereaved, not only by death but the loss caused by separation or the sense of loss and pity engendered by the birth
of a mentally handicapped child.

Western society reacts to a death by providing varying
amounts of solace for the bereaved. The relief of guilt
may be simply informal words of comfort and exculpation,
as in reassurances like 'nobody could have done more than
you did'. Some communities have more formal procedures.
Maori tribes, for example, had a complex and magical procedure: they used professional mourners who symbolically
accepted the sorrows and grief of the bereaved and in
their turn were treated as outcasts by the rest of the
tribe. It is surprising how often the prescribed rituals
lasted between nine and 12 months, the time which psychologists accept a normal person needs to come to terms with
grief, although some would say it takes longer.

As it is used in everyday conversation, grief usually
refers to an extreme degree of sorrow associated with loss
or separation. We grieve the departure of a dear friend to
another country; the child grieves when left in hospital
by the mother; we feel grief when we lose a loved one's
love or when we lose our illusions about him or her. Psychoanalysts have emphasized that the identification of the
bereaved person with the deceased is the main process
involved in mourning: part of the self, an extension of
the ego, has died. Let us look more closely at these
processes.

Bowlby (1969) formulates a theory of mourning which
distinguishes three main phases. During the first phase,
the individual's attachments are still focused on the lost

object, but because of the deceased's absence they cannot
be resolved. As a result, the bereaved individual experiences repeated disappointment, the anxiety of persistent
separation and, insofar as reality can be accepted, grief.
So long as the affections and dependencies are focused on
the deceased, there are strenuous and often angry efforts
to recover him or her.

In the second stage, before the final resolution,
there is a disorganization of the personality accompanied
by pain and despair. In the first two stages, feelings
often fluctuate between an angry demand for, or an expectancy of, the loved one's return, to a despair expressed
in subdued pining, to total lack of any expression. Though
hope and despair may alternate for a long time, there
evolves, at last, a degree of emotional detachment from
the deceased.

During the third stage, the function of mourning is
complete, and a new and different state has come about: a
reorganization of attitudes and feelings, partly in relation to the image of the lost person, partly in connection
with a new object or objects. Children show this pattern
of mourning when separated early in life from their
mothers. The consequences can be serious if adequate substitute care is not provided.

Bowlby claims that the pattern of mourning behaviour
in higher animals is similar to that of humans. He concludes that the evidence, fragmentary though it is, makes
it fairly certain that each of the main behavioural features alleged to be characteristic of human mourning is
essentially shared by humans with lower animals. Members
of animal species protest at the loss of a loved object
and do all in their power to seek and recover it. Externally directed hostility is frequent; withdrawal, rejection of a potential new object, apathy and restlessness
are the rule. And, given time and opportunity, a reorganization of behaviour in connection with a new object, as
well as recovery, often follows.

This theory has received support from the zoologist
Konrad Lorenz in his studies of jackdaws, geese, dogs,
orang-outangs, and chimpanzees (1961, 1966). A greylag
goose which had lost its mate at first began a frantic
searching and calling. Then, in the phase of depression,
there was a lack of energy, movements were slow, eyes
seemed smaller, feathers were loose and slightly fluffed,
head and neck were less erect, and there was a noticeably
decreased readiness to fly. These deserted, solitary geese
also exhibit a disinclination for social contacts: they
are generally ignored by other geese, and 'grief-stricken
widows of this type are hardly ever courted by males, even
if a quite considerable shortage of females prevails in
the goose society ... The general picture of grief is just
as clearly marked in a widowed goose as it is in a dog'.

A chimpanzee reacting to the death of his mate made

repeated efforts to arouse her; he manifested yells of rage and expressed his anger by snatching the short hairs of his head, subsequently giving way to crying and moaning. Later he tended to become more attached to his keeper than he had been before the death and would become angry when the keeper left him.

All this does not mean that there are not features of mourning which are specific to humans; there obviously are uniquely human responses. Perhaps the most significant of these is the intimate relationship between grief and the intense emotional anxiety caused by separation. There is evidence that suggests that when infants or young children lose their mother they habitually show responses comparable to a process of mourning in the adult. This observation is also based on studies of healthy children undergoing limited separation experiences in residential nurseries or hospital wards. A predictable sequence of behaviour appeared in the separated child; again we see the three-stage response. At first, with tears and anger the child demands the return of the mother and seems hopeful of success. This phase of protest may last several days. In the subsequent periods of despair the child becomes quieter but is clearly still preoccupied with the absent mother and still yearns for her return; the child's hopes, nonetheless, have faded.

Often the first two phases alternate: hope turns to despair and despair to renewed hope. Eventually, however, a greater change occurs. The child seems to forget the mother and when she does come back, remains curiously uninterested in her, perhaps not even recognizing her. This is the phase of detachment. In each of these phases the child is prone to tantrums and episodes of destructive behaviour, often of a disquietingly violent kind. Bowlby believes that there is good reason to believe that the sequence of responses described - protest, despair, and detachment - is, in one variant or another, characteristic of all forms of mourning. (This formulation has not escaped criticism and the observation that these patterns are not invariable.) For example, the prediction that, if the loss of a loved one is experienced in early childhood, decisive changes in the personality structure often follow requires a qualification. What is critical is the way the matter of the death is handled and what substitute care (in the case of maternal death) of a loving and continuous kind is available. The emotional scars from such traumatic occurrences appear to be more profound the younger the age of the bereaved (not counting the earliest months) but they are not necessarily irreversible (see Rutter, 1977).

Many parents tend to avoid the unpleasant subject of death. They say, 'There's plenty of time to worry about that later'. But all children who lose a parent or a brother or sister or a beloved relative or playmate can be spared unnecessary or serious emotional repercussions later if they are encouraged to express their feelings at the time, if they are helped to mourn the loss and thus eventually come to accept the death.

In chapter 16, Carr deals with not only the reactions to death, but also the dying.

References

Bigner, J.J. (1979)
Parent-Child Relations: An Introduction to Parenting. New York: Macmillan.

Biller, H.B. (1971)
Father, Child and Sex Role. Lexington, USA: Heath Lexington Books.

Bowlby, J. (1951)
Maternal Care and Mental Health. Geneva: WHO.

Bowlby, J. (1969)
Attachment and Loss, Vol. 1.
London: Hogarth Press.

Brown, F. (1966)
Childhood bereavement and subsequent psychiatric disorder. British Journal of Psychiatry, 112, 1035-41.

Bruch, H. (1954)
Parent education or the illusion of omnipotence. American Journal of Orthopsychiatry, 24, 723.

Chess, S. (1964)
Editorial, in American Journal of Orthopsychiatry, 34, 613-614.

Clarke, A. and Clarke A.D.B. (1976)
Early Experience: Myth and reality. London: Open Books.

Erikson, E.H. (1965)
Childhood and Society (rev. edn) Harmondsworth: Penguin Books.

Harlow, H.F. (1960)
Primary affection patterns in primates. American Journal of Orthopsychiatry, 30, 676.

Herbert, M. (1974)
Emotional Problems of Development in Children. London: Academic Press.

Herbert, M. (1980a)
Behavioural social work in families. In D.S. Freeman (ed.), Perspectives on Family Therapy. Western Canada: Butterworths.

Herbert, M. (1980b)
Socialization for problem resistance. In P. Feldman and J. Orford (eds), The Social Context. Chichester: John Wiley & Sons Ltd.

Herbert, M. (1985)
Caring for Your Children. Oxford: Basil Blackwell.

Lee, S.G.M., Wright, D.S. and Herbert, M. (1972)
Aspects of the development of social responsiveness in children. Unpublished report to the Social Science

Research Council, Psychology Department, University of Leicester.

Lidz, T. (1968)
The Person. London: Basic Books

Lorenz, K. (1961)
Imprinting. In R.C. Birney and R.C. Teevan (eds), Instinct. London: Van Nostrand.

Lorenz, K. (1966)
On Aggression. New York: Harcourt, Brace & World.

Mead, M. (1935)
Sex and Temperament in Three Primitive Societies. London: Routledge & Kegan Paul.

Montagu, M.F.A. (1962)
Prenatal Influences. Springfield, Ill.: Thomas.

Orford, J. (1980)
The domestic context. In P. Feldman and J. Orford (eds), Psychological Problems. Chichester: John Wiley & Sons Ltd.

Rheingold, H.L. (ed.) (1963)
Maternal Behaviour in Mammals. Chichester: John Wiley & Sons Ltd.

Robson, K.M. and Kumar, R. (1980)
Delayed onset of maternal affection after childbirth. British Journal of Psychiatry, 136, 347-353.

Rutter, M. (1972)
Maternal Deprivation Reassessed. Harmondsworth: Penguin Books.

Rutter, M. (1977)
Other family influences. In M. Rutter and L. Hersov (eds), Child Psychiatry: Modern approaches. Oxford: Blackwell Scientific Publications.

Sluckin, W., Herbert, M. and Sluckin, A. (1983)
Maternal Bonding. Oxford: Basil Blackwell.

Sluckin, W. and Herbert, M. (eds) (in press)
Parental Behaviour in Humans and Animals. Oxford: Basil Blackwell

Thomas, A., Chess, S. and Birch, H.G. (1968)
Temperament and Behaviour Disorder in Children. London: University of London Press.

Watson, J.B. and Watson, R.R. (1928)
Psychological Care of Infant and Child. New York: Norton.

Whiten A. (1977)
Assessing the effects of perinatal events on the success of the mother-infant relationship. In H.R. Schaffer (ed.), Studies in Mother-Infant Interaction. London: Academic Press.

Yarrow, M.R., Campbell, J.D. and Burton, R.V. (1968)
Child Rearing: An inquiry into research and methods. San Francisco: Jossey-Bass.

Further
reading

Manor, O. (ed.) (1984)
Family Work in Action. London: Tavistock.

5
Stages of development and life tasks

Human beings have aways entertained theories about the nature of development. One of the ancient notions was called 'preformationism'; human beings' tendencies and attributes were thought to exist preformed at birth. The 'homunculus' view of human development was an elaboration of preformationism; this theory proposed that the sperm contains a fully formed, miniature human, who simply develops, once conception has taken place, in an incremental way, until maturity is reached. These things have their modern and more sophisticated (but also dubious) counterparts in concepts such as human instincts and innate ideas.

Theologians and philosophers speculated about human nature and motives. Some of the explanations of the mainsprings of human actions were profoundly optimistic views, while others involved extremely pessimistic ideas; some suggest that humans are self-centred and driven by what is good for themselves and their egos. This is the theory of 'egoism'. In this tradition Thomas Hobbes, the seventeenth-century philosopher, believed that human beings are basically selfish and (incidentally) brutish and destructive. Freudian psychology contains elements of the pessimistic view as can be seen in the emphasis on instincts which have to be repressed. Freud argued in 'Civilization and its Discontents' that every advance of civilization is bought at the cost of a communal (and therefore individual) renunciation of instinctual gratification. Some theorists believe humans always choose to do what is basically pleasurable: the theory of 'hedonism'. Freud made a great deal of this motive, which he called the 'pleasure principle'. It also shows itself in modern learning theories.

Others again (like the seventeenth-century philosopher John Locke) feel that humans are not basically selfish. They are driven by a fundamental inclination to co-operate peacefully with their fellows. This theory of 'altruism' (formulated, among others, by Rousseau) maintains that nature knows best. The child is like the noble savage, pure and unspoilt until corrupted by society interfering with natural processes.

One of the controversies in developmental psychology concerns the concept of 'stage', and its importance in describing the development of psychological processes such as thinking and personality. Mussen, Conger and Kagan (1979) illustrate the problem by contrasting the growth of a butterfly with that of a leaf. Once a leaf has grown from its form as a seed, it never changes its basic shape or organization while it grows larger; growth seems to be continuous, with no transformations in shape. By contrast, the butterfly passes through several dramatically different forms - or stages - before it reaches its adult organization. The theorists point out that the mature form of a maple leaf can be predicted easily from an early version, but it would be difficult to guess that the caterpillar and the butterfly are part of the life history of the same creature. Psychologists debate which psychological systems grow continuously without marked transformations, and which pass through different stages in growing towards maturity.

Psychosexual stages of development

Sigmund Freud (1932) believed that the development of a normal sex life involves the successful traversing of various psycho-sexual stages. The basic drives, according to Freud, remain the same throughout life. What changes is the manner of the expression of our motives. There are shifts in the zones of the body (and the associated psychological attitudes) through which gratification is sought and obtained, and in the objects which satisfy our needs. Freud noted that three sensitive areas of the body - the mouth, anus and genitals - are particularly associated with sexual or libidinous gratification. He described certain character traits which are associated with either too great frustration or overly indulged gratification at each of these stages. Certain children, according to the theory, become fixated at one or other of these developmental stages, and the residues of this fixation show themselves in the adult personality.

The development of cognitive functions

Another proponent of stages of development - this time with regard to the growth of cognitive functions - is Jean Piaget. On the basis of his observations and questioning of his own and other children he delineated several successive stages in the development of intelligent behaviour in infancy. Piaget's basic orientation is biological. He proposed that intelligence is an aspect of adapting to the environment; in other words, adaptation is the cognitive striving of the thinking child to find an equilibrium between himself and his or her milieu.

Adaptation depends upon two interrelated processes which Piaget calls assimilation and accommodation (1932).

Assimilation involves a person's adaptation of the environment to the self and represents the individual's use of the environment as it is perceived. Accommodation is the converse of assimilation and involves the impact on the individual of the actual environment itself. To accommodate is to perceive and to incorporate the experience provided by the environment as it actually is.

The whole span of development from birth to maturity is classified into major stages which can be related to approximate age ranges. Although there are qualitative differences between the stages, the movement from one to the next is continuous. Piaget would claim that the order is fixed.

The complexity of the child's schematic structure - which reflects the development of intelligence - depends upon the variety of the environmental objects which are available for the child to assimilate and which simultaneously induce accommodation. The Piagetian description of cognitive development in terms of an interplay of accommodatory and assimilatory processes is analogous (according to Danziger, 1971) to the interplay of ego and alter in personality development: namely, the achievement of a balance between the poles of recognizing and adapting to the needs of others and imposing self-centred demands on the social environment. An extreme lack of balance in reciprocity between self and others in either direction gives rise to unsatisfactory social relationships. Children (for example) demand parental support and they try to limit the restraints parents put upon their pleasures. The balance, therefore, is about a compromise between sometimes incompatible mutual demands, and about a style of life which maximizes the mutually rewarding possibilities of the parent-child relationship.

Developmental discontinuity

The periods in which qualitatively new and discontinuous (inter-stage) changes in personality organization are being formulated are described by Ausubel and Sullivan (1970) as transitional phases or developmental crises. During these transitional periods the individual is in the marginal position of having lost an established and accustomed status, and of not yet having acquired the new status towards which the factors impelling developmental change are driving him. Knowledge of 'sensitive periods' in personal development could alert the social worker to the developmental tasks which put a heavy burden on adjustive capacities. Each stage of development corresponds to a particular form of social demand: the person must deal with and master a central problem, a potential crisis. At each of eight stages a conflict (as Erikson, 1965, sees it) between opposite poles in a pattern of reciprocity between self and others, has to be resolved.

From birth to about four years of age, to illustrate

one of the developmental tasks described by Erik Erikson, the child needs to develop a sense of trust and, later, a growing independence. A lasting sense of trust, security, confidence or optimism (as opposed to distrust, insecurity, inadequacy or pessimism) is thought to be based upon affection, a degree of continuity of care-giving and the reasonably prompt satisfaction of the infant's needs. The major hazards to the development of a perception of a benign, trustworthy and predictable world in which the child initiates independence-seeking, are neglect, abuse, indifference, extreme inconsistency and other conditions - social and physical - which interfere with the child's sense of personal adequacy or which hinder the acquisition of skills.

Life tasks: attachment
In becoming 'civilized' the child, who is basically 'self-centred' (being concerned only with the immediate gratification of individual needs and desires), must give up much. He or she must accept many restraints in order to fit into society; the wishes of others have to be taken into account. Children's love for their parents (in large part) is what makes many of these sacrifices possible. The psychoanalyst Otto Fenichel (1945) believes that the small child loses self-esteem when love is lost and attains it when love is regained. That is what makes children educable. They need supplies of affection so badly that they are ready to renounce other satisfactions if rewards of affection are promised or if withdrawal of love is threatened.

If a major task to be achieved during infancy is the internalization of a sense of trust (derived from parental affection and the prompt satisfaction of needs), mistrust and a sense of insecurity are the emotional problems which potentially have their origins in the neglect of the child's needs during this phase of life. If parents are neglectful, the child may see the world not as a manageable and benign place, but as threatening and insecure. The contrasting attitudes of trust and mistrust are very like the adult attitudes of optimism and pessimism: they colour the child's entire outlook on life and, indeed, personality. A lasting sense of security or insecurity, self-confidence or inadequacy - as well as many other social and self attitudes of vital importance for positive mental health - are thus, in this view, laid down in the early months and years.

All infants need to become attached to a parent in order to survive. The child's growing bond of love and loyalty are a great source of joy to the parents: but such ties of affection also serve a utilitarian function. The respect and goodwill the child feels (including that towards teachers) enhances all the adults' efforts to teach him or her. The fact that the child is 'on their side', so to speak, makes the task of teaching - and learning - much easier.

What, then, is the source of this bond of love, of social 'attachment', as psychologists refer to it?

The first year of life is the critical one to look at, because within 12 months of birth almost all babies have developed a strong attachment to the mother or a mother-figure. And it is fortunate that this is so! The long period of helpless infancy of the human species entails serious risks, so looked at from an evolutionary point of view it is of crucial importance for the survival of the human species that the child and its parent should become attached to one another for the protection of the young. An interesting theory with regard to early human infant attachment behaviour suggests that the infant demonstrates a primary need (not so much for proximity to other people) but for stimulation. At first infants seek optimal arousal from all aspects of the environment. In time they learn that humans are a particularly satisfying source of stimulation and that they are also often sources of non-social stimulation. A need for proximity to other people develops when the infant has learned about their particular characteristics. Eventually, a narrowing down occurs and attachments are formed to specific people.

Other theorists have postulated that an infant is born with a primary 'need' or 'drive' for social contact. Not all would accept this idea of an instinctual response. According to social learning theorists, it is the mother's function to provide the child with positive reinforcing stimuli (i.e. stimuli such as food, water, warmth and many others which meet primary motivations and needs); they follow upon and strengthen the responses of the infant. General characteristics of the mother, such as her attention, her affection and her proximity to the infant, which often precede or are presented at the same time as such reinforcing stimuli, acquire positive reinforcing value.

Here then are the concepts of drive and motivation. What happens, according to some theorists, is the development of a fundamental need for the mother - a dependency - which becomes more compelling than such physical needs as hunger and thirst. The child's early love, in other words, is a form of 'cupboard love', which it learns. More recently, John Bowlby in Britain and Mary Salter Ainsworth (1973) in the USA and other research workers, have rejected this as an oversimplified picture of early social responsiveness. The child is not just a passive recipient of love and stimulation.

Researchers have remarked on the way children often seem to dictate their parents' behaviour by the insistency of their demands. Infants do not wait passively for things to be done to them; they reach out actively to their surroundings for stimulation and social contact. Early on the baby smiles, laughs, reaches out and coos at its mother.

71

Later, when able to, the baby greets and approaches her and does delightful things which ensure that she will continue to do the things it likes, such as making funny noises tickling, and so on. The mother has a powerful influence on her child's behaviour, and by encouraging some activities and discouraging others she 'shapes' the child's personality. But in all sorts of subtle ways her behaviour is also shaped by the child. There is a two-way traffic in the relationship between mother and child in the crucial business of the child's becoming a person.

This observation has meant that psychologists have found it useful to conceive of the mother and child as a single 'attachment system' while they are interacting with each other. We cannot describe attachment (or dependency) in the child without describing the attributes and behaviour of the mother. Psychologists have observed and analysed the attachment system in the laboratory and the natural setting of the youngster's home. What evidence we have - and it is still incomplete - has been interpreted by Bowlby, the author of 'Attachment and Loss' (1969), as supporting the view that the child's attachment can occur (as it does in animal species) without the rewards of food, warmth and the like. It is suggested that the child is 'programmed' by its heredity so that it is sensitive to certain types of stimulation in its surroundings. The human face in movement, for example, is one of the most dependable 'triggers' of a smile in young babies. And as all mothers know, her baby's smile binds her to the child with a deep feeling of joy and love.

Failure to master previous developmental tasks is thought to hinder the individual in the next social endeavour. All these formulations are difficult to prove or disprove, although they are articles of faith for many psychologists.

We have referred to the interplay of ego and alter in personality development: the balance between a self-centred and altruistic point of view in social interactions. The family, like other socializing agents of society, uses various techniques to teach and control the child in its care, and not least to encourage the 'alter' component of personality. Among those used are material and psychological rewards, praise, reproof, corporal and psychological punishment, examples, giving or withholding love, approval and explanation of rules.

One may say that all children in all societies are socialized in numerous behaviours by many agents, using a wide variety of techniques and practices. The emphasis on particular social behaviour patterns and the means for developing them often varies from culture to culture, but certain systems of behaviour are universally brought under social control: eating, elimination, dependency and aggression. In the Tarongan child, from the Philippines, cooperativeness is a culturally desirable characteristic. Mani-

festations of this quality are rewarded even during the
child's earliest years. Rewards are predominantly verbal
or edible. Sharing toys or food with other children is
highly approved, as is helping another child who needs
assistance. Either will gain lavish praise for the child,
and perhaps a biscuit or a bit of fruit.

References

Ainsworth, M.D. (1973)
  The development of infant-mother attachment. In B.M.
  and H.N. Ricciuti (eds), Review of Child Development
  Research. Chicago: University of Chicago Press.
Ausubel, D.P. and Sullivan, E.V. (1970)
  Theory and Problems of Child Development (2nd edn).
  London: Grune & Stratton.
Bowlby, J. (1969)
  Attachment and Loss, Volume 1. London: Hogarth Press.
Danziger, K. (1971)
  Socialization. Harmondsworth: Penguin Books.
Erikson, E.H. (1965)
  Childhood and Society (rev. edn). Harmondsworth:
  Penguin Books.
Fenichel, O. (1945)
  The Psychoanalytic Theory of Neurosis. London:
  Routledge and Kegan Paul.
Freud, S. (1932)
  New Introductory Lectures on Psychoanalysis. London:
  Hogarth Press.
Mussen, P.H., Conger, J.L. and Kagan, J. (1979)
  Child Development and Personality. New York: Harper &
  Row.
Piaget, J. (1932)
  The Moral Judgement of the Child. New York: Harcourt
  Brace.
Schaffer, H.R. (1971)
  The Growth of Sociability. Harmondsworth: Penguin
  Books.
Schaffer, H.R. (1977)
  Mothering. London: Fontana/Open Books.

Annotated reading

Herbert, M. (1974) Emotional Problems of Development in
Children. London: Academic Press.
  This book provides the reader with a normal framework
  within which to look at problems. At each stage of
  development there is information about what to expect
  of the child's social, emotional, moral intellectual
  and ego development.

Herbert, M. (1985) Caring for Your Children: A Practical
Guide. Oxford: Basil Blackwell.
  This book does the same thing but is suitable to give
  to parents and child care staff.

6

Personality and intellect

In trying to understand differences in the characteristic
but varied responses individuals make to life situations,
psychologists have developed theories of personality.
Margaret Mead's work (1935) among the South Sea Islanders
showed the huge variation in patterns of adjustment which
can be produced in humans by different styles of upbringing. The Arapesh of New Guinea are gentle, peace-loving
people, among whom self-assertion is so rare as to be
regarded as abnormal. For their periodic celebrations they
persuade some of their members, much against their will,
into the role of organizers. Passivity and selflessness
form an essential part of the nurture and education of
each individual. From birth, children are exposed to
traits like these in the behaviour of those about them; in
the course of development, they assimilate many of them
into their own personality.

Another island group, the Mundugumor, in complete
contrast, fosters aggression from infancy. If a suckling
baby does not take a firm grip on the mother's breast she
will pull the nipple away and the infant will go hungry.
As children grow up their early experience is shaped by
training in warlike pursuits.

Cultural influences
The cultural milieu into which a child is born is highly
significant in determining many aspects of the life style
and characteristics the individual will adopt. The process
of socialization is a sometimes pleasurable, sometimes
painful route, which children travel in their own unique
way, acquiring those minimal social and personality attributes regarded as desirable by the community. Of course,
they do not become an exact replica of fellow group members. As we saw in chapter 4, many influences operate to
make each individual quite unique; Kluckhohn and Murray
(1953) put it in this way: 'every man is in certain respects like all other men, like some other men, like no
other man'. Even identical twins - sharing precisely the
same genetic endowment - can be socialized in different
ways to become very different persons.

Personality represents the enduring properties of individuals which tend to separate them from other individuals. It expresses consistency and regularity. Personality includes both structure and dynamics, in the sense that it is characterized both by parts and by relationships among the parts. In this sense it can be viewed as a system. Indeed Allport (1937), in a classical text, definedperson-ality as a dynamic organization within individuals of those psycho-physical systems which determine their unique adjustments to the environment.

This rather technical-sounding definition emphasizes certain important features of personality. It stresses the changing (dynamic) nature of personality. Personality is less a finished product than a transitive process. It has some stable features; at the same time, it is continually undergoing change. Allport (1955) described this course of change, or 'individuation', as a process of 'becoming'. It is one of the paradoxes of social case work that social workers spend much of their time delving into clients' past experiences, whereas clients themselves are preoccupied with the present and in projecting their life towards the future.

The definition also stresses the inter-relatedness (organization) of different personal traits. In other words, humans are not simply a static aggregation of qualities. Allport emphasizes the psychological and physical bases (psychophysical systems) of human attitudes, habits, values, emotions, beliefs, motives and sentiments. These in turn determine the unique adjustments individuals will make to any situation (family, school, work or community) in which they find themselves. They, in turn, are shaped by the environment, so there is a continuing transaction between the individual and the environment.

A transactional model stresses the changing character of the environment and of the organism as an active participant in its own development. The child's response to events, for example, is thought to be more than a simple reaction to the environment. The child is thought to be actively engaged in attempts to organize and structure the world. He or she is not a 'tabula rasa' passively accepting the etchings of experience. The infant is already something of an individual at birth, reaching out in its own way to 'shape' the environment. Among the idiosyncracies which have been demonstrated in early infancy are autonomic response patterns, social responsiveness (cuddliness), regularity of sleeping, feeding and other biological patterns, and perceptual responses (Thomas et al., 1968).

Temperament   There are others to take account of, in particular the 'temperamental' factors related to the child's general level of activity, sensory threshold, intensity of response and the general affective tone of the child's transactions with the environment. Emphasis is on the 'how' rather than the 'why' or 'what' of behaviour. Any social worker who has worked on the maternity ward of a hospital so as to be able to contrast babies knows that they differ markedly in temperament. This term is essentially applied to the inherited (or innate) aspects of personality and is used to describe the person's characteristic behavioural style independently of the content of his or her specific behaviour.

Historically, the psychological notion of temperament originated with Galen, the Greek physician of the second century AD, who developed it from an earlier theory based on the assumption of four basic fluids (humours) which were supposed to produce four types of temperament: the warm and pleasant (sanguine), slow-moving (apathetic), sad and depressed (melancholic) and the hot-tempered and quick to react (choleric). His theory was one of the first of many attempts to classify people into types.

Personality types

Among the many factors which are thought to predispose a client to one sort of problem rather than another are the basic combinations of such personality attributes as extraversion-introversion and neuroticism (also known as emotionality or instability). The psychologist Hans Eysenck (1963), among others, has systematically studied the traits making up these personality types. He described the typical extravert as sociable, a person who likes parties, needs to have people to talk to and does not like reading or studying alone. This type tends to crave excitement, takes chances, is impulsive, sticks his or her neck out, and behaves on the spur of the moment. Extraverts are care-free, easy-going, fond of practical jokes, like change, and always have a ready answer. They tend to be optimistic, laugh a lot and prefer to keep on the move. They are inclined to be aggressive and lose their temper rather swiftly.

Eysenck's characterization of the typical introvert encompasses a very different sort of person. This type tends to be shy, quiet and retiring, introspective and more attracted to books than people at large. Introverts tend to plan ahead, being cautious rather than impulsive. They avoid excitement, take matters of everyday life with some seriousness and prefer a well-ordered style of life. They keep their feelings under tight control, are not aggressive and not hot-tempered. They are more reliable than the extravert, and more pessimistic. They place a lot of emphasis on ethical issues.

These descriptions are, of course, profiles of 'pure' types and do not necessarily fit people who tend to be extraverted or introverted in only some respects. It is a matter of degree. The term 'personality dimension' has been introduced to represent the fact that people can be assigned a position (depending on a personality test score) somewhere along a scale, such as extraversion-introversion.

These personality dimensions are thought to arise from genetic and environmental causes. There are thought to be differences in certain nervous processes in the brain which determine some of the characteristic behaviour patterns and traits of the extravert and introvert. Because of their hereditary make-up, some individuals have more sensitive or reactive central nervous systems than others. Experimental studies and comparisons of identical and fraternal twins provide the evidence for this claim. Although it is commonly said that a person is a 'born' extravert or 'born' introvert, early family and other environmental experiences also have their effect. Happy social experiences encourage the child to want to repeat them. By comparison, too many miserable social experiences tend to reinforce negative attitudes towards social experiences and towards other people. Children are particularly impressionable during their formative years and can therefore be influenced in the direction of being sociable, unsociable or antisocial more easily in early childhood than later on.

The nomothetic approach

Here is a theory that was derived from the study of large numbers of subjects (people and their test results). The approach emphasizes common principles of functioning across individuals. Such a theory involves the systematic recording of responses and is usually associated with structured, objective tests (see Pervin, 1970, who provides a detailed account of how psychologists assess individual differences in personality, temperament, mood, motivation, aptitude, interests, intelligence and perception of people). Raymond Cattell (1946) also presents this kind of theory formulation. Both Cattell and Eysenck emphasize the structural elements of personality based on a statistical (factorial) analysis of test results. The basic element for Cattell is the trait. Traits are distinguishable along the traditional lines in psychology of emotion (temperament), motivation (dynamic) and cognition (ability).

Three other theories of personality social workers should be acquainted with might be called clinical theories; they are derived to a great extent from observations of individuals in treatment. The theorists Sigmund Freud (1932), Carl Rogers (1951, 1959, 1961: see Hopson, chapter 12), and George Kelly (1955: see Bannister, chapter 8), share an emphasis on individual differences and on the total, holistic functioning of the organism. All are valuable (along with others described by Hopson) in the social worker's vital role as a counsellor. The psychologist Lawrence A. Pervin provides an excellent text relating personality theory to practice in his book, 'Personality: Theory, assessment and research' (1970).

Emotionality
What of that dimension of personality referred to earlier, known as neuroticism? Clients who have a high degree of this attribute are often referred to as being 'nervous', 'timid', 'emotional', or 'highly-strung', because their emotions seem to be so labile, so volatile. It has been demonstrated by experimental investigation that emotional people display a variety of related traits. They tend to be anxious, worried, unhappy, ego-centric and quickly and easily aroused. Such traits set them apart from 'calm' individuals. But we must remember that it is all a matter of degree, not an absolute distinction. The calm person tends to be persistent, steadfast, carefree, hopeful and contented. The client who shows intense emotionality and anxiety is susceptible to neurotic breakdown. Such a vulnerability implies a low tolerance for stress, whether it be physical, as in painful situations, or psychological, as in conflict or frustration situations. There is some evidence that highly-strung over-reactive attributes are in part the consequences of inherited factors.

The issue of emotion is an important one to social workers; they ascribe great significance to 'feelings': that is, the affective tone and content of their clients.

Emotion
The word 'emotion' comes from the Latin word 'movere', meaning 'to move'. Children and adults alike often feel that they are driven or moved by their feelings and, in fact, the study of emotion is closely linked to the investigation of 'motivation', a subject discussed in detail by Allport (1937, 1955). Scientists have investigated different aspects of emotion. Some define it in terms of the feelings experienced by the person, others define it in terms of the bodily changes which always accompany these feelings. Most emphasize the reaction as the main aspect of emotion, but others stress the way in which people perceive situations that arouse emotion or the effect that emotion has on ordinary behaviour.

The term emotion has now become rather vague and there are many feelings and reactions to which the label 'emotion' is given. Some are predominantly negative states such as rage, horror, fear, agony, anxiety, disgust, embarrassment, boredom or grief. Others are more positive: love, joy, pleasure, amusement, ecstasy and so on. It has been theorized that there are eight basic emotional reactions: anticipation, anger, joy, acceptance, surprise, fear, sorrow and disgust. There are patterned bodily reactions and it is thought that the primitive prototypes for these can be found in animals.

In a classic book, 'The Expression of the Emotions in Animals and Man', written in 1872, Charles Darwin proposed three principles for interpreting emotional manifestations: among them was the utility of the behaviour which appears during emotional excitement. He gave the example of the hostile animal baring the canine teeth in preparation for biting; when angry humans curl their lip and show the canine teeth they do not intend to bite but the expression is a vestige of a biologically useful act. Walter Cannon (1932) elaborated this principle of utility to include internal bodily changes that occur during the so-called 'emergency emotions': rage, fear, excitement and pain. Cannon demonstrated that during a crisis the physical changes mobilize the energies of an individual in preparation for a vigorous fight or a flight for one's life. These issues are taken up again in a section on stress in chapter 17.

Emotional development
There is an important link between social and emotional development. The sorts of emotions called delight, love, anger and jealousy depend upon social awareness: a consciousness of 'me' and 'mine' and 'other people'. Newborn infants gradually learn to perceive themselves as separate individuals, and to distinguish 'things out there' from internal impressions or feelings. We have been referring to emotion (in the form of a noun) as if it were an entity. This is the reification fallacy. Emotion is no more a thing than is intelligence, or mind. It is a complete set of psycho-physiological processes, partly learned, partly inherited. What do seem to be inherited are certain physiological structures which enable a child to react with a particular degree of sensitivity to stimulating events in the environment, and to act with a particular level of intensity of emotion. This 'emotional tone' means that some children live at a relatively high and consistent level of activity and passivity, elation and depression. Neonates (new-borns) - as we have seen - differ quite markedly in their senstivity, susceptibility and responsiveness to all kinds of stimulation.

In this volume, as is the practice of many psychologists, we started with behaviour. As Murray puts it in 'Explorations in Personality': 'upon behaviour and its results depends everything which is generally regarded as important: physical wellbeing and survival, development and achievement, happiness and the perpetuation of the species' (Murray, 1938). However, as was made clear in chapter 1, we are not interested in overt behaviour to the complete exclusion of such psychological phenomena as feelings, fantasies, inner conflicts, emotions, attitudes, beliefs, needs and motives. The analysis of individuals' motives helps the psychologist to understand their behaviour by clarifying what is reinforcing to them. It helps the psychologist to predict how the person may act in future situations.

Motivation   Motivation has three aspects:

* motivating states (called needs, drives or motives);
* motivated behaviour;
* the conditions that satisfy or alleviate the motivating conditions.

The American psychologist Robert Woodworth introduced the term 'drive' in 1918 to describe the energy which impels an animal into some action as opposed to the habits that guide its behaviour in one direction or another. The term 'drive' came to be used to describe specific urges such as sex, hunger, and so on.

Biologically-based 'drives' are motives which originate in some organic or tissue need. They are best described as 'homeostatic needs'. What does this mean? The term 'homeostasis' (steady state) is used for a situation in which internal environment fluctuations are held within certain tolerable limits; the body has to maintain a steady internal environment because humans are exposed to widely fluctuating external conditions. If the blood-sugar concentration increases above its normal level, homeostatic mechanisms (functioning like thermostats) cause it to decrease. Body temperature, too, must not be too high or too low. In any homeostatic system (think of the thermostat in the central heating boiler) a response is fed back into the system as a stimulus for homeostasis: that is, the reaching of a certain temperature is the stimulus for a reverse in the direction of change. Such systems are called 'feedback systems'; these concepts have found their way into contemporary social work jargon in relation to systems theory and family therapy.

As we saw, physiological mechanisms take care of many of the problems of maintaining a homeostatic equilibrium, but the body also makes use of what is called 'regulatory behaviour'. It motivates the regulatory behaviour that is instrumental in satisfying the physiological needs. Since homeostasis is necessary for life and since a primary goal of behaviour is to maintain life at an optimal level, it is scarcely surprising that a secondary goal of behaviour is the maintenance of what might be called 'psychological homeostasis': a form of tension reduction. To give an example, someone with a reputation as an up-and-coming executive reacts to the arrival of a highly experienced newcomer in the firm by extra endeavour in order to maintain status. This behaviour might be described as analogous to a homeostatic mechanism, and is designed to restore mental equilibrium. Biological needs and psychological (or social) needs are accompanied by feelings of tension or disequilibrium. Much of our psychological adjustive behaviour can be thought of as reducing tension.

Social motives

There are many social motives (or needs). To mention but a few:

* security;
* approval;
* power;
* affiliation (companionship);
* sympathy;
* self-actualization (self-fulfilment).

These secondary motives, as they are called, are learned as a result of the unique experiences of the individual in various environments. There are several theories which try to explain social/psychological motives as derivatives of more basic physiological ones, hence terms such as secondary or acquired motives/drives. None are totally convincing.

Needs

This is a familiar term in the social worker's vocabulary; for example, the 'needs' of the child have to be considered in adoption or care proceeding decisions. A social need is usually defined as a state of disequilibrium, for instance, a need for love and affection, which drives the individual in a direction which will restore equilibrium (e.g. looking for a marital partner). Although some psychologists have rejected the directional (that is, motivational) aspects of living processes, most sciences have accepted such tendencies.

Needs and motives usually manifest themselves in relation to particular kinds of stimulus situations. The stimulus situation is that part of the total environment to which the individual attends and reacts. The environment as it appears in a psychological description occurs not most often as a physical or chemical agent impinging on the body or sense organs, but in terms of its meaning for the individual. Notcutt (1953) states that the same stimulus may have many different meanings, and many different stimuli may have the same meaning. It is the meanings that are important and not the stimulus in its own nature as a physical or chemical process. This notion of 'meaning' - mediating stimulus and response - takes us to the cognitive aspects of personality.

Cognitive learning

According to Albert Bandura and many other theorists, the processes that govern human adjustment (and maladjustment) are cognitive in nature. Bandura (1977) points out that if human behaviour could be fully explained in terms of external stimulus conditions, there would be no need to postulate any additional regulating mechanisms. Reviews of the evidence on operant and classical conditioning in adult humans seem to indicate that awareness (a cognitive process) mediates the so-called conditioning processes. Behaviour is not always predictable from external sources of influence; cognitive factors, in part, determine what we observe, feel, and do at any particular point in time.

Cognitive learning is a generic term for learning about the world by the use of reasoning, judgement, imagination, and various perceptual and conceptual abilities. Such learning makes use of images, symbols, concepts and rules. Cognitive processes involved in cognitive learning include attentional processes, the encoding of information, the storage and retrieval of information in memory, the positing of hypotheses, their evaluation, and inductive and deductive reasoning. These are some of the attributes which are measured in estimates of a person's intelligence.

Intelligence

There is no definitive statement to be made about the nature of intelligence. To begin with, it is a multi-faceted phenomenon; intellectual activity takes many forms. Psychologists have found the term useful to summarize many mental activities which underlie behaviour we choose to call 'intelligent' or 'unintelligent' in everyday life. We talk of verbal intelligence (a facility with words and verbal problems) and spatial intelligence (a facility with spatial relationships) and so on.

Intelligence matures rapidly during childhood until about 12. The rate of growth slows down until, for the majority of the population, maximum intellectual capacity in the biological sense is reached somewhere between the ages of 15 and 25. Early investigations of intellectual changes associated with ageing suggested (as we saw) that full intellectual capacity is reached by the early twenties, followed by a more or less static period (a plateau) and then by a slow, long decline. Early studies were concerned with different age cross-sections of the population which meant that older groups were not always as well-educated, quick or highly motivated and confident to do intelligence tests as younger groups. Consequently, the early reports were in error in significant ways. More recent studies have been of the longitudinal kind, which is to say that the same individuals are followed up and re-tested over long periods of time. The first longitudinal reports that showed continuing intellectual gains in older adults were from investigations of gifted individuals, and as a result continued gains were thought to be characteristic only of people of superior intelligence. Later studies included individuals of more average abilities and even in these circumstances, gains in adult intellectual activity have been observed.

Theoreticians have divided intelligence into an un-specified type of intellectual ability (Type A), also referred to as 'fluid ability', or 'g' (general ability), which involves abstract thinking, capacity for perceiving and discriminating between things, discerning relation-ships and groupings and working out implications. It reveals itself in new situations where successful adapta-tion cannot rely on the person's existing repertoire of intellectual skills. This ability reaches its maximum growth at the same time as general biological maturity, at adolescence. The subsequent decline is not noticeable until after the age of about 25. Another type of intellec-tual ability is postulated. This is Type B, a specialized ability sometimes referred to as 'crystallized ability' or 'verbal and educational ability'. It consists of cognitive skills and conceptual categories which allow the indivi-dual to assimilate and learn from new experiences. Crystal-lized intelligence reveals itself in those tests which require learned habits or thinking. This ability may con-tinue to develop (particularly in individuals who use their minds) throughout adult life. The psychologist Dennis Bromley makes the point that during maturity and old age, intellectual activity is concerned mainly with the application of acquired techniques and the assimila-tion of experience to established frames of reference. The wisdom of the older person is the wisdom of experience because, as unspecialized mental ability declines with age, the older person relies more on what has been learn-ed. The wisdom of the younger person is the wisdom of insight because, as specialized mental ability is lacking for want of experience, the younger person must think things out from first principles (Bromley, 1968).

Personality also changes and develops. It is the execu-tive processes of personality which come to prominence in middle age: self-awareness, selectivity, manipulation and control of the environment, mastery, competence, and a wide array of strategies for coping with life. The middle-aged individual places more importance on, above all, the restructuring of experience: that is, the processing of new information in the light of past experience. Forty-year-olds often seem to see the environment as one that rewards boldness and the taking of risks, and they per-ceive themselves as having the energy to deal with the opportunities they see around them.

There is another important component of mind to con-sider: the self-concept.

The self-concept　　Common sense would seem to demand concepts such as 'self' to account for, and unify, the complex elements which make up personality. It seems, on the face of it, essential to postulate the self as the integrating core of the indivi-

dual's personality, the reference point around which thinking and feeling, attitudes, experiences and reactions are
organized. Could there be any alternative way of explaining the apparent coherence, unity and purposiveness of
personality?

In fact, for several decades, many psychologists attempted to study personality without resorting to these
allegedly circular and question-begging terms. The objec-
tion of the early experimental psychologists to the term
self is seen in their appeal for 'a psychology without a
soul'. They saw clearly the scientific dangers of invoking
a convenient 'homunculus', or ghost in the machine (labelled 'ego' or 'self') to explain away awkward or discrepant
facts about personality, or to produce consistencies where
there were none. Since the 1950s many psychologists have
embraced the 'heresy' of yesteryear. Allport (1955) believes that the primary requirement of an adequate psychological approach to the person are matters of fact to the
individual; between what the person feels to be significant, vital and central in becoming a person and what be-
longs to the periphery of his or her being. He suggests
that use of the term 'proprium' for those aspects of personality, those areas of life, that have powerful personal
relevance and which we regard as peculiarly ours.

The description 'propriate' certainly applies to our
term 'self-image' (see Bannister, chapter 9). The self-
image is a crucial propriate function, and is referred to
by some writers as the phenomenal self. Allport describes
two aspects of the self-image: the way individuals perceive their present abilities, status and roles and what
they would like to become, their aspirations for themselves: their idealized self-image. Various researchers
have marshalled evidence from various sources to demonstrate that even very young babies exhibit a need to be
competent, to master or deal effectively with their own
environment. This need is referred to as 'effectance
motivation' and is thought to be related to such motives
as mastery, curiosity and achievement.

Martin Seligman (1975) suggests that what produces
self-esteem and a sense of competence in a child (two
crucial attributes for positive mental health) and what
immunizes him or her against depression and helplessness,
is (in part) the actual quality of the child's experience.
But what is also crucial is the child's perception that
his or her own actions controlled the experience. Seligman
states that to the degree that uncontrollable events
occur, either traumatic or positive, depression will be
predisposed and ego strength undermined.

The love and affection of parents for children and
their unfolding attitudes toward them as they grow up are
of continuing importance in the more and more sophisticated evolution of the self-image. But beyond the early
years of childhood, many other persons outside the family

assume an increasingly important role in forming the self-concept: teachers, classmates, playmates and friends. In adult years, work associates, spouse and children contribute to this process. It is the process of identification which is important in incorporating aspects of other persons into the self. Once a person (consciously or unconsciously) is chosen for this significance, the individual not only models overt behaviour after him or her, but also takes on his or her thoughts and feelings and ways of looking at things; in other words, takes on the attitude of the other.

References

Allport, G.W. (1937)
Personality: A psychological interpretation. New York: Holt, Rinehart & Winston.
Allport, G. (1955)
Becoming. New Haven, Conn.: Yale University Press.
Bandura, A. (1977)
Social Learning Theory. Englewood Cliffs, NJ: Prentice-Hall.
Bromley, D.B. (1968)
The Psychology of Human Ageing. Harmondsworth: Penguin Books.
Cannon, W.B. (1932)
The Wisdom of the Body. New York: Norton.
Cattell, R.B. (1946)
The Description and Measurement of Personality. Yonkers, NY: World Book Co.
Darwin, C. (1872)
The Expression of the Emotions in Animals and Man. New York: John Murray.
Eysenck, H.J. (1963)
Uses and Abuses of Psychology. Harmondsworth: Penguin Books.
Freud, S. (1932)
New Introductory Lectures on Psychoanalysis. London: Hogarth Press.
Kelly, G.A. (1955)
The Psychology of Personal Constructs. New York: Van Nostrand Reinhold.
Kluckhohn, C. and Murray, H.A. (eds) (1953)
Personality in Nature, Society and Culture. New York: Knopf.
Mead, M. (1935)
Sex and Temperament in Three Primitive Societies. London: Routledge and Kegan Paul.
Murray, H.A. (1938)
Explorations in Personality. New York: Oxford University Press.
Notcutt B. (1953)
The Psychology of Personality. New York: Philosophical Library.

Pervin, L.A. (1970)
Personality: Theory, assessment and research. New York: Wiley.
Rogers, C.R. (1951)
Client-Centered Therapy. Boston: Houghton-Mifflin.
Rogers, C.R. (1959)
A theory of therapy, personality and interpersonal relationships, as developed in the client-centred framework. In S. Koch (ed.), Psychology: The study of a science, 3. New York: McGraw-Hill.
Rogers, C.R. (1961)
On Becoming a Person: A therapist's view of psychotherapy. Boston: Houghton-Mifflin.
Seligman, M.E.P. (1975)
Helplessness. San Francisco: Freeman.
Thomas, A., Chess, S. and Birch, H.G. (1968)
Temperament and Behaviour Disorder in Children. London: University of London Press.
Woodworth, R.S. (1918)
Dynamic Psychology. Milford, USA: Jesup Lectures, 191 1917.

7

Psychopathology: models of causation and change

Psychopathology is the study of 'diseases of the mind'
(see Shapiro, chapter 17). Humans have always suffered
from mental illness. Studies carried out in this century
indicate that the members of primitive, pastoral societies
suffered from all the mental diseases that are known in
modern industrial nations, even though the manifestations
and treatment were sometimes different. For centuries the
bizarre behaviour of the mentally ill aroused the cruel
hostility and prejudice of ignorance.

Very early in the development of medicine societies
devised ways to treat mental disorders. Skulls have been
found with holes cut carefully in them - an operation
carried out while their owners were alive - showing that
trepanning, as this procedure is called, was used by far-
flung cultures. More recently, patients were made to walk
along dark corridors with trap-doors, through which they
fell into ice-cold water below, to shock them back to
normality.

In the twentieth century increasing numbers of people
have suffered from various forms of mental illness; now-
adays, with the improvement in standards of physical
health, their problems have received greater attention.

Definitions

The terms 'insanity' and 'madness' are the colloquial expressions often applied to psychological disturbance in
adults. In the very old Hollywood films, the scheming villain tried to drive his heiress wife crazy by a series of
nefarious tricks, like her counterpart, the heroine from
even earlier movies, who teetered on the edge of a preci-
pice while the dastardly villain tried to push her over.
The victim, nearly 'terrified out of her wits', or 'driven
out of her senses', teeters on the edge of the chasm of
insanity. For the authors of these melodramas and the fascinated audiences who watched them, the issue was quite
simple: there was a clear-cut dividing line between sanity
and insanity. The popular view, even today, is that there
is a breaking point - a fairly precise point - at which
some overwhelming emotion, or profound physical illness,

or excessive fatigue might lead to 'a nervous breakdown'. It is, in fact, much more complicated than this. How does one recognize that a change - which would be labelled insanity (or to use the correct psychiatric term, psychosis) - has actually taken place? As far as the public are concerned, they can tolerate a great deal of peculiar behaviour, eccentric ideas and strange manners and speech, as long as the individual does not threaten or attempt to do anything which threatens his own or other people's safety. It is basically the loss of self-control which is the distinguishing mark of what the public regards as insanity, and it is very much the same for the individual. It is at that point when they have to admit, 'I have lost my self-control, I am no longer master of my own mind' that people doubt their own sanity. To establish the insanity of a person in a court of law it must be demonstrated that the person does not know the difference between right and wrong, or is unable to exercise that control over his or her actions generally expected and observed in the average individual.

Psychiatrists have moved away from legal definitions and would tend to diagnose mental illness by the presence of 'symptoms'. Individuals' mental functions are so profoundly disturbed that they are incapacitated from participating in everyday activities. They usually show signs of thought disorder, including delusions and hallucinations and disturbed motor behaviour, all of which give the bizarre, irrational colouring to their behaviour. Essentially, there is an alteration of that central aspect of his personality: his ego, or self. Sometimes it is the disintegration or fragmentation of the various aspects of self which usually work harmoniously together. But there are many mentally ill patients who do not show such extreme symptoms. Here is one of the most trying problems o deciding upon the presence or absence of mental abnormality; the symptoms of mental illness are so often only the exaggeration of traits occurring in normal people. When does a sense of injustice or resentment or suspicion become paranoid: that is to say, a delusion of persecution? When does shyness and solitariness or imaginative introspection become schizoid? These are not easy questions to answer. Certainly the issue of mental health and mental ill-health are not simple matters or straight opposites like black and white.

Every society has certain patterns of behaviour which it expects from its members. The eminent psychiatrist Karl Menninger (1963) defined normality of behaviour as the adjustment of human beings to the world and to each other with a maximum of effectiveness and happiness. A reading of popular literature shows that wisdom - that pinnacle of our social ideals - is perceived as adapting oneself to nature or to one's environment, an effort after harmony, a striving for self-control. It is not surprising that society should expect a 'wise person' to be well-balanced, someone in harmony with the world, someone with self-possession.

What is this concept of 'adjustment' or 'adaptation' which psychologists are so fond of using?

The nature of adjustment

Living creatures can exist only within rather narrow limits of pressure and temperature and under a limited variety of chemical conditions. Adjustment is biologically and psychologically fundamental to life. As beings that consume energy, they must adjust their input of energy to their output at all times. This effort, with its particular and often precise demands, is termed adaptation. Adaptation is a concept which is central to Charles Darwin's theory of evolution. Over countless thousands of years, new species appeared and flourished because genetic mutations allowed some forms of life to adapt better than others to their often harsh circumstances.

The fascinating subject, of course, is the person who, because of the complexity and flexibility of his or her adjustive equipment (complex brain, flexible fingers, upright position, etc.), has attained a pre-eminent position on earth. Human living is a matter of give-and-take, a continuous transaction between individuals and their surroundings, one which takes place on the physical and psychological level. Throughout life the individual is required to adjust to a never-ending stream of changing events, situations and people. Many of the physical adaptations are reflex in nature, mediated by inherited physical processes; but the majority of the psychological strategies for coping with life-situations are learned, many of them during childhood.

There are great difficulties in defining effective adjustment. If adjustment is efficient, that is, favourable in its consequences, psychologists tend to call it normal. The word normal comes from the Latin 'norma' meaning a 'standard' or 'rule'. A norm is a standard prescribed by society, in the case of social norms. The word normal is usually taken to mean three things: that behaviour is understandable, predictable and controllable. Thus the child who does bizarre things, who is inconsistent - being one way one day and another way the next - and whose behaviour is difficult to control, would seem abnormal and cause a parent to worry. The majority of human problems are a matter of degree. All people are aggressive to some extent, all individuals are fearful to some degree, all of us show relatively bizarre, difficult behaviour at certain times. Many ordinary citizens have problems like phobias, nightmares, obsessions and compulsions. Generally the expert will apply the following criteria to answer questions about a person's mental health. What are the consequences - favourable or unfavourable - of this individual's patterns of traits and ways of behaving? Does the person's general style of life and mode of adjusting to situations, or his or her particular tensions and conflicts, prevent him or her from leading a happy life in which he or she is able to enjoy social and loving relationships, and work (and play or relax) effectively?

Even in the psychological realm the slogan might be 'adapt or perish'. Those whose adjustive mechanisms are defective (e.g. the severely subnormal or the mentally ill) have to be taken care of in special institutions because they cannot survive in the outside world. Many, who cannot make the necessary adjustments to life, opt out of it by committing suicide.

Recent advances in the treatment of the mentally ill have virtually all been in the realm of physical methods. Physical treatment, mainly by electro-convulsive therapy and drugs, has radically changed the whole outlook over the range of psychiatric disorders. Many people with mental illnesses can be treated as out-patients and for those who have to be admitted to hospital, the length of stay is now usually measured in weeks rather than in months or years, as used to be the case.

There are countless others who survive, but whose survival is so restricted and in some cases marginal that they can only be said to be existing. Feeling as they do - alienated, unloved, unreal and aimless - they cannot be said to be living life to the full. Some of these people would be diagnosed as suffering from a psychoneurosis (or neurosis). Neurosis is a shorthand term for something as pervasive as emotional disturbance or life problems; it can be applied to a set of attitudes (Horney, 1947); and it can also be defined narrowly and technically (see Fenichel, 1945; Wolpe, 1973). The neurotic person is invariably a suffering person.

The generic term 'neurosis' can encompass:

* feelings of unhappiness, distress, misery;
* vague feelings that life is not being lived as mean- ingfully, effectively or joyfully as it should be;
* a feeling of having lost control;
* a loss of the ability to make decisions;
* a loss of the ability to make choices;
* a loss of the feeling of being real, vital, committed to or enthusiastic about life;
* a sense of conflict, apathy, aimlessness;
* a sense of alienation (with self and/or society);
* a sense of being compelled to do things against one's will;
* an avoidance of situations/people/objects one should not have to avoid;
* a sense of emotional turmoil (anger, fear, anxiety, dread, guilt, depression, disgust);
* a feeling of helplessness, of not being fully in control of one's life.

Many of these problems afflict (for a variety of reasons) the clients of social workers and they rank among the alleviating tasks (helping, healing) social work sets itself. The theories about the nature of neurosis have ranged from the neurological ('nerves'), through the intrapsychic (Freud), to the social-cultural (Mead).

Transition and change are common themes in social workers' problem caseloads. It is important that they should understand how people react during periods of transition and how to recognize the symptoms of transitional stress. This knowledge of coping techniques could offer invaluable assistance to clients in time of need. Crisis intervention is concerned with the short-term treatment of individual clients or families who are undergoing some form of crisis - perhaps an illness, loss, or the birth of a handicapped child - which precipitates a state of emotional disruption and in which the customary repertoire of problem-solving or coping mechanisms fails to suffice. An introduction to various ideas about psychotherapy, counselling and other forms of helping is provided by Hopson in chapter 12. The author could be addressing himself particularly to social workers when he says:

> Today, more than any other time in our history, people have to cope with an often bewildering variety of transitions: from home to school; from school to work; from being single to being married and - increasingly - divorced; from job to job; from place to place and friend to friend; to parenthood and then to children leaving home; and finally to bereavements and death. Alongside these and other major life events people are happy to learn to cope with the passage from one stage of personal development to another - adolescence, early adulthood, stabilization, mid-life transition, old age.

The personality adjustments and 'maladjustments' of adolescent (Herbert) and of the elderly (Coleman) are detailed in chapters 11 and 15 respectively.

During several decades, British social work has incorporated components from various psychotherapy and counselling approaches which have added depth to the person-oriented individual service which has always been its raison d'etre.

Theories of practice: psychoanalysis and the psychodynamic approach

Let us now look at some of the particular theories and ideas which inform micro-level social work. Many of the theories of practice and particularly the ideas about child rearing in social work, come from psychoanalysis. Since the 1950s psychoanalytic theory (founded by Sigmund Freud) has formed an important part of the knowledge normally acquired by the social worker on basic and post-professional courses in Britain. On basic courses it is most often incorporated in sequences on human growth and development (often forming the core of such a course) and to some extent in casework teaching.

Psychoanalysis Psychoanalysis is a motivationally (instinct) based theory which assumes determinism in all human behaviour, the exis tence and significant influence of unconscious mental processes, and the centrality of psychological conflict, anxiety and defence mechanisms in both normal personality development and in the evolution of psychopathology (e.g. neuroses). Sigmund Freud (1856-1939) set up models of underlying entities and mechanisms, the former exemplified by his division of the personality into id, ego and super-ego. He wished to account for the whole of human mentatic at the psychological level of explanation. While he did not deny the possibility - indeed, probability - of physiological accompaniments for all mental phenomena, he did not concern himself with these in any detail. He was concerned with the experience of the neurotic patient and with the meaning of his symptoms (in a semantic sense). He was not concerned (despite his eminence as a neurologist) with the functioning of the patient's cells or nerves.

Most of Freud's thinking was inductive in character. He was not an experimentalist and did not use, formally, the hypothetico-deductive method in this work. Steadily, through a long life, he added further findings and theoretical formulations to the huge body of psychoanalytic statements. This accounts partly for the contradictions and changes of mind in the writing of Freud. While it is a tribute to his flexibility of mind that he was able to modify his ideas over so long a time, this makes the social workers' task even harder, in that they have to spend time trying to pin down a Freudian dictum to its definitive form before even beginning to try to verify its truth. For the experimentalist, there is an additional difficulty in that Freud did not specifically set out his formulations in the form of specific, experimentally testable hypotheses (see Farrell, in Lee and Herbert, 1970).

Freud was essentially a proponent of 'verstehende' or 'understanding' psychology; he wished to answer the 'whys' of human conduct. It is impossible to do more than hint at the discoveries Freud made about the human psyche. It was empirical fact (brilliant clinical observation) that led to Freud's views which, indeed, he changed when he came u against discrepant facts. It may be true that in later years the distinction between observation and interpretation became somewhat blurred. Most critics admit to Freud's genius, and many to his insights.

Freud continues (decades after his death) to generate controversy. Psychoanalysis is one of the most controver-

sial systems introduced to professional social work practice and education. Many psychologists, psychiatrists and
social workers are now questioning the place of psychoanalysis in these helping professions. There is no question of the status of Freud himself. He has had an enduring effect upon the intellectual and cultural ethos of
this century.

Lee and Herbert (1970), introducing an account of
Freud's work, had this to say:

> Three thinkers, probably more than any others, have
> contributed to the dethronement of Man's confidence in
> himself as being of unique importance in the Universe.
> In physical and cosmological terms, Copernicus dis-
> placed him from the central place in that Universe.
> Charles Darwin showed clearly that he had much in
> common with 'lower' animals and that he did not owe
> his existence as a species to an act of special
> creation by an omniscient deity, but that the press-
> ures to selective evolution had been brought to bear,
> through millenniums, on him as on others. Freud,
> against a background of the surge of 'progress' and
> technical development in the nineteenth century sowed
> grave doubts about the rationality of man and about
> his ability to solve his problems - particularly
> individual ones - by conscious ratiocination alone.

The best introduction to Freud is to read Freud himself, in the original. A surprising number of people who
have strong opinions about Freud and psychoanalysis depend
upon secondary sources - someone else's exegesis of Freudian psychology - for their criticisms. However, a fine
account of the evolution of his thinking is provided by
Wollheim, (1971; see also Shapiro, chapter 17).

From psychoanalysis comes an accent on the one-to-one
(dyadic) situation, on long-term intensive casework and a
choice of methods involving the development of insight.
What have come to be called psychoanalytically or (more
popularly and more vaguely) psychodynamically-based theories and methods, represent a significant theoretical and
ideological strand in social work; but it is misleading
(certainly as far as basic courses are concerned) to
imagine that social workers receive rigorous training in
psychodynamic psychotherapy.

Yet many social workers describe their orientation as
being 'psycho-dynamic'. The term encompasses theories of
personality and therapies which assume the existence of unconscious mental processes, which concern themselves with
the elucidation of motives, and which assume the significance of transference relationships. It is the 'verstehende' (understanding) aspect of psychoanalytically-based
theories rather than the application of analytic treatment
techniques which has contributed to social work practice

and which has been stressed in training.

Neo-Freudians

The psychoanalytic movement has evolved over the years and there is now a recognized school of 'ego psychology'. The ego psychologists postulate an autonomous ego which is a rational institution responsible for intellectual and social achievements, and whose functioning is not solely dependent on the wishes of the id. Among the concepts of ego psychology which have particular relevance for social work practice are the defence mechanisms and coping strategies: the ways in which the ego characteristically deals with threat, pain and loss by mobilizing anger, denial, displacement, emotional insulation and so on.

The humanistic approach

Ego psychology has generated a multitude of diverse thera-peutic - 'human potential' and 'training' - movements. The offspring range from the academically respectable and serious to the rather dubious and raffish. Some of the more cultish groups are decidedly bizarre and esoteric.

Among the most thoughtful and well-researched and pro-ductive 'therapies' is the client-centred approach develop-ed by Carl Rogers (1951, 1959, 1961). The goal of therapy is to intervene in such a way as to increase positive self-regard and self-direction.

Rogers comes from an academic background in counsel-ling and is less influenced by psychoanalytic thinking than most others in the humanist/existential traditions of ego psychology.

Framework for therapy

Rogers has a clear notion of the wholeness of the self; the basic assumptions about the nature of man are not pessimistic like Freud's.

Humans are essentially good, rational, realistic, social and forward-looking; however, they may need help with their basic impulse to grow. Rogers states that it has been his experience that individuals have a basically positive direction: that is, constructive, moving towards self-actualization, growing towards maturity and evolving towards socialization.

Therapy is akin to good education and, essentially, to the basic process of socialization. The therapist is encouraged to feel positive towards the client, accepting him or her, experiencing what the client is experiencing and manifesting 'unconditional positive regard'. The necessary and sufficient conditions for therapeutic change in Rogers' opinion are: empathic understanding, positive regard, genuineness, acceptance and non-possessive warmth.

The human relationship factor

These qualities in the therapist are associated with 'heal-

ing' properties. Whether a trained professional has special access to these qualities (or some unique development
of them) is thrown into doubt (surely even for those who
give most weight to the relationship factor in therapy) by
the absence of substantive differences in the results of
professional as opposed to non- or paraprofessional 'therapists' (Durlak, 1979).

**Behavioural
social work**

The behavioural approaches based on theories of learning
are variously called behaviour therapy, behavioural psychotherapy, behaviour modification and behavioural casework
(Iwaniec and Herbert, 1985). These highly systematized
theories and methods are growing in influence. People may
not yet realize the challenge they pose to the psychodynamic orientation which strongly coloured training perspectives in the fifties and early sixties.

What is most poignant (not to say paradoxical) about
the particular points of criticism of social casework
raised by Joel Fischer (1973, 1978), is that they
precisely indicate areas of relative strength of behaviour
modification. It is this fact that makes so bewildering
the profession's failure to embrace behavioural social
work with even half-open arms. There is little evidence
that social workers and social work educators have
enquired seriously (i.e. critically) into its potential
value as one social work method among others. Here are
some of the points made by Fischer (1978) about casework:

* it is inefficient, even where successful, in terms of
  the professional time invested;
* it is not oriented (in the sense of having a relevant
  knowledge base) toward social-environmental change;
* it does not make adequate use of people in the client's
  natural environment;
* it gives disproportionate attention to diagnosis and
  assessment while paying insufficient attention to
  intervention, this situation being encouraged by a
  lack of techniques for changing behaviour and a low
  correlation between the assessment and choice of treatment techniques;
* a reliance on talking (interview) therapies is mis-
  placed as the outcomes are doubtful (most clients
  being treated in the same way whatever the problem);
* a focus on a revelatory approach, that is, client self-
  understanding, rather than on changes in social
  functioning, seldom changes the disruptive environmental patterns which instigate and maintain the
  problems;
* clients are minimally involved in any active sense in
  the change process, and there is a neglect of presenting complaints in favour of more remote, internal
  inferred disorders. The paradox here is that the vast

95

majority of clients describe their problems in terms of maladaptive social functioning;
* high drop-out rates are wasteful of resources. These are exacerbated by disagreements between the social workers and clients over what has to be accomplished during contacts, and ignorance about what the process is about;
* most damning of all is the claim that social work research on traditional approaches reveals, at best, questionable results.

It should be a source of concern that at this relatively late date and despite the availability of such excellent texts as those of Jehu (1972), Fischer and Gochros (1975) Gambrill (1977) and Sheldon (1982), so many social workers and social work educators hold ideas about behaviour modification and behavioural theories that go back to the 1930s or, at best, the 1950s! Some cover their ignorance of behavioural theory and practice by a dismissive comment (usually couched in humanistic terminology) about not being interested in the field because it is dehumanizing, mechanistic, and so on.

What is behaviour modification?
We need to begin by clarifying the nature of behaviour modification; it has grown and diversified considerably since its formal beginnings in the late 1950s and early 1960s. There are certain distinguishing features of behaviour modification and these are succinctly listed by O'Leary and Wilson (1975):

* behaviour modification is based on a model in which abnormal behaviour is viewed not as symptomatic of some kind of underlying quasi-disease process but as the way a person has learned to cope with the stress and difficulties of living in a changing and increasingly more complex physical and social environment;
* since abnormmal behaviour is learned and maintained in the same manner as normal behaviour, as opposed to being a manifestation of hypothetical intrapsychic conflicts, it can be treated directly through the application of social learning principles rather than indirectly by 'working through' presumed underlying personality conflicts;
* behaviour modification entails the rejection of psychodynamic and personality trait labels to describe people and their behaviour. It is assumed that individuals are best described and understood by determining what they think, feel and do in particular life situations;
* behaviour modification emphasizes the principles of classical and operant conditioning but is not restricted to them; it draws upon principles from other

branches of experimental psychology such as social and developmental psychology. The importance of 'private events' or the cognitive mediation of behaviour is recognized, and a major role is attributed to vicarious and symbolic learning processes, for example modelling;

* reliance upon basic research in psychology as a source of hypothesis about treatment and specific therapy techniques;
* specificity in defining, treating, and measuring the target problems in therapy;
* the goal of behaviour modification is eventually to help individuals to control their own behaviour and achieve self-selected goals.

Behaviour modification represents an optimistic ideology
The higher species, as we saw earlier, are able to learn how to solve problems, to change, and to adapt to novel situations. It is this human flexibility, the potential to learn afresh new ways of living or to unlearn self-defeating behaviours, that should allow behaviour modification to command the attention of social workers (see Kazdin, 1978).

Attempts to identify and modify environmental conditions which control problem behaviour are very much in line with the renewed emphasis in social work on social and environmental (rather than individual) change. The behaviour of clients is assessed and changed - if change is thought desirable - at the places and in the situations where they find themselves. Behaviourists, by recognizing interior cognitive events, seem to be losing some of their previous rigidity. Thus contemporary behaviour modifiction belatedly makes room for such concepts as self-control, self-observation, and observational learning. Of course, all social workers are in the business of trying to produce change, no matter what their orientation. But one of the dimensions along which therapies differ is that of direction/indirection. Behaviour modification is highly directive - although that statement requires a good deal of qualifying in the case of behavioural casework. The possibilities of client-choice, a democratic negotiation of treatment objectives and the opportunity for introspective discussion (especially in self-management work) are increasingly allowed for in current practice. Herbert (1981) notes that far from assuming an authoritative posture and considering the art of therapy as a secret cult, behaviour modification is more willing to rally the support of the non-professionals like parents, housewives, siblings and peers, than most others.

Behavioural casework
One variant of behaviour modification, the behavioural casework approach (Herbert and O'Driscoll, 1978; Herbert

and Iwaniec, 1979, 1981; Herbert, 1980a and b, 1981), is anchored in the natural environment: the community. The triadic model, as it is called, is crucial to the social work task, be it in residential settings (Child Treatment Research Unit Reports 1-7), natural home settings (Herbert, 1978, 1981, Iwaniec and Herbert, 1985) and hospitals (ibid). Indeed, there is growing evidence that effective assessment and treatment of many emotional and behavioural disorders requires observation and intervention in the natural environment. Furthermore, the systematic and successful involvement of parents, and particularly mothers, in work with children has increased considerably (Iwaniec and Herbert, 1985). The value of this approach is nicely illustrated by reference to the literature on conduct-disordered and delinquent youngsters - perennial problems for hard-pressed social workers (see chapter 11).

Where else can behaviour modification help?
The areas are too many to enumerate in detail (however, see Gambrill, 1977). They include:

* anxiety reduction;
* conflict resolution;
* antisocial behaviour;
* addictive behaviour and substance abuse;
* poor self-esteem and related problems;
* social skill deficits;
* stress inoculation;
* development.

Over recent years methods such as family therapy, crisis intervention, task-centred casework, contract work and systems theory have all been incorporated into casework practice. These are all ways of approaching particular problems and can be adapted for use with whichever theoretical model one adheres to, be it sociological, psychodynamic or behavioural. Behavioural theory is particularly congruent with, and nourishing of, these ideas (see Yelloly, 1980).

References

Child Treatment Research Unit (undated)
Reports 1-7. Available from the Psychology Department, University of Leicester.
Durlak, J.A. (1979)
Comparative effectiveness of paraprofessional and professional helpers. Psychological Bulletin, 86, 80-92.
Fenichel, O. (1945)
The Psychoanalytic Theory of Neurosis. London: Routledge and Kegan Paul.
Fischer, J. (1973)
Is casework effective? A review. Social Work (US), 18, 5-20.

Fischer, J. (1978)
Effective Casework Practice: An eclectic approach. New
York: McGraw-Hill.

Fischer, J. and Gochros, H.L. (1975)
Planned Behaviour Change: Behaviour modification in
social work. London: Collier Macmillan.

Gambrill, E. (1977)
Behaviour Modification: Handbook of assessments,
intervention and evaluation. San Francisco: Jossey-
Bass.

Herbert, M. (1978)
Conduct Disorders of Childhood and Adolescence: A
behavioural approach to assessment and treatment.
Chichester: John Wiley & Sons Ltd.

Herbert, M. (1980a)
Behavioural social work in families. In D.S. Freeman
(ed.), Perspectives on Family Therapy. Western Canada:
Butterworths.

Herbert, M. (1980b)
Socialization for problem resistance. In P. Feldman
and J. Orford (eds), The Social Context. Chichester:
John Wiley & Sons Ltd.

Herbert, M. (1981)
Behavioural Treatment of Problem Children: A practice
manual. London: Academic Press; New York: Grune &
Stratton.

Herbert, M. and Iwaniec, D. (1979)
Managing children's behavioural problems. Social Work
Today, 10, 12-14.

Herbert, M. and Iwaniec, D. (1981
Behavioural psychotherapy in natural homesettings: an
empirical study applied to conduct disordered and
incontinent children. Behavioural Psychotherapy, 9, 55-
76

Herbert, M. and O'Driscoll, B. (1982)
Behavioural casework - a social work method for family
settings. In A.W. Clare & R.H. Corney (eds) Social
Work and Primary Health Care. London: Academic Press.

Horney, K. (1947)
The Neurotic Personality of Our Time. London:
Routledge and Kegan Paul.

Iwaniec, D. and Herbert, M. (1985)
Social work with failure-to-thrive children and their
families. Part I: Psychosocial Factors; and Part II:
Behavioural Casework. British Journal of Social Work,
15, Nos 3 (June) and 4 (August) respectively.

Jehu, D. (1972)
Behaviour Modification in Social Work. Chichester:
John Wiley & Sons Ltd.

Kazdin, A.E. (1978)
History of Behavior Modification. Baltimore:
University Park Press.

Lee, S.G.M. and Herbert, M. (eds) (1970)
Freud and Psychology. Harmondsworth: Penguin.
Menninger, K. (1963)
The Vital Balance: The life process in mental health
and illness. New York: The Viking Press.
O'Dell, S. (1974)
Training parents in behavior modification: a review.
Psychological Bulletin, 81, 7, 418-433.
O'Leary, K.D. and Wilson, G.T. (1975)
Behaviour Therapy: Application and outcome. London:
Prentice-Hall.
Rogers, C.R. (1961)
On Becoming a Person: A therapist's view of
psychotherapy. Boston: Houghton-Mifflin.
Sheldon, B. (1982)
Behaviour modification. London: Tavistock.
Wollheim, R. (1971)
Freud. London: Fontana.
Wolpe, J. (1973)
The Practice of Behaviour Therapy (2nd edn). Oxford:
Pergamon Press.
Yelloly, M.A. (1980)
Social Work Theory and Psychoanalysis. London: Van
Nostrand Reinhold.

**Further
reading**

Boulougouris, J. (ed.) (1982)
Learning Theory Approaches to Psychiatry. Chichester:
John Wiley & Sons Ltd.
Caldwell, B.M. (1964)
The effects of infant care. In L.W. Hoffman (ed.),
Review of Child Development Research. New York:
Russell Sage Foundation.
Goldstein, H. (1981)
Social Learning and Change. London: Tavistock.
Rycroft, C. (1966)
Causes and meaning. In C. Rycroft (ed.),
Psychoanalysis Observed. London: Constable.

Part two

Psychological Theory for Social Work Practice

8

Knowledge of self
Don Bannister

Definition is a social undertaking. As a community we
negotiate the meaning of words. This makes 'self' a
peculiarly difficult term to define, since much of the
meaning we attach to it derives from essentially private
experiences of a kind which are difficult to communicate
about and agree upon. Nevertheless, we can try to abstract
from our private experience of self qualities which can
constitute a working definition. Such an attempt was made
by Bannister and Fransella (1980) in the following terms.

**Each of us entertains a notion of our own separateness from
others and relies on the essential privacy of our own
consciousness**
Consider differences between the way in which you communicate with yourself and the way in which you communicate
with others. To communicate with others involves externali-
zing (and thereby blurring) your experience into forms of
speech, arm waving, gift giving, sulking, writing and so
on. Yet communicating with yourself is so easy that it
seems not to merit the word communication: it is more like
instant recognition. Additionally, communicating with specific others involves the risk of being overheard, spied
upon or having your messages intercepted and this contrasts with our internal communications which are secret
and safeguarded. Most importantly, we experience our internal communications as the origin and starting point of
things. We believe that it is out of them that we construct communications with others. We know this when we
tell a lie because we are aware of the difference between
our experienced internal communication and the special
distortions given it before transmission.

**We entertain a notion of the integrity and completeness
of our own experience in that we believe all parts of it
to be relatable because we are, in some vital sense, the
experience itself**
We extend the notion of me into the notion of my world. We
think of events as more or less relevant to us. We distinguish between what concerns and what does not concern us.

In this way we can use the phrase 'my situation' to indicate the boundaries of our important experience and the
ways in which the various parts of it relate to make up a
personal world.

We entertain the notion of our own continuity over time; we possess our biography and we live in relation to it

We live along a time line. We believe that we are essentially the 'same' person now that we were five minutes ago
or five years ago. We accept that our circumstances may
have changed in this or that respect, but we have a feeling of continuity, we possess a 'life'. We extend this to
imagine a continuing future life. We can see our history
in a variety of ways, but how we see it, the way in which
we interpret it, is a central part of our character.

We entertain a notion of ourselves as causes; we have purposes, we intend, we accept a partial responsibility for the consequences of our actions

Just as we believe that we possess our life, so we think
of ourselves as making 'choices' and as being identified
by our choices. Even those psychologists who (in their professional writing) describe humankind as wholly determined, and persons as entirely the products of their environments, talk personally in terms of their own intentions
and purposive acts and are prepared to accept responsibility, when challenged, for the choices they have made.

We work towards a notion of other persons by analogy with ourselves; we assume a comparability of subjective experience

If we accept for the moment the personal construct theory
argument (Kelly, 1955, 1969) and think not simply of
'self' but of the bipolar construct of self versus others,
then this draws our attention to the way in which we can
only define self by distinguishing it from and comparing
it to others. Yet this distinction between self and others
also implies that others can be seen in the same terms, as
'persons' or as 'selves'. Our working assumption is that
the rest of humankind have experiences which are somehow
comparable with, although not the same as, our own and
thereby we reasonably assume that they experience themselves as 'selves'.

We reflect, we are conscious, we are aware of self

Everything that has been said so far is by way of
reflecting, standing back and viewing self. We both
experience and reflect upon our experience, summarize it,
comment on it and analyse it. This capacity to reflect is
both the source of our commentary on self and a central
part of the experience of being a 'self'. Psychologists
sometimes, rather quaintly, talk of 'consciousness' as a
problem. They see consciousness as a mystery which might

best be dealt with by ignoring it and regarding people as mechanisms without awareness. This seems curious when we reflect that, were it not for this problematical consciousness, there would be no psychology to have problems to argue about. Psychology itself is a direct expression of consciousness. Mead (1925) elaborated this point in terms of the difference between 'I' and 'me', referring to the 'I' who acts and the 'me' who reflects upon the action and can go on to reflect upon the 'me' reflecting on the action.

Do we or do we not know ourselves

The question 'do you know yourself?' seems to call forth a categorical 'yes' by way of answer. We know, in complete and sometimes painful detail, what has happened to us, what we have to contend with and what our thoughts and feelings are. We can reasonably claim to sit inside ourselves and know what is going on.

Yet we all have kinds of experience which cast doubt on the idea that we completely know ourselves. A basic test (in science and personal life) of whether you understand someone is your ability to predict accurately what they will do in a given situation. Yet most of us come across situations where we fail to predict our own behaviour; we find ourselves surprised by it and see ourselves behaving in a way we would not have expected to behave if we were the sort of person we thought we were.

We also sense that not all aspects of ourselves are equally accessible to us. There is nothing very mysterious in the notion of a hidden storehouse. We can confirm it very simply by reference to what we can readily draw from it. If I ask you to think about what kind of clothes you wore when you were around 14 years old you can probably bring some kind of image to mind. That raises the obvious question: where was that knowledge of yourself a minute ago, before I asked you the question? We are accustomed to having a vast knowledge of ourselves which is not consciously in front of us all the time. It is stored. It is not a great step to add to that picture the possibility that some parts of the 'store' of your past may not be so easily brought to the surface. We can then go one stage further and argue that although parts of your past are not easily brought to the surface they may nevertheless influence the present ways in which you feel and behave.

The best known picture of this kind of process is the Freudian portrait of the unconscious. Freud portrayed the self as divided. He saw it as made up of an id, the source of our primitive sexual and aggressive drives; a super-ego, our learnt morality, our inhibitions; and an ego, our conscious self, struggling to maintain some kind of balance between the driving force of the id and the controlling force of the super-ego. Freud argued that the id is entirely unconscious and a great deal of the superego is also unconscious, and that only very special strategies such as those used in psychoanalytic therapy can give access to the contents of these unconscious areas of self. We do not have to accept Freud's particular thesis in order to accept the idea of different levels of awareness, but it may well be that the enormous popularity of Freudian theory is due to the fact that it depicts what most of us feel is a 'probable' state of affairs; namely, that we have much more going on in us than we can readily be aware of or name.

Indeed, if we examine our everyday experience then we may well conclude that we are continually becoming aware of aspects of ourselves previously hidden from us.

A great deal of psychotherapy, education and personal and interpersonal soul-searching is dedicated to bringing to the surface hitherto unrecognized consistencies in our lives.

How do we know ourselves?

There is evidence that getting to know ourselves is a developmental process: it is something we learn in the same way that we learn to walk, talk and relate to others. In one study (Bannister and Agnew, 1977), groups of children were tape-recorded answering a variety of questions about their school, home, favourite games and so forth. These taperecordings were transcribed and rerecorded in different voices so as to exclude circumstantial clues (names, occupations of parents and so forth) as to the identity of the children. Four months after the original recording the same children were asked to identify their own statements, to point out which statements were definitely not theirs and to give reasons for their choice. The children's ability to recognize their own statements increased steadily with age, and the strategies they used to pick out their own answers changed and became more complex. Thus, at the age of five, children relied heavily on their (often inaccurate) memory or used simple clues such as whether they themselves undertook the kinds of activity mentioned in the statement; 'That boy says he plays football and I play football so I must have said that'. By the age of nine, they were using more psychologically complex methods to identify which statements they had made and which statements they had not made. For example, one boy picked out the statement 'I want to be a soldier when I grow up' as definitely not his because 'I don't think I could ever kill a human being so I wouldn't say I wanted to be a soldier'. This is clearly a psychological inference of a fairly elaborate kind.

Underlying our notions about ourselves and other people are personal psychological theories which roughly parallel those put forward in formal psychology.

A common kind of theory is what would be called in formal psychology a 'trait theory'. Trait theories hinge on the argument that there are, in each of us, enduring

106

characteristics which differentiate us from others, who have more or less of these characteristics. The notion that we are, or someone else is 'bad-tempered' is closely akin to the notion in formal psychology that some people are constitutionally 'introverted' or 'authoritarian' and so forth. The problem with trait descriptions is that they are not explanatory. They are a kind of tautology which says that a person behaves in a bad-tempered way because he is a bad-tempered kind of person. Such approaches tend to distract our attention from what is going on between us and other people by firmly lodging 'causes' in either us or the other person. If I say that I am angry with you because I am 'a bad-tempered person' that relieves me of the need to understand what is going on specifically between you and me that is making me angry.

Environmental and learning theories in psychology have their equivalents in our everyday arguments about our own nature. The fundamental assertion of stimulus-response psychology, that a person can be seen as reacting to the environment in terms of previously learnt patterns of response, is mirrored in our own talk when we offer as grounds for our actions that it is all 'due to the way I was brought up' or 'there was nothing else I could do in the circumstances'. Those theories and approaches in formal psychology which treat the person as a mechanism echo the kinds of explanation which we offer for our own behaviour when we are most eager to excuse it, to deny our responsibility for it and to argue that we cannot be expected to change.

Any theory or attempt to explain how we come to be what we are and how we change involves us in the question of what kind of evidence we use. Kelly (1955) argued that we derive our picture of ourselves through the picture which we have of other people's picture of us. He was arguing here that the central evidence we use in understanding ourselves is other people's reactions to us, both what they say of us and the implications of their behaviour towards us. He was not saying that we simply take other people's views of us as gospel. Obviously this would be impossible because people have very varying and often very disparate reactions to us. He argued that we filter others' views of us through our view of them. If someone you consider excessively rash and impulsive says that you are a conventional mouse, you might be inclined to dismiss their estimate on the grounds that they see everyone who is not perpetually swinging from the chandelier as being a conventional mouse. However, if someone you consider very docile and timid says that you are a conventional mouse, then this has quite different implications. You do not come to understand yourself simply by contemplating your own navel or even by analysing your own history. You build up a continuous and changing picture of yourself out of your interaction with other people.

**Do we change
ourselves?**

That we change in small ways seems obvious enough. Looking at ourselves or others we readily notice changes in preferred style of dress, taste in films or food, changes in interests and hobbies, the gaining of new skills and the rusting of old and so forth.

Whether we change in large ways as well as small involves us in the question of how we define 'large' and 'small' change. Kelly (1955) hypothesized that each of us has a 'theory' about ourselves, about other people, and about the nature of the world, a theory which he referred to as our personal construct system. Constructs are our ways of discriminating our world. For many of them we have overt labels such as nice-nasty, ugly-beautiful, cheap-expensive, north-south, trustworthy-untrustworthy and so forth. He also distinguished between superordinate and subordinate constructs. Superordinate constructs are those which govern large areas of our life and which refer to matters of central concern to us, while subordinate constructs govern the minor detail of our lives.

If we take constructs about 'change in dress' at a subordinate level then we refer simply to our tendency to switch from sober to bright colours, from wide lapels to narrow lapels and so forth. If we look at such changes superordinately then we can make more far-reaching distinctions. For example, we might see ourselves as having made many subordinate changes in dress while not changing superordinately because we have always 'followed fashion'. Thus at this level of abstraction there is no change because the multitude of our minor changes are always governed and controlled by our refusal to make a major change: that is, to dress independently of fashion.

Psychologists differ greatly in their view of how much change takes place in people and how it takes place. Trait psychologists tend to set up the notion of fixed personality characteristics which remain with people all their lives, which are measurable and which will predict their behaviour to a fair degree in any given situation. The evidence for this view has been much attacked (e.g. Mischel, 1968). Direct examination of personal experience suggests that Kelly (1955) may have been right in referring to 'man as a form of motion and not a static object that is occasionally kicked into movement'.

Psychological measurement, to date, suggests that people change their character, if only slowly, and have complex natures so that behaviour is not easily predictable from one situation to another. Psychologists have also tended to argue that where change takes place it is often unconscious and unchosen by the person. The issue of whether we choose change or whether change is something that happens to us is clearly complex. One way of viewing it might be to argue that we can and do choose to change ourselves, but that often we are less aware of the direction which chosen change may eventually take.

A person in a semi-skilled job may decide to go to nightschool classes or undertake other forms of training in order to qualify themselves for what they regard as more challenging kinds of work. They might be successful in gaining qualifications and entering a new field. Up to this point they can reasonably claim to have chosen their direction of personal change and to have carried through that change in terms of their original proposal. However, the long-term effect may be that they acquire new kinds of responsibility, contacts with different kinds of people, new values and a life style which, in total, will involve personal changes not clearly envisaged at the time they went to their first evening class.

On the issue of how we go about changing ourselves, Radley (1974) speculated that change, particularly self-chosen change, may have three stages to it. Initially, if we are going to change, we must be able to envisage some goal; we must have a kind of picture of what we will be like when we have changed. He argued that if we have only a vague picture or no picture at all then we cannot change; we need to be able to 'see' the changed us in the distance. He went on to argue that when we have the picture then we can enact the role of a person like that. That is to say, we do not at heart believe that we are such a person but we can behave as if we were such a person, rather like an actor playing a role on stage or someone trying out a new style. (This may relate to the old adage that adolescence is the time when we 'try out' personalities to see which is a good fit.) He argued that if we enact in a committed and vigorous way for long enough then, at some mysterious point, we become what we are enacting and it is much more true to say that we are that person than that we are our former selves. This is very much a psychological explanation, in that it is about what is psychologically true, rather than what is formally and officially true. Thus the student who qualifies and becomes a teacher may officially, in terms of pay packet and title, be 'a teacher'. Yet, in Radley's terms, the person may still psychologically be 'a student' who is enacting the role of teacher, who is putting on a teaching style and carrying out the duties of a teacher but who still, in his heart of hearts, sees himself as a student. Later, there may come a point at which he becomes, in the psychological sense, a teacher.

However, we are also aware that there is much that is problematic and threatening about change. The set expectations of others about us may have an imprisoning effect and restrict our capacity to change. People have a picture of us and may attempt to enforce that picture. They may resist change in us because it seems to them unnatural, and it would make us less predictable. Phrases such as 'you are acting out of character', or 'that is not the true you', or 'those are not really your ideas' all reflect the difficulty people find and the resistance they manifest to change in us. Often the pressure of others' expectations is so great that we can only achieve change by keeping it secret until the change has gone so far that we can confront the dismay of others.

This is not to argue that we are simply moulded and brainwashed by our society and our family so that we are merely puppets dancing to tunes played by others. We are clearly influenced by others and everything, the language we speak, the clothes we wear, our values, ideas and feelings, is derived from and elaborated in terms of our relationships with other people and our society. But the more conscious we become of how this happens, the more likely we are to become critical of and the less likely automatically to accept what we are taught (formally and informally), and the more we may independently explore what we wish to make of ourselves as persons.

Equally, when we attempt to change we may find the process personally threatening. We may lose sight of the fact that change is inevitably a form of evolution: that is to say, we change from something to something and thereby there is continuity as well as change. If we lose faith in our own continuity we may be overwhelmed by a fear of some kind of catastrophic break, a fear of becoming something unpredictable to ourselves, of falling into chaos. Whether or not we are entirely happy with ourselves, at least we are something we are familiar with, and quite often we stay as we are because we would sooner suffer the devil we know than the unknown devil of a changed us. Fransella (1972) explored the way in which stutterers who seem to be on the verge of being cured of their stutter often suddenly relapse. She argued that stutterers know full well how to live as 'stutterers'; they understand how people react and relate to them as 'stutterers'. Nearing cure they are overwhelmed with the fear of the unknown, the strangeness of being 'a fluent speaker'.

Monitoring of self

One of the marked features of our culture is that it does not demand (or even suggest) that we formally monitor our lives or that we record our personal history in the way in which a society records its history. True, a few keep diaries, and practices such as re-reading old letters from other people give us glimpses into our past attitudes and feelings. For the most part, our understanding of our past is based on our often erratic memory of it. Moreover, our memory is likely to be erratic, not just because we forget past incidents and ideas but because we may actively 're-write' our history so as to emphasize our consistency and make our past compatible with our present.

Psychologists have tended to ignore the importance of personal history. The vast majority of psychological tests designed to assess the person cut in at a given point in

110

time; they are essentially cross-sectional and pay little heed to the evolution of the person. It would be a very unusual psychology course that used biography or autobiography as material for its students to ponder. There are exceptions to this here-and-now preoccupation. In child psychology great emphasis is laid on the notion of 'development' and a great deal of the research and argument in child psychology is about how children acquire skills over a period, how they are gradually influenced by social customs and how life within the family, over a period of years, affects a child's self-value. Additionally, clinical psychologists involved in psychotherapy and counselling very often find themselves engaged in a joint search with their clients through the immediate and distant past in order to understand present problems and concerns. This does not necessarily argue that a person is simply the end product of their past. We need to understand and acknowledge our past, not in order to repeat it but in order either to use it or to be free of it. As Kelly (1969) put it, 'you are not the victim of your autobiography but you may become the victim of the way you interpret your autobiography'.

Obstacles to self-knowledge and self-change

To try and understand oneself is not simply an interesting pastime, it is a necessity of life. In order to plan our future and to make choices we have to be able to anticipate our behaviour in future situations. This makes self-knowledge a practical guide, not a self-indulgence. Sometimes the situations with which we are confronted are of a defined and clear kind so that we can anticipate and predict our behaviour with reasonable certainty. If someone asks you if you can undertake task X (keep a set of accounts, drive a car, translate a letter from German and so forth) then it is not difficult to assess your skills and experience and work out whether you can undertake the task or not. Often the choice or the undertaking is of a more complex and less defined nature. Can you stand up in conflict with a powerful authority figure? Can you make a success of your marriage to this or that person? Can you live by yourself when you have been used to living with a family? The stranger the country we are entering the more threatening the prospect becomes; the more we realize that some degree of self-change may be involved, the more we must rely upon our understanding of our own character and potential.

In such circumstances we are acutely aware of the dangers of change and may take refuge in a rigid and inflexible notion of what we are. Kelly (1955, 1969) referred to this tendency as 'hostility'. He defined hostility as 'the continued effort to extort validational evidence in favor of a type of social prediction which has already been recognized as a failure'. We cannot lightly

111

abandon our theory of what we are, since the abandonment of such a theory may plunge us into chaos. Thus we see someone destroy a close relationship in order to 'prove' that they are independent or we see teachers 'proving' that their pupils are stupid in order to verify that they themselves are clever.

Closely connected to this definition of hostility is Kelly's definition of guilt as 'the awareness of dislodgement of self from one's core role structure'. Core constructs are those which govern a person's maintenance processes; they are those constructs in terms of which identity is established and the self is pictured and understood. Your core role structure is what you understand yourself to be.

It is in a situation in which you fail to anticipate your own behaviour that you experience guilt. Defined in this way guilt comes not from a violation of some social code but from a violation of your own personal picture of what you are.

There are traditional ways of exploring the issue of 'what am I like?' We can meditate upon ourselves, ask others how they see us, or review our history. Psychologists have devised numerous tests for assessing 'personality', though in so far as these are of any use they seem to be designed to give the psychologist ideas about the other person rather than to give the people ideas about themselves. Two relatively recent attempts to provide people with ways of exploring their own 'personality' are offered by McFall (in Bannister and Fransella, 1980) and Mair (1970).

McFall offers a simple elaboration on the idea of talking to oneself. His work indicated that if people associate freely into a tape-recorder and listen to their own free flow then, given that they erase it afterwards so that there is no possible audience other than themselves at that time, they may learn something of the themes, conflicts and issues that concern them; themes that are 'edited out' of most conversation and which are only fleetingly glimpsed in our thinking. Mair experimented with formalized, written conversation. Chosen partners wrote psychological descriptions of each other (and predictions of the other's description) and then compared and discussed the meaning and the evidence underlying their written impressions.

Although we have formal ways of exploring how we see and how we are seen by others (the encounter group), and informal ways (the party), it can be argued that there is something of a taboo in our society on direct expression of our views of each other. It may be that we fear to criticize lest we be criticized, or it may be that we are embarrassed by the whole idea of the kind of confrontation involved in telling each other about impressions which are being created. Certainly if you contemplate how much you know about the way you are seen by others, you may be struck by the limitations of your knowledge, even on quite simple issues. How clear are you as to how your voice tone is experienced by other people? How often do you try and convey to someone your feelings and thoughts about them in such an oblique and roundabout way that there is a fair chance that they will not grasp the import of what you are saying?

Psychologists are only very slowly seeing it as any part of their task to offer WAYS to people in which they may explore themselves and explore the effect they have on others.

Role and person

Social psychologists have made much use of the concept of 'role'. Just as an actor plays a particular role in a drama it can be argued that each of us has a number of roles in our family, in work groups, in our society. We have consistent ways of speaking, dressing and behaving which reflect our response to the expectations of the group around us. Thus within a family or small social group we may have inherited and developed the role of 'clown' or 'hardheaded practical person' or 'sympathizer'. Jobs often carry implicit role specifications with them so that we perceive different psychological requirements in the role of teacher from the role of student or the role of manager from the role of worker. We are surprised by the randy parson, the sensitive soldier, the shy show-business person. Society also prescribes very broad and pervasive roles for us as men or women, young or old, working-class or middle-class and so forth. It is not that every word of our scripts is prewritten for us, but the broad boundaries and characteristics of behaviour appropriate to each role are fairly well understood. These social roles can and do conflict with personal inclinations and one way of defining maturity would be to look on it as the process whereby we give increasing expression to what we personally are, even where this conflicts with standard social expectations.

Kelly chose to define role in a more strictly personal sense in his sociality corollary which reads: 'to the extent that one person construes the construction processes of another he may play a role in a social process involving the other person'. He is here emphasizing the degree to which, when we relate to another person, we relate in terms of our picture of the other person's picture of us. Role then becomes not a life style worked out by our culture and waiting for us to step into, but the ongoing process whereby we try to imagine and understand how other people see the world and continuously to relate our own conception to theirs.

113

**The paradox
of self-
knowing**

We reasonably assume that our knowledge of something does
not alter the 'thing' itself. If I come to know that Guatemala produces zinc or that the angle of incidence of a
light ray equals its angle of reflection, then this new
knowledge of mine does not, of itself, affect Guatemala or
light. However, it alters me in that I have become 'knowing' and not 'ignorant' of these things. More pointedly,
if I come to know something of myself then I am changed,
to a greater or lesser degree, by that knowledge. Any
realization by a person of the motives and attitudes underlying their behaviour has the potential to alter that behaviour.

Put another way, a person is the sum of their understanding of their world and themselves. Changes in what we
know of ourselves and the way in which we come to know it
are changes in the kind of person we are.

This paradox of self-knowledge presents a perpetual
problem to psychologists. An experimental psychologist may
condition a person to blink their eye when a buzzer is
pressed, simply by pairing the buzzer sound with a puff of
air to the person's eyelid until the blink becomes a response to the sound of the buzzer on its own. But if the
person becomes aware of the nature of the conditioning process and resents being its 'victim' then conditioning may
cease, or at least take much longer. Knowledge of what is
going on within that person and between the person and the
psychologist has altered the person and invalidated the
psychologist's predictions. Experimental psychologists
seek to evade the consequences of this state of affairs by
striving to keep the subject in ignorance of the nature of
the experimental process or by using what they assume to
be naturally ignorant subjects: for example, rats. But
relying on a precariously maintained ignorance in the
experimental subject creates only a mythical certainty in
science. Psychotherapists, on the other hand, generally
work on the basis that the more the person (subject,
patient, client) comes to know of themselves, the nearer
they will come to solving, at least in part, their personal problems.

This self-changing property of self-knowledge may be a
pitfall for a simple-minded science of psychology. It may
also be the very basis of living, for us as persons.

References

Bannister, D. and Agnew, J. (1977)
The Child's Construing of Self. In A.W. Landfield
(ed.), Nebraska Symposium on Motivation 1976.
Nebraska: University of Nebraska Press.

Bannister, D. and Fransella, F. (1980)
Inquiring Man (2nd edn). Harmondsworth: Penguin.

Fransella, F. (1972)
Personal Change and Reconstruction. London: Academic
Press.

114

Kelly, G.A. (1955)
The Psychology of Personal Constructs, Volumes I and
II. New York: Norton.
Kelly, G.A. (1969)
Clinical Psychology and Personality: The selected
papers of George Kelly (ed. B.A. Maher). New York:
Wiley.
Mair, J.M.M. (1970)
Experimenting with individuals. British Journal of
Medical Psychology, 43, 245-256.
Mead, G.H. (1925)
The genesis of the self and social control.
International Journal of Ethics, 35, 251-273.
Mischel, W. (1968)
Personality and Assessment. New York: Wiley.
Radley, A.R. (1974)
The effect of role enactment on construct alternatives.
British Journal of Medical Psychology, 47, 313-320.

Questions

1. Examine the way in which a person's idea of 'self' is affected by the nature of their work.
2. Discuss the nature of sex differences in ideas about 'self'.
3. Describe some way in which you have increased your knowledge of yourself.
4. How do parents influence their children's ideas about 'self'?
5. To what extent is our picture of our self influenced by our physical state and appearance?
6. We come to understand ourselves through our relationship with others. Discuss.
7. Examine the way in which social customs inhibit our revealing of 'self'.
8. People are born with a fixed character which they cannot alter. Discuss.
9. 'He is not himself today.' What triggers off this kind of comment, and does it say more about the speaker than the person of whom it is said?
10. Your job enables you to express yourself. Your job prevents you being yourself. Discuss.

Axline, V.M. (1971) Dibs: In search of self.
Harmondsworth: Penguin.
A finely written description of a withdrawn and
disturbed child who in the process of psychotherapy
comes vividly to life. It casts light on our early
struggles to achieve the idea of being a 'self'.

Bannister, D. and Fransella, F. (1980) Inquiring Man: The
psychology of personal constructs. Harmondsworth: Penguin.
The second edition of a book which sets out the way

Kelly sees each of us as developing a complex personal view of our world. The book describes two decades of psychological research based on the theory and relates it to problems such as psychological breakdown, prejudice, child development and personal relationships.

Bott, M. and Bowskill, D. (1980) The Do-It-Yourself Mind Book. London: Wildwood House.
A lightly written but shrewd book by a psychiatrist on the ways in which we can tackle serious personal and emotional problems without recourse to formal psychiatry.

Fransella, F. (1975) Need to Change? London: Methuen.
A brief description of the formal and informal ways in which 'self' is explored and change attempted.

Rogers, C.R. (1961) On Becoming a Person. Boston: Houghton-Mifflin.
Sets out the idea of 'self-actualization' and describes the ways in which we might avoid either limiting ourselves or being socially limited, and come to be what Rogers calls a fully functioning person.

9

The family
Neil Frude

Psychology and the family

The psychologist may regard the family as a background against which to view the individual, asking perhaps how the parents influence the development of a child or how families of alcoholics may help the individual to overcome his or her difficulties, or alternatively the family itself may be the unit of study. The family is a small group and we can observe the patterns of communication within it, the process of mutual decision making, and so forth. It is a system, with individuals as sub-units or elements within. Typically, psychologists have focused their interests on the biological and social nature of the individual, but they are now becoming increasingly concerned not only with individuals or even 'individuals in relationships' but with the relationships themselves.

Clinical and educational psychologists, for example, are increasingly working within the family context and some problems which were initially identified as 'belonging' to the individual adult or child are now seen, more appropriately, as problems of the 'family system'. Also, psychologists working, for example, with handicapped children have come to recognize that the powerful influence and involvement of the parents means that they can be harnessed as highly potent sources of training, and such clinicians are increasingly using these strategies to establish a far more effective educational programme than they themselves could possibly provide. But the needs of parents, and the stresses which such a high level of involvement may place upon them, are also recognized and so the psychologists may well regard themselves as involved with the problems of the family as a whole.

So there are vital problems in the area and there are some impressive results. Let us look at some of these, choosing some of those areas which relate to major social problems and some innovations which suggest methods for their alleviation.

Family planning

Current surveys of the plans of young married couples for families have shown a high level of conscious control and

117

The family

active planning, a reflection of the wide availability of
highly effective contraceptive techniques. The number and
spacing of children are controlled with varying degrees of
skill and success. The number of couples who opt for voluntary childlessness seems to be increasing. In about half
of such cases the couple have planned from the start not
to have children, while the other half postpone pregnancy
and eventually decide to remain childless.

Contraceptive use varies greatly. Despite the numerous
methods available, none is perfect, for various reasons.
Some men and women find that the sheath reduces pleasurable sensation; the pill may have side effects on health
or mood; and a number of women find methods such as the
cap bothersome and distasteful. The coil may involve a
painful initial fitting and an extensive gynaecological
involvement which some find embarrassing and disturbing.
Sterilization or vasectomy may be advisable for the older
and highly stable couple, but a number of people who have
undergone such surgery later change their partners. They
may then request reversal surgery and in many cases
successful reversal will not be possible. The solution to
the contraception problem is thus by no means always
simple and family planning counselling, and the tailoring
of recommendations to the particular needs and life stage
of the couple, is a task requiring considerable skill and
insight as well as knowledge of the technical features of
the particular methods.

Different couples have different 'ideal family structures', often specifying not only the number of children
but also their spacing and sex. There is still some prefer-
ence, overall, for boys, and current research makes it
likely that in the near future couples will be able, with
some accuracy, to determine the sex of their baby. Many
will prefer to 'leave it to nature' but others will choose
one option or the other. This is likely to result in a
relative excess of boys, with longer-term social results
which can only be guessed.

Reactions to pregnancy range from unqualified delight
to profound despair. The option of abortion is now increasingly available. Reactions to this also vary from relief
to regret and while, overall, the evidence is that there
are rarely long-term negative consequences for the women,
several studies have suggested the need for pre-and for
post-termination counselling. A number of women miscarry,
some repeatedly, and again this can be a very stressful
experience requiring skilled intervention.

**Birth and
early
interaction**

The process of birth is biological, but the importance of
social variables is also apparent. The pregnant woman may
anticipate the sex and looks of her baby, but initial acceptance is by no means inevitable. Premature babies, for
example, may look very unlike the baby-food advertisements
which may have conditioned the mothers' expectations.

118

Fathers are now often present at the delivery and there is evidence that this helps the woman in the birth process itself and also helps the couple to feel that the baby is part of both of them. The demands which the baby makes may not have been fully anticipated and the initial period with the infant may call for a difficult process of adaptation and adjustment, just as the first period of the couple living together calls for give and take and the setting-up of new norms of interaction.

Not all babies are the same: they differ in their activity level, their crying and their patterns of sleep and wakefulness. Some are not easy to care for, and may be unresponsive and difficult to soothe. Baby-care makes great demands and the mother may be totally unprepared for the energy and level of skill required. Surveys show that many of them find the period of early childhood highly stressful. They may be tired and feel inadequate and, at times, very angry. If they fail to understand and control the baby their treatment of him or her may be poor and, sometimes, harsh.

The level of medical care in pregnancy and around the time of the birth may be high, but many mothers then feel isolated with the baby, unsure about such matters as feeding, toileting and weaning.

In assuming that a 'mother's instinct' will aid her in these tasks we may have seriously under-estimated the extent to which, in earlier times, the informal training opportunities offered to the young girl by larger family units and the close neighbourhood community helped her in her own parenting.

The developing child

In the early years interactions with parents form the major social background for the child. There is a good deal of informal teaching and the child learns by example. Guidance and discipline help the infant to establish a set of internal rules and encouragement and praise help to develop skills and intellectual abilities. Overhearing conversations between adults enables the child to learn about the structure of language and conversation and the rules of social interaction. Watching the parents' interactions and reactions enables children to develop their own emotional repertoire and social skills, and they will experiment and consciously imitate the behaviour of their parents. The child may identify strongly with a particular parent. Games of pretence enable youngsters to practise complex tasks and build a repertoire of interactive styles, and in collaboration with other young children they may rehearse a number of roles. In both competitive and co-operative play social interaction patterns are devised and perfected, children learn about rule-following and discover their strengths and weaknesses relative to their peers.

Different parents treat their children differently, and there are many styles of parenting. Some parents are warm and affectionate, others are more distant, and some are openly hostile. Some give the child a lot of freedom and exercise little control while others are very restrictive. Not surprisingly, the children reared in such atmospheres develop somewhat differently. The children of highly restrictive parents tend to be well-mannered but lack independence, the children of warm parents come to have a confident high regard for themselves, and the children of hostile parents tend to be aggressive. There are various ways in which such findings can be explained. Do the aggressive children of hostile parents, for example, behave in that way because they are reacting against the pressures which their parents put on them, are they simply imitating the behaviour of the adults around them and picking up their interactive styles, or is there perhaps some hereditary biological component which makes both parents and children hostile?

Probably, as in so many cases of such overall correlations, there is a combination of such factors. It is also possible, of course, that hostility originating in the children themselves causes a parental reaction. We must be wary of the conclusion that children simply respond to the atmosphere of their home. They also help to create that atmosphere and the relationship between parents' behaviour and the child's behaviour is a fully interactive one. Children are not shapeless psychological forms capable of being moulded totally in response to their social environment, but have dispositions and levels of potential of their own which they bring into the family.

Children have certain psychological needs which the family should be able to provide. They need a certain stability, they need guidance and a set of rules to follow and the feeling needs to be conveyed to them that they are 'prized' by their parents. In the traditional system with two parents there may be a certain safeguard for the constant provision of these needs by one or other of the parents, and for the prevention of total lack of interest or of rejection. But if the natural family with two parents is ideal in many ways as an arrangement in which to provide for the child's development, this is not to say that the child's best interests cannot also be met in alternative contexts. Most children in single-parent households fare well and develop happily. For the child living apart from the natural parents adoption seems a better option than does fostering (though long-term fostering seems to share many of the positive features of adoption) and fostering seems to be better for the child than a continued stay in an institution. Even this context, however, can provide reasonably well for the child's needs if there is stability, a high level of staffing, high intimacy between staff and children and the provision of high levels of verbal and other types of stimulation.

The family and stress

Just as the family is a principal source of a person's happiness and well-being, it can also be the most powerful source of stress. Research has now been done to try to establish inventories of the life stresses which people experience and in even a cursory glance through such a list it is difficult not to be struck by the extent to which the relationships within the family are bound up with personal change. Some of these events, like the birth of a handicapped child or the death of a child, happen to only a few people, but others, such as the older child leaving home, marital conflict, sexual problems, and the death of a parent happen to many or most. Stress precipitated by such life events has been shown to have a marked effect on both physical and mental health, and if illness is the result then this in turn will provide added hardship.

It is not only particular events which cause stress. The constant presence of ill-health, handicap or marital conflict can similarly take its toll over the years. On the other hand, the stability and comfort of the family setting and the constant presence of others seems to provide much that is beneficial. Marriage reduces the risk of alcoholism, suicide and many forms of psychological ill-health, and interviews with separated and widowed people reveal the elements which they feel they are now missing in their lives, and which in turn may help to explain why living in relative isolation tends to be associated with a greater risk of experiencing psychological problems. As well as providing the opportunity to discuss problems and providing stability, the presence of a spouse reduces loneliness. It also facilitates discussion of a variety of issues and so enables the partners to forge a consensus view of the world: it provides extra interest and social contact, the opportunity to give love and express concern, and provides constant feedback to the individuals about themselves, their value and their role. Practical tasks may be shared and the person may be aware of being prized by the other. This then fosters the sense of self-worth which has been found to be very important for overall well-being.

Of course, not all marital relationships are good and some may lead to far greater problems than those of living in isolation. Certainly recent family changes and conflict seem, in many cases, to be a trigger factor leading to subsequent admission to a psychiatric hospital. Overall, however, it seems that the emotional impact of an intimate relationship, in adult life as in childhood, is likely to involve many more gains for the individual than losses, that people value the protection which such relationships provide and that they often suffer when such support ends.

**Schizo-
phrenia,
depression
and the
family**

There is a popular notion that schizophrenic illness ori-
ginates in family relationships, and that certain forms of
family communication, in particular, may cause an adolescent or young adult to become schizophrenic. A considerable number of studies have now been carried out to establish whether or not there is a firm evidential basis for
such an assumption and, at this point, it looks as if the
decided lack of positive evidence should lead us to
abandon the hypothesis that such relationship problems
constitute the major cause of the illness. While no strong
data have been forthcoming to support the family interaction claim, a great deal of evidence implicating the
role of genetics in schizophrenia has been found and it
now looks as if a predominantly biological explanation may
eventually be given. But while there is no good evidence
that family relationships are formative in schizophrenia,
there is strong support for the notion that family interaction markedly influences the course of a schizophrenic
illness and the pattern of relapses and remission from
symptoms over the years. It seems that the emotional climate in the home and particular family crisis events often
trigger renewed episodes of schizophrenic breakdown.

On the other hand, it seems that depression often has
its origin in severe life events and difficulties and that
the family context provides many of these. In a recent
study conducted in London, Brown and Harris (1978) found
that depression was more common in those women in the
community who had recently experienced a severe event or
difficulty. Many of the events involved loss. Women with
several young children were more vulnerable than others,
as were the widowed, divorced and separated. Social contact seemed to provide a protective function against the
effects of severe life events and the rate of depression
was lower in those women who had a close relationship
with their husbands. Women without employment outside the
home were found to be more vulnerable and the loss of a
mother in childhood also seemed to have a similar effect.
Brown and Harris suggest that such early loss through the
death of a parent may change the way in which the person
comes to view the world and attempts to cope with the
problems that arise. The study provides clear evidence
that family relationship factors may make a person more or
less susceptible to clinical depression, and again illustrates how the contribution of family life to personal
problems is two-sided. The family may be the source of
much stress, but a close supportive marital relationship
will enable the individual to cope with many problems
without succumbing to the threat of clinical depression.

**Sexual
behaviour
and sexual
problems**

Married couples vary greatly in the frequency of their
sexual contact and in the style and variety of their
sexual interaction. The rate of intercourse does not seem
to be related to overall satisfaction with the marriage,

except that where a marriage is failing for other reasons sexual contact may be low or absent. If there is a marked discrepancy between the expectations or needs of the partners then this may lead to conflict and dissatisfaction. Sex is also one of the factors which can cause problems in the early stages of adjustment to marriage.

Although several medical men and women wrote 'marriage manuals' during the nineteenth century and in the early part of this century, our knowledge of human sexuality was very limited before the studies of people such as Kinsey and Masters and Johnson. Using interviews, and later observational and physiological techniques, researchers have now provided us with extensive information about sexual practices. Masters and Johnson (1966, 1970), in particular, have supplied a thorough and detailed account of human sexual behaviour, and they have also provided insights into such questions as sexuality in the older person and sexual behaviour during pregnancy.

It has become clear that problems of sexual dysfunction affect a great many people at some stage in their marriage. Masters and Johnson have produced a range of therapies which has been shown to be highly effective, and many of these have now been adopted by other psychologists, psychiatrists and marriage counsellors. The couple, rather than the individual man or woman, is considered to be the most appropriate treatment unit, and discussion and detailed advice are followed up with 'homework assignments' which the partners carry out in the home. Anxiety about sexual performance can have a serious effect on behaviour and a vicious circle can easily form, for example, between anxiety and failure to achieve erection. Awareness of the female orgasm has increased considerably in recent years and it appears that the pattern of problems for which advice is sought has changed. Whereas the majority of sexual problems encountered by counsellors some decades ago involved a mismatch of sexual appetites, with the woman complaining about her husband's excessive demands, a dominant problem now seems to be that of the woman's dissatisfaction with her husband's ability to bring her to orgasm.

Opinions differ about how much the 'couple unit' is always the appropriate focus for treatment and how far deep-seated relationship difficulties, rather than specific sexual skills and attitudes, underlie the problems presented. It does appear that in about half of the cases seen there are other serious marital difficulties in addition to the sexual dysfunction being treated by sex therapy, which is aimed at improving other aspects of the relationship.

Family conflicts and violence

There is open conflict at times in most families. Sometimes the focus of disagreements is easily apparent; it may centre, for example, on matters concerning money, sex

123

or the handling of children; but at other times the row seems to reflect underlying resentments and difficulties in the relationship. Studies have been made of how arguments start, how they escalate and how they are resolved, and some research in this area has been successful in identifying patterns of conflict which seem to predict later marital breakdown. It appears that there are right ways and wrong ways to fight with other family members. In some marriages there may be constant conflict which, however, is successfully worked through and which does not endanger the basic relationship.

Inter-generational conflict is also common. In the early years the parents have the power and may use discipline to settle matters of disagreement. Again, the way in which this is done is important and it seems that parents should not use their power in such a way that the child feels rejected. Children should be made to feel that their behaviour, rather than their whole personality, is the target of the parents' disapproval. In the adolescent years, the child's struggle for power and independence is often the focus of conflict. Adolescence is frequently a period of stress and young people may have doubts about their status and future. It is also a time when peer-influence may conflict with that of the parents.

Marital conflict sometimes leads to physical assault and a number of wives have to receive medical attention for injuries inflicted by their husbands. Many such wives choose to return to the home after such an incident although some seek the haven of a women's refuge. Even where there is repeated violence, the wife often feels that her husband is not likely to treat her badly in the future; she may feel that drinking or stress triggered the assault, and such wives often report that the man is generally caring and responsible and that his violent outbursts are out of character. Jealousy and sexual failure or refusal are also associated with attacks on the wife, though it is also true that for some couples physical assault or restraint represents a modal response in conflict situations, and that in some marriages (and indeed in some sub-cultures) there are few inhibitions against the couple hitting one another.

Violence against children also occurs with alarming frequency in families, and it is estimated that about two children die each week in England and Wales as a result of injuries inflicted by their parents. The children involved are often very young, and it does not take much physical strength to seriously injure a small child or baby. Only a small proportion of the parents involved in these attacks have a known psychiatric history and, contrary to one popular image, they often provide well for the general needs of their children. Sadistic premeditated cases do occur but they are relatively rare. Generally the attack occurs when a child is crying or screaming or has committed some 'crime' in the eyes of the parent. The mother or father involved is often under considerable stress, and there are frequently severe marital difficulties. The parents involved are often young and may have little idea of how to cope with the crying child, and there is evidence that many abused children are themselves difficult to handle. They may be disturbed, over-active or unresponsive although, of course, many such problems may themselves be the result of longer-term difficulties in the family.

Family therapy

There has recently been a considerable growth of interest in 'family therapy'. This is practised in a variety of ways and with a number of alternative theoretical under-pinnings but it claims, in all its forms, that when there is a psychological disturbance it is useful to work with the 'family system' rather than with the individual identified client. The view is often expressed that the symptom should properly be seen as an attribute not of the individual but of the family as a whole. By focusing on the structure of the group, on the emotional climate and on the pattern of relationships and communication, an attempt is made to bring about a fundamental change which will result in a well-functioning family and an alteration in the circumstances which have maintained the symptom.

Thus a child who is truanting from school may be presented as the only problem by a family who, in fact, have a number of difficulties. By focusing on or scape-goating the child in this way, the family system may preserve itself from serious conflict between other members or between the family group and another part of the wider social system. The child's problem with school is therefore in some way 'useful' to the family and any direct attempt to deal with the truanting may be directed at reducing the underlying conflict or at changing a disordered style of communication which has led to the family 'needing' the child's symptom.

In the therapeutic sessions family members are seen together. The focus is largely on the group processes operating and involves the observations of such inter-actional elements as coalitions, stratagems and avoid-ances. As these are further analysed, they may be revealed to the family or they may be simply 'corrected' by the direct authoritative action of the therapist. The periods intervening between treatment sessions are seen as being of primary importance for the family, who may then revert to original dysfunctional patterns or may continue in the direction of therapeutic change.

The role of the therapist is varied. Some therapists regard themselves primarily as analysts and concentrate on making the family aware of its interactional style, where-as some regard themselves as mediators or referees or may take sides with one or more family members to provide a necessary balance of power. If two or more therapists work as a team then they may present their own relationship as a model of open communication and in this way try, for example, to illustrate the constructive potential of conflict.

The professional background of family therapists is highly varied and their original training may be in psychology, social work or psychiatry. The theoretical concepts used similarly cover a wide range including psychoanalysis, communications theory and behavioural analysis. Concepts have also been borrowed freely from general systems theory, which is predominantly a mathematical theory with applications in cybernetics and biology. In behavioural family therapy the focus is on the manipulation of the family consequences of individual behaviour and the attempt is made to analyse and modify social reinforcement patterns and observational learning.

Because family therapy involves a varied and often subtle set of procedures, it is very difficult to carry out satisfactory studies to measure its effectiveness. Many of the variables said to be involved are rather intangible and the processes underlying changes in social systems are highly complex. Preliminary evidence suggests that it is often useful but this can also be said of many other forms of therapy, and the 'cost-effectiveness' considerations which play a part in treatment choice sometimes make it difficult to support a strong case for the use of family therapy. Many critics would return a general verdict of 'not proven', but the level of interest by professionals is undoubtedly high and growing. One special difficulty has been the failure of those working in this area to provide an adequate means of identifying the cases which may be most appropriately treated in this way. Any attempt to treat all conditions with a uniform approach is unlikely to return a high overall rate of effectiveness. With a more limited set of identified problems this mode of treatment may in future prove to be the optimal means of effective intervention for a range of cases. At present, family therapy reflects just one aspect of the increasing awareness of the importance of understanding the social context when dealing with a presented psychological symptom.

The effects of marital breakdown

Divorce statistics represent a very conservative estimate of marital failure and a still more conservative estimate of marital unhappiness and disharmony, but the rates are high and increasing. There are various estimates of the likely divorce rate of currently made marriages but one in four is a frequently encountered figure. There are certain known predictors of marital breakdown. It is more frequent, for example, when the couple married at an early age, when they have few friends, when they have had relatively little education and when their life style is unconventional. The marital success or failure of their own parents also bears a direct statistical relationship to the couple's chances of breakdown.

Psychological studies have shown that certain measures of personality and social style are also predictors of failure. If the wife rates her husband as being emotionally immature, if the husband's self-image is lacking in coherence and stability, or if either of the partners is emotionally unstable then marital breakdown is more likely than if the reverse holds. Good communication, a high level of emotional support and the constructive handling of conflict situations are, not surprisingly, features of relationships which are associated with high levels of marital happiness and low rates of breakdown. In many of these studies it is, of course, difficult to disentangle cause and effect.

The process of adjustment to a marriage may be a long and difficult one, and some marriages never successfully 'take'. The highest rates of breakdown therefore occur in the first years, but many relationships are stable and satisfactory for a while and are then beset with difficulties at a later stage. Divorce is usually preceded by months or years of intense conflict and may eventually come as a relief, but the evidence suggests that generally the whole process is a very painful one for many members of the family involved, both adults and children.

Research with divorcees has revealed a high degree of stress and unhappiness which may last for a very long time. On the whole, it appears that the experiences of women in this situation result in rather more disturbance than those of men, but for both sexes the status of divorce is associated with higher risk of clinical depression, alcoholism and attempted suicide. The psychological effects of a marriage breakdown may stem largely from lack of social support, the absence of an intimate relationship and a loss of self-esteem, but there are often additional pressures relating to the loss of contact with the children or of having to bring them up alone. There is a high rate of remarriage among the divorced; and divorce itself, for all the apparent risks which it brings, is still often preferable to continuing in a marriage which has failed.

The 'broken home' is associated with increased aggressiveness and delinquency in children, but there seems to be only a weak association with neurotic and other psychiatric problems of childhood. While the rate of conduct problems in the children of divorce is considerably higher than that for children of stable marriages, there is apparently little increase in such antisocial behaviour for children whose homes have been broken by the death of a parent. This suggests that it is the discord in the home which produces the effect rather than the mere absence of one parent. This is supported by the finding that conduct

The family

problems also occur with increased frequency in homes with continual discord, even when there is no separation or divorce.

Single-parent families

Children are raised in single-parent families when the mother has not married, when there has been a divorce or separation, or when one parent has died. 'Illegitimacy' is a somewhat outmoded term and an increasing number of single women now feel that they want to rear their child on their own. Social attitudes against illegitimacy and single parenthood have softened over the years and this has encouraged more mothers to keep the baby rather than have it adopted.

Single parenthood appears to be more stressful for the remaining parent than sharing the responsibilities with a partner. Lack of emotional support and of adult company are some of the reasons for this but there are also likely to be increased financial hardships, and the homes of single parents have been shown to be overcrowded and often lack both luxuries and basic amenities. During times of parental illness there may be few additional social resources to call upon, and the single parent is less likely to be able to organize a social life for herself (about 90 per cent of single parents are women). A number of self-help organizations have now been formed to fulfil some of the special needs of the single parent.

One-parent families are viable alternatives to the more traditional nuclear families, and most of the children raised in such circumstances do not appear to show any signs of disturbance or impaired development. There have been suggestions that the boy without a father might tend to be more effeminate but it has been found that most boys brought up by their mothers are as masculine as the rest. If anything, they tend to make fewer sex-identity based assumptions about tasks and roles. We could say that they seem to be less 'sexist' than other boys. Similarly, the girl brought up with the father alone does not seem to lack feminine identity. These findings reflect a more general conclusion that children seem to base their own stereotypes on the wider world around them rather than on the conditions prevailing in their own immediate family.

The family life of old people

Old age is marked by declining health and mobility and by a process of disengagement from several life enterprises, notably employment. There may be low income and financial difficulties, contemporaries are likely to die, and the old person may find it difficult to replace such contacts with the result that they live in a shrinking social world. The high emphasis which some old people place on privacy may reduce the uptake of potential neighbourhood and community resources.

128

The major exception made to such concern with privacy is with the immediate family. Typically, contacts with children and grandchildren are highly prized and may be a major focus of interest in their lives. While there is likely to be an increase in dependency, however, this is often recognized by the old and they often respect the independence of the younger family and feel a crushing sense of obligation if they are forced through circumstance to accept aid from them. In some families there is an informal 'exchange of services' between generations with the older person, for example, looking after the grandchildren while parents are working or having a short holiday.

Recent social change has resulted in fewer three-generation households, but with increasing age and decreasing health, and perhaps the death of one of the parents, the younger couple may want to offer the surviving partner a place in their home. There may be doubts about how well this will work out and conflict may be initiated between the marital partners over how far feelings of duty should lead to changes which might disrupt the family. As the children become older the pressure on space may build up, and with increasing health difficulties the burden of the older person may become too great. Deafness may become an irritation, there may be restricted mobility and the elderly parent may become incontinent.

The increased strain on the family may lead to harsh feelings or even violence towards the old person as well as to a detrimental effect on the health of other members of the family. Eventually the pressure may become unmanageable and the old person may be forced to enter an institution. For many elderly people, living with a child is a halfway stage between having a home of their own and living in an old people's home. Both moves may involve their giving up possessions and pets. The quality of institutions varies greatly, but a frequent reaction is one of withdrawal, depression and depersonalization. Despite having many people around the old person may suffer from a deep sense of loneliness and isolation.

While it seems inevitable that old age will always bring unhappiness to some people, for many it is a time of contentment and fulfilment and in a number of cases the positive aspects centre on activities and memories of relationships within the family. Older women, for example, may play a major role in organizing family get-togethers and may act as a social secretary for members of the extended family, and grandmothers and grandfathers may gain great satisfaction from their relationships with their grandchildren. Many of the recent social changes in housing organization and mobility, it is true, militate against a high level of interaction between the generations, and there seems as yet little awareness by policymakers of the social costs which such changes entail.

**The future
of intimate
lifestyles**

Contact with intimates in the family group seems to provide the individual, overall, with considerable benefits.
Significant relationships are highly potent and there may
be dangers, but generally the benefits far outweigh the
costs. A variety of psychological needs are very well
fulfilled in the traditional family setting. The child
growing in the caring and stable family setting can generally develop skills and abilities and achieve a potential for happiness better than in any other setting, and
the adult can fulfil with the marital partner the needs of
emotional support, freedom from loneliness, sex, stability, and the building of a mutually comfortable 'social
reality'. When the basic family pattern is disturbed there
can be grave consequences for each of the people
involved.

There is no uniform change in western society to a
single alternative life style arrangement but there is
rather an increasing diversity. There are now fewer children in families, more single-parent families, more
divorces and separations, and there is a high incidence of
transitory relationships and less contact between generations. Several lines of evidence suggest that children are
valued less than in the recent past; that women, in particular, are looking more outside the family for their role-
orientation and their life satisfactions; that there is
now less 'family feeling'; and that family duties and
responsibilities impinge upon individual decision making
less than was the case some decades ago.

We may expect this variety to increase further as
ideas regarding the roles of men and women evolve, as
changes in biological and 'hard' technology take place and
as patterns of employment and leisure alter. It would be
premature to forecast, at this stage, what effects such
changes will bring to interpersonal relationships and personal life styles. What does seem certain, however, is
that there will be important effects. To some extent these
can be affected by direct social intervention and some undesirable effects may be prevented.

Family life, then, is a key variable in society and
adverse changes may inflict an enormous social bill. For
this reason the effects on individuals must be carefully
monitored. Psychologists are just one of the groups which
will be involved in this vitally important enterprise.

References

Brown, G.W. and Harris, T. (1978)
Social Origins of Depression. London: Tavistock
Publications.
Masters, W. and Johnson, V. (1966)
Human Sexual Response. Boston: Little, Brown.
Masters, W. and Johnson, V. (1970)
Human Sexual Inadequacy. London: Churchill.

1. Consider some of the factors which might lead a couple to decide to remain childless.
2. Many mothers find looking after a young baby a difficult and stressful experience. Why is this?
3. Hospital births may be medically the safest, but are there likely to be psychological dangers in treating birth more as a biological than as a social and family process?
4. Some people have maintained that schizophrenia arises as a result of problems within the family. Critically assess the evidence relating to this issue.
5. Write an essay on alcoholism in the context of the family.
6. The family seems to be the context for a good deal of violence, particularly towards children and wives. Why should this be so?
7. Consider the special problems of the single-parent family.
8. 'The natural social setting for old people is with their younger family.' How true is this statement? Consider the problems that may arise in a three-generation family.
9. Are there 'experts' in child-rearing? Is this process too important to be left to parents?
10. Some authors have claimed that the family is oppressive and that people should be liberated from the limits that it places on them. How far do you share this view? Give reasons.

Annotated reading

Belliveau, F. and Richter, L. (1971) Understanding Human Sexual Inadequacy. London: Hodder & Stoughton.
Non-technical report of the work of Masters and Johnson on sexual behaviour and sexual problems, including details of treatment methods.

Herbert, M. (1975) Problems of Childhood. London: Pan.
A comprehensive account of the problems of the early years, their treatment and prevention.

Kellmer Pringle, M. (1980) The Needs of Children (2nd edn). London: Hutchinson.
Important review of children's needs and how they may be met both inside and outside the family. Readable and authoritative book with important implications for social policy.

Kempe, R. and Kempe, E. (1978) Child Abuse. London: Fontana/Open Books.
The nature of treatment of violence and sexual assault on children in the family, with an account of methods of treatment and prevention.

Rutter, M. (1976) Helping Troubled Children.
Harmondsworth: Penguin.
    Leading British child psychiatrist examines the nature
    of the more severe problems of childhood. Provides
    good coverage of the importance of family factors and
    related methods of treatment.

10

Transition: understanding and managing personal change
Barrie Hopson

In the ongoing flux of life, (the person) undergoes
many changes. Arriving, departing, growing, declining,
achieving, failing - every change involves a loss and
a gain. The old environment must be given up, the new
accepted. People come and go; one job is lost, another
begun; territory and possessions are acquired or sold;
new skills are learnt, old abandoned; expectations are
fulfilled or hopes dashed - in all these situations
the individual is faced with the need to give up one
mode of life and accept another (Parkes, 1972).

Today, more than at any other time in our history, people
have to cope with an often bewildering variety of transitions: from home to school; from school to work; from
being single to being married and - increasingly -
divorced; from job to job; from job to loss of employment;
retraining and re-education; from place to place and
friend to friend; to parenthood and then to children
leaving home; and finally to bereavements and death.
Alongside these and other major life events people are
having to learn to cope with the passage from one stage of
personal development to another: adolescence, early adulthood, stabilization, mid-life transition and restabil-
ization.

What is a transition?
We define a transition as a discontinuity in a person's
life space (Adams, Hayes and Hopson, 1976). Sometimes the
discontinuity is defined by social consensus as to what
constitutes a discontinuity within the culture. Holmes and
Rahe (1967) provide evidence to show the extent of cultural similarity in perceptions of what are important
discontinuities, in the research they conducted to produce
their social readjustment rating scale. The life changes
represented here (see table 1), along with their weighted
scores, were found to be remarkably consistent from
culture to culture: Japan, Hawaii, Central America, Peru,
Spain, France, Belgium, Switzerland and Scandinavia. For
example, death of a spouse requires about twice as much

133

change in adjustment worldwide as marriage, and ten times
as much as a traffic violation. The correlation between
the items ranged from 0.65 to 0.98 across all the
cultures.

Another way of defining a discontinuity is not by
general consensus but by the person's own perception.
These two may not always coincide: for example, adoles
cence is considered to be an important time of transition in most western cultures, whereas in other cultures
like Samoa it is not considered to be a time of stressful
identity crisis. Also, in a common culture some children
experience adolescence as a transition while others do
not. Consequently it cannot be assumed that everyone
experiences a transitional event (e.g. a change of job) in
the same way.

Table 1

The Holmes and Rahe social readjustment rating scale

LIFE EVENT	Mean value
1. Death of a spouse	100
2. Divorce	73
3. Marital separation from mate	65
4. Detention in jail or other institution	63
5. Death of a close family member	63
6. Major personal injury or illness	53
7. Marriage	50
8. Being fired at work	47
9. Marital reconciliation with mate	45
10. Retirement from work	45
11. Major change in the health or behaviour of a family member	44
12. Pregnancy	40
13. Sexual difficulties	39
14. Gaining a new family member (e.g. through birth, adoption, oldster moving in, etc.)	39
15. Major business readjustment (e.g. merger, reorganization, bankruptcy, etc.)	39
16. Major change in financial state (e.g. a lot worse off or a lot better off than usual)	38
17. Death of a close friend	37
18. Changing to a different line of work	36
19. Major changes in the number of arguments with spouse (e.g. either a lot more or a lot less than usual regarding childbearing, personal habits, etc.)	35

20. Taking on a mortgage greater than $10,000 (e.g. purchasing a home, business, etc.)   31
21. Foreclosure on a mortgage or loan   30
22. Major change in responsibilities at work (e.g. promotion, demotion, lateral transfer)   29
23. Son or daughter leaving home (e.g. marriage, attending college, etc.)   29
24. In-law troubles   29
25. Outstanding personal achievement   28
26. Wife beginning or ceasing work outside the home   26
27. Beginning or ceasing formal schooling   26
28. Major change in living conditions (e.g. building a new home, remodelling, deterioration of home or neighborhood)   25
29. Revision of personal habits (dress, manners, associations, etc.)   24
30. Trouble with the boss   23
31. Major change in working hours or conditions   20
32. Change in residence   20
33. Changing to a new school   20
34. Major change in usual type and/or amount of recreation   19
35. Major change in church activities (e.g. a lot more or a lot less than usual)   19
36. Major change in social activities (e.g. clubs, dancing, movies, visiting, etc.)   18
37. Taking on a mortgage or loan less than $10,000 (e.g. purchasing a car, TV, freezer, etc.)   17
38. Major change in sleeping habits (a lot more or a lot less sleep, or change in part of day when asleep)   16
39. Major change in number of family get-togethers (e.g. a lot more or a lot less than usual)   15
40. Major change in eating habits (a lot more or a lot less food intake, or very different meal hours or surroundings)   15
41. Vacation   13
42. Christmas   12
43. Minor violations of the law (e.g. traffic tickets, jaywalking, disturbing the peace, etc.)   11

For an experience to be classed as transitional there should be:

* PERSONAL AWARENESS of a discontinuity in one's life space; and
* NEW BEHAVIOURAL RESPONSES required because the situation is new, or the required behaviours are novel, or both.

A person can sometimes undergo a transitional experience without being aware of the extent of the discontinuity or that new behavioural responses are required. This at some point will probably cause the person or others adaptation problems. For example, following the death of her husband the widow may not be experiencing strain - she might even be pleased that he is dead - but suddenly she becomes aware that no house repairs have been done, and a new dimension or loss becomes evident along with the awareness of new behavioural responses required.

Why is an understanding of transitional experience important?
Life in post-industrial society is likely to bring more and more transitions for people in all arenas of living. Any transition will result in people being subjected to some degree of stress and strain. They will be more or less aware of this depending upon the novelty of the event and the demands it makes upon their behavioural repertoires. Thus, there is likely to be a rise in the number of people experiencing an increased amount of stress and strain in the course of their daily lives.

Many practitioners in the helping professions are dealing directly with clients who are in transition. It is vital for them to understand how people are likely to react during transition, and to recognize the symptoms of transitional stress. Professionals also need helping techniques to ensure that individuals cope more effectively with their transitions, and to make organizations and social groups more aware of what they can do to help people in transition.

Is there a general model of transitions

As we began to discover other work on different transitions, a general picture increasingly began to emerge. It appeared that irrespective of the nature of the transition, an overall pattern seemed to exist. There were differences, of course, especially between those transitions that were usually experienced as being positive (e.g. marriage and desired promotion) and those usually experienced negatively (e.g. bereavement and divorce). But these differences appeared to reflect differences of emphasis rather than require a totally different model.

The major point to be made in understanding transitions is that whether a change in one's daily routine is an intentional change, a sudden surprise that gets thrust upon one, or a growing awareness that one is

136

moving into a life stage characterized by increasing or decreasing stability, it will trigger a cycle of reactions and feelings that is predictable. The cycle has seven phases, and the identification of these seven phases has come about through content analysis of reports from over 100 people who have attended transition workshops for the purpose of understanding and learning to cope more effectively with transitions they were experiencing and through extending the findings reported above.

Immobilization
The first phase is a kind of immobilization or a sense of being overwhelmed; of being unable to make plans, unable to reason, and unable to understand. In other words, the initial phase of a transition is experienced by many people as a feeling of being frozen up. It appears that the intensity with which people experience this first phase is a function of the unfamiliarity of the transition state and of the negative expectations one holds. If the transition is not high in novelty and if the person holds positive expectations, the immobilization is felt less intensely or perhaps not at all. Marriage can be a good example of the latter.

Minimization
The way of getting out of this immobilization, essentially, is by movement to the second phase of the cycle, which is characterized by minimization of the change or disruption, even to trivialize it. Very often, the person will deny that the change even exists. Sometimes, too, the person projects a euphoric feeling. Those readers who recall seeing Alfred Hitchcock's film 'Psycho' will remember that Tony Perkins spent considerable time shrieking at his mother in the house on the hill. It is not until the end of the film that one learns the mother has been dead for some time, and it is her semi-mummified body with which he has been carrying on his 'dialogue'. That is an extreme example of denying or minimizing the reality of a major change in one's life. Denial can have a positive function. It is more often a necessary phase in the process of adjustment. 'Denial is a normal and necessary human reaction to a crisis which is too immediately overwhelming to face head-on. Denial provides time for a temporary retreat from reality while our internal forces regroup and regain the strength to comprehend the new life our loss has forced upon us' (Krantzler, 1973).

Depression
Eventually, for most people - though not for Tony Perkins in 'Psycho' - the realities of the change and of the resulting stresses begin to become apparent. As people become aware that they must make some changes in the way

they are living, as they become aware of the realities involved, they sometimes begin to get depressed: the third phase of the transition cycle. Depression is usually the consequence of feelings of powerlessness, of aspects of life out of one's control. This is often made worse by the fear of loss of control over one's own emotions. The depression stage has occasional high energy periods often characterized by anger, before sliding back into a feeling of hopelessness. They become depressed because they are just beginning to face up to the fact that there has been a change. Even if they have voluntarily created this change themselves, there is likely to be this dip in feelings. They become frustrated because it becomes difficult to know how best to cope with the new life requirements, the ways of being, the new relationships that have been established or whatever other changes may be necessary.

Letting go
As people move further into becoming aware of reality, they can move into the fourth phase, which is accepting reality for what it is. Through the first three phases, there has been a kind of attachment, whether it has been conscious or not, to the past (pre-transition) situation. To move from phase three to phase four involves a process of unhooking from the past and of saying 'Well, here I am now; here is what I have; I know I can survive; I may not be sure of what I want yet but I will be OK; there is life out there waiting for me.' As this is accepted as the new reality, the person's feelings begin to rise once more, and optimism becomes possible. A clear 'letting go' is necessary.

Testing
This provides a bridge to phase five, where people become much more active and start testing themselves vis-a-vis the new situation, trying out new behaviours, new life styles, and new ways of coping with the transition. There is a tendency also at this point for people to stereotype, to have categories and classifications of the ways things and people should or should not be relative to the new situation. There is much personal energy available during this phase and, as they begin to deal with the new reality, it is not unlikely that those in transition will easily become angry and irritable.

Search for meaning
Following this burst of activity and self-testing, there is a more gradual shifting towards becoming concerned with understanding and for seeking meanings for how things are different and why they are different. This sixth phase is a cognitive process in which people try to understand what all of the activity, anger, stereotyping and so on have

Figure 1

Self-esteem changes during transitions

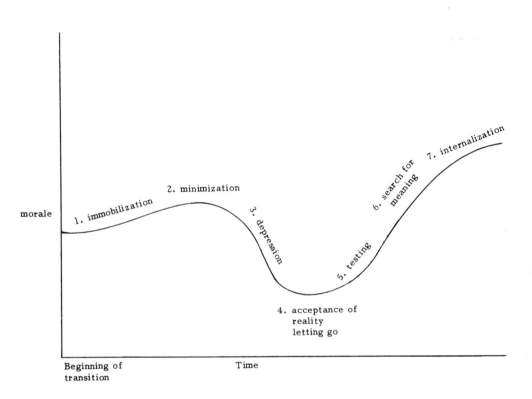

morale

1. immobilization

2. minimization

3. depression

4. acceptance of
reality
letting go

5. testing

6. search for
meaning

7. internalization

Beginning of
transition

Time

meant. It is not until people can get out of the activity
and withdraw somewhat from it that they can begin to understand deeply the meaning of the change in their lives.

Internalization

This conceptualizing, in turn, allows people to move into
the final phase of internalizing these meanings and incorporating them into their behaviour. Overall, the seven
transition phases represent a cycle of experiencing a
disruption, gradually acknowledging its reality, testing
oneself, understanding oneself, and incorporating changes
in one's behaviour. The level of one's morale varies
across these phases and appears to follow a predictable
path. Identifying the seven phases along such a morale
curve often gives one a better understanding of the nature

of the transition cycle. This is shown in figure 1.

Interestingly, the Menninger Foundation's research on Peace Corps volunteers' reactions to entering and experiencing training (a transition for each person) produced a very similar curve. More recently, Kubler-Ross and those who joined her death and dying seminars have also charted a very similar curve of the reaction cycle people go through upon learning they are terminally ill, which is the ultimate transition.

Before proceeding, it is necessary to make it clear that seldom, if ever, does a person move neatly from one phase to another as has been described above. It can help someone in distress, however, to be made aware that what they are experiencing is not uncommon, that it will pass, and that they have a great deal they can do in determining how quickly it will pass.

It is also important to point out that each person's experience is unique and that any given individual's progressions and regressions are unique to their unique circumstances. For example, one person may never get beyond denial or minimization. Another may end it all during depression. Yet another might experience a major failure just as things begin to look up, and slip back to a less active, more withdrawn posture.

What is important is the potential for growth arising from any major disruption or calamity. One realizes this potential and moves toward it when one lets go and fully accepts the situation for what it is; one dies a 'little death' to become larger.

What effects do transitions have on people? It is important to note here that all transitions involve some stress, including those considered by society to be positive changes, such as being left large sums of money, parenthood or marriage (Holmes and Rahe, 1967). Our own studies investigating this relationship show the following results:

* transitions are most stressful if they are unpredictable, involuntary, unfamiliar, of high magnitude (degree of change), and high intensity (rate of change);
* the incidence of illness is positively correlated with the amount of life change one undergoes;
* lack of feedback on the success of attempts to cope with strain-inducing events causes more severe stress-related diseases than when relevant feedback is present;
* interpersonal warmth and support during stressful periods seems to reduce the impact of the stress;
* viruses alone do not cause illnesses. The incidence of bad emotional experiences seems to upset the body and allow the viruses to take over;
* hypertension occurs more often in environments charac-

terized by high stressors and few ways of responding to
those stressors;
* the more major the life changes the higher the risk of
coronary heart disease.

**Every
transition
contains
'opportunity
value' for the
mover**

However undesirable a particular transition may be for the
mover, there is always opportunity for personal growth and
development contained within it. If one takes a severe
example such as death of a spouse, for the majority of
those bereaved nothing will compensate for that loss. On
the other hand, given that the loss is out of their
control, what is under their control is what they decide
to do with their lives from there on. There are opportunities for new relationships, travel, career change, new
interests, etc. Obviously, during the grief process -
which is essential - the opportunities are difficult and
often obnoxious to contemplate but part of the 'letting
go' stage involves doing exactly that. The Chinese have
two symbols for the concept of 'crisis': one means
'danger' while the other signifies 'opportunity'.

**What are the
coping tasks
relevant to all
transitional
events**

We believe that there are common elements in any
transition, which enable us to talk generally about
transitional behaviour. We also assert that in dealing
with any transitional event a person has two tasks to
perform when moving through the phases of the model:

* MANAGEMENT OF STRAIN: to manage the degree of
strain generated by the stress in such a way that the
individual can engage with the external problems
caused by the transition.
* COGNITIVE COPING TASKS: a transition will always
necessitate adjustment. Any adjustment requires
decisions to be made about the appropriateness of new
and old behaviour patterns. The individual will be
asking questions such as: (i) how can I accept this
situation?; (ii) what behaviour is expected of me?;
(iii) what do I want from this situation?

How successfully he manages these two tasks determines the
speed with which he completes the transition.

**What are the
coping skills
relevant to
transitions?**

At the Counselling and Career Development Unit at Leeds
University we have been working for a number of years on
developing training programmes to help adults in transition and to teach transition coping skills to young
people in schools and colleges.
We have developed a questionnaire to be used to help
people identify the transition coping skills they already
possess and which simultaneously highlights the deficits

141

in their coping repertory. Table 2 reproduces the questionnaire designed for use with adults. People are asked to answer 'yes' or 'no' to all the questions. Each time they reply 'no', it suggests an area where they are lacking in some theoretical understanding of the nature of transitions, or deficient in cognitive or behavioural skills. Each of the items is dealt with briefly below, along with some teaching points we make to participants. In a workshop, this learning would take place experientially and participants would have an opportunity to develop and practise their skills. The language used is written to convey the flavour of the workshop approach. The text which follows should be read in conjunction with the questionnaire below.

Table 2

Coping skills questionnaire

1. KNOW YOURSELF
a. Would I have chosen for this to have happened?
b. Am I proactive in new situations: do I take initiatives, have a purpose as opposed to sitting back and waiting on events?
c. Do I know what I want from this new situation?
d. Do I know what I don't want from this new situation?
e. If I feel under stress do I know what I can do to help myself?
f. Do I know how to use my feelings as indicators of where I am?

2. KNOW YOUR NEW SITUATION
a. Can I describe the transition?
b. Do I know how I'm expected to behave?
c. Can I try out the new situation in advance?

3. KNOW OTHER PEOPLE WHO CAN HELP: do I have other people:
a. To depend on in a crisis?
b. To discuss concerns?
c. To feel close to - a friend?
d. Who can make me feel competent and valued?
e. Who can give me important information?
f. Who will challenge me to sit up and take a good look at myself?
g. With whom I can share good news and good feelings?
h. Who will give me constructive feedback?

4. LEARN FROM THE PAST
a. Is there anything similar that has happened to me?
b. Can I identify what I did which helped me get through that experience?
c. Can I identify what I would have done differently?

5. LOOK AFTER YOURSELF
a. Do I know how to use supportive self-talk?
b. Do I get regular exercise or have a personal fitness programme?
c. Am I eating regularly and wisely?
d. Do I know how to relax?
e. Am I keeping to a regular schedule?
f. Do I know my 'personal anchor points'?
g. Do I give myself 'treats' when under stress?
h. Do I have other people who will take care of me?
i. Can I survive?
j. Do I know when my low points are likely to be?

6. LET GO OF THE PAST
a. Do I easily let go of old situations?
b. Do I continually feel that this should not happen to me?
c. Do I know how to vent my anger constructively?

7. SET GOALS AND MAKE ACTION PLANS
a. Do I know how to set goals?
b. Do I know what my goals are for this transition and for my life generally?
c. Do I know how to make and implement action plans?
d. Do I know how to set priorities?
e. Do I know how to make effective decisions?
f. Do I know how to generate alternatives, because there is always an alternative?

8. LOOK FOR THE GAINS YOU HAVE MADE
a. Can I find one thing which is positive about this experience?
b. Can I list a variety of new opportunities that did not exist before or that I would not have thought of previously?
c. Have I learnt something new about myself?

Know yourself
1. WOULD I HAVE CHOSEN FOR THIS TO HAVE HAPPENED? You may not have chosen this situation. This could make it more difficult for you to accept the transition. But it has happened. You now have three options:

(A) accept it and put up with it
(B) refuse to accept
(C) accept it and try to benefit from it

(A) will help you to survive. (B) will bring you nothing but bad feelings and worse; you will be less able to cope with the tasks facing you in the new situation. (C) will help you to grow in addition to merely surviving.

Given the inevitable, ask yourself the key question:

'What is the worst thing that could happen?' Having identified it, ask yourself if you can cope. Is it really so
terrible?

It is essential to remember that problematic situations constitute a normal aspect of living. It is also
useful to recall the variety of transitions that you have
encountered and survived up until now. Through having
survived you will probably have developed some skills. If,
on looking back, you feel dissatisfied with how you managed a transition, it is important to ask yourself whether
you had all the skills needed to deal effectively with
that situation. More than likely you did not. Do not
berate yourself for not having these skills. Instead be
glad that you have identified the need for additional
skills, for that in itself is the first stage of skill
development.

2. AM I PROACTIVE IN NEW SITUATIONS: DO I TAKE
INITIATIVES, HAVE A PURPOSE, AS OPPOSED TO SITTING
BACK AND WAITING ON EVENTS? To be proactive involves
certain sequence of behaviour:

*   knowing what you want;
*   knowing alternative ways of achieving this;
*   choosing one alternative;
*   evaluating the results against your original objective.

The essence of proactive behaviour is that there is a
REASON for it, even if the end result involves no action.
The reason, however, must stem from what Maslow (1968)
calls a 'growth' need as opposed to a 'deficiency' need.
Deciding not to give a public talk (objective), and
knowing various ways of avoiding this (knowing alternatives), choosing one, and thereby achieving the objective
at first glance seems to fit the description of 'proactive
behaviour'. However, if the reason is based on fear of
making a fool of oneself, this would not be classed as
proactive. If it were due to over-commitment, or the
feeling that you are not the best equipped person to do
it, that would be proactive.

3. DO I KNOW WHAT I WANT FROM THIS NEW
SITUATION?

4. DO I KNOW WHAT I DO NOT WANT FROM THIS NEW
SITUATION? If you are unclear as to what you want or do
not want from a new situation this usually signifies a
lack of knowledge about your own values or about what the
new situation has to offer. There is an entire educational
technology designed to help young people and adults to
crystallize their needs and values. It has been developed
in the USA and is known generically as 'values clarification' (Simon, Howe and Kirschenbaum, 1972; Simon, 1974;

Howe and Howe, 1975; Kirschenbaum, 1977). Obtaining more information about the new situation is dealt with in the next section.

5. IF I FEEL UNDER STRESS DO I KNOW WHAT I CAN DO TO HELP MYSELF? Avoid situations where you might over-react. If you have recently separated from your spouse and it is still painful, do not accept an invitation to an event where you know you will encounter your spouse again. Make as few decisions as possible as you will not be think-ing clearly enough. Do not make more than one transition at a time. It is amazing how often people choose one trans-ition to be the stimulus for a host of others. If you have changed your job, do not change your spouse, residence and/or life style all at the same time. A new broom can sometimes sweep you over!
    Look after yourself (see below).
    Do not waste time blaming yourself (see below).
    Remember that time itself will not eliminate the stress or heal you, it is what you do with that time. There are a variety of cognitive shielding techniques that you can use to minimize the strain. These all involve controlling the amount of stimulation in the environment. Some examples are:

*   time management: making priorities;
*   making lists;
*   queuing: delaying decisions during a difficult period by queuing them up, dealing with them one at a time, and not thinking about future decisions until the time to make them arrives. Writing down a decision in a diary to be made at a future date is a good way of queuing.
*   temporary drop-out: refusing to resolve decisions until after a recuperation period. This can appear initially as reactive; however, it is correctly termed proactive as the mover is deliberately opting out of the situation temporarily as part of a strategy to move in later and thereby more effectively.

There are now some excellent resources available for techniques of preventing and managing stress (e.g. Lamott, 1975; Sharpe and Lewis, 1977; Forbes, 1979).

6. DO I KNOW HOW TO USE MY FEELINGS AS INDICATORS OF WHERE I AM? Many people, especially men, as a result of their upbringing are emotionally illiterate: that is, they have not developed the skills of 'reading' their own emotions. One's 'gut' feelings are the surest indicator of how one is coping at any particular time. The skill is in learning to recognize the changes in feelings when they occur and then having an emotional vocabulary to be able to label them correctly. Often when people are asked what they are feeling they will answer you in terms of only

what they are thinking (see Hopson and Scally, 'Lifeskills Teaching Programmes no. 1 - How to manage negative emotions', 1980a; Johnson's 'Reaching Out', 1972).

Know your new situation

1. CAN I DESCRIBE THE TRANSITION? An essential prerequisite to successful transition coping is to know that you are in one. It is essential to be aware of when the transition began, where you are in relation to it and what are all the variables involved. For example, considering changing your job might involve geographical change, relationship changes, financial implications, holiday plans for this year, etc.

2. DO I KNOW HOW I AM EXPECTED TO BEHAVE? Transitions are naturally accompanied by stress even if they are desired. Anxiety certainly increases the less information you have about your new situation. Collect as much data as you can about what others expect of you, what society expects and how you are to behave. You may decide not to live up to or down to those expectations, but again you need the initial data before you can make that decision. You also need to know the consequences of any decision before you make it.

You can ask people who have made a similar transition or indeed are presently going through the same transition. A variety of self-help and special interest groups have developed in recent years to provide mutual support and information to people undergoing similar transitions: ante-natal classes, induction courses, orientation programmes, women's and men's 'rap' groups for people redefining their sex roles, widows' clubs, singles' clubs, one-parent family groups, and so on.

It is important to remember that other people often forget, or in some cases are not even aware, that this is a new situation for you. They may need reminding. For example, one new day at the end of your first week at a new job constitutes 20 per cent of the time you have worked there. For people who have been here for five years, one new day represents less than 0.4 per cent of the time they have been there. Consequently, his feelings about that day are likely to be quite different from your feelings about the same day.

3. CAN I TRY OUT THE NEW SITUATION IN ADVANCE? Some transitions can be 'sampled' in advance, for example, starting a new job, moving to another country; even a divorce or death can sometimes be anticipated. Reading books about anticipated transitions can be valuable, as can talking to others who have experienced it, while remembering that no one will experience it just like you. Where appropriate you can visit places, meet people, watch films, etc., prior to your transition.

146

Knowing other people who can help
There is now considerable evidence to show the beneficial
effects on stress reduction of talking problems through
with people: friends, colleagues, even strangers.

We often make the mistake of expecting too few people,
typically a spouse and children, to satisfy too great a
proportion of our needs. Check the list in the questionnaire. How many categories of person do you have available
to you in your life? Are there any gaps? How many different people make up your 'support' group? How dependent
are you on one or two?

We are also better at developing some forms of support
at the expense of others. For example, people are often
better at developing friendships than relationships with
people who challenge us. The challengers in most people's
support systems are about as abrasive as a marshmallow.
Yet sometimes challengers are exactly what we require to
shift us out of stereotyped thinking. Who are the challengers in your support systems? Remember, you may not even
like them.

Learn from the past
Our past is an important part of our present. Our past is
the history of our successes and our failures and is
thereby a record of our learning. As such, we can continue
to learn from our past experiences. 'Mistakes' are another
way of labelling 'opportunities for learning'. If we can
identify times in the past when we have had similar feelings or experienced similar transitions, we have an opportunity to monitor those chapters of our history and evaluate our performances against the criteria of our own
choosing. What did we do that really did not help the
situation? What would we avoid if we were to have that
experience again? Can we learn from that experience and
generalize it to the new transition? A sense of one's own
history is a prerequisite to a fully functioning present
and a portent for one's range of possible futures.

Look after yourself
1. DO I KNOW HOW TO USE SUPPORTIVE SELF-TALK?
Many of the problems we create for ourselves and much of
the support that we give ourselves derives from the same
source: our internal dialogue with ourselves. This dialogue continues throughout most of our waking hours. These
'cognitions' are vital to our survival and growth. They
enable us to adapt to new situations, to learn, to feel
and to enact cognitively a variety of scenarios without
having to perform any of them. Ellis, with his RATIONAL
EMOTIVE THERAPY, for years has claimed that the way we
think determines what we feel, with the corollary that if
we can change how we think we can also change how we feel
(Ellis and Harper, 1975). His therapeutic method involves
retraining people to talk internally to themselves to

147

minimize the negative emotions which they otherwise would create. Ellis claims that most people carry a variety of 'irrational beliefs' in their heads unfounded in reality, but which result in their creating bad feelings for themselves as a infallible. These beliefs usually belong to one of three categories, which Ellis calls the 'Irrational Trinity' on the road to 'mustabation':

* A belief that I should be a certain sort of person, or a success, or perfect, or loved by everyone, and if I'm not, I'm a failure and worthless;
* a belief that you, or other people, should do as I want them to do: love me, work for me, understand me, etc., and if they do not, it is terrible, and I deserve to be miserable or they should be made to suffer;
* a belief that things should be different; there should not be racial hatred, this organization should run better, our parents should not have to die, etc., and if things are not as I want them to be it is awful and either I cannot cope and deserve to be miserable, or I have every right to be furious.

Since it takes years to develop our patterns of self-talk, changing them involves practice. There are a variety of programmes now available for helping people to restructure their self-talk into more supportive statements. Mahoney and Mahoney (1976) call this process 'cognitive ecology': cleaning up what you say to yourself.

2. DO I GET REGULAR EXERCISE OR HAVE A PERSONAL FITNESS PROGRAMME? Physical fitness is related to one's ability to cope with stress. It has also been shown to be related to the ability to create effective interpersonal relationships (Aspy and Roebuck, 1977) which in turn is related to stress reduction.

You need to be fit to cope effectively with transitions. Yet, of course, it is often when we are most in need of fitness that we are often least inclined to make time for it. There are a number of well-researched fitness programmes available (Health Education Council, 1976; Carruthers and Murray, 1977; Cooper, 1977; Royal Canadian Air Force, 1978).

3. AM I EATING REGULARLY AND WISELY? Now is not the time for a crash diet. Your body needs all the help it can get. People in transition often have neither the time nor inclination to eat wisely. There is sometimes a reliance on quick junk foods, take-away meals or eating out. Remember to eat something every day from the four major food groups: meat, fish, poultry; dairy products; fruits and vegetables; bread and cereals.

Do not replace food with alcohol or smoking. Obviously there may be times when alcohol will help you get through a lonely evening. You need a holiday from self-work as much as from any other kind of work. The danger signs are when alcohol or a cigarette is used as a substitute for meals.

Be wary of developing a dependence on drugs at this time. Sleeping tablets can sometimes be helpful during a crisis, but get off them quickly. They can serve to prevent you from developing healthier coping strategies.

It is a good idea to acquire an easy to read book on diet but one that is critical of food fads. The Health Education Council's booklet, 'Look After Yourself' (1976), contains a simple introduction to good nutrition, and Breckon's 'You Are What You Eat' (1976) is a fascinating survey of dietary facts and fiction, arguing strongly against overdosing oneself with vitamins and dealing in a balanced way with the hysteria over additives.

4. DO I KNOW HOW TO RELAX? There are two ways of reducing stress. One is to organize your life to minimize the number of stressors working on you. The other concerns how to reduce the effect of stress when it hits you. The latter is typically the biggest problem when coping with a transition. Unfortunately, the very people who are most prone to stress illnesses often exacerbate the problem by packing their lives with transitions.

There are numerous relaxation methods, each of which have their advocates. A brief guide follows.

*   Learn a relaxation technique. Progressive relaxation is simple and easy to learn. It is described in Hopson and Hough (1973) as a classroom exercise. Transcendental meditation is now well researched and strong claims are made for it as a technique which directly affects the body's physiology. Most cities have a TM centre. You could also read Russel (1977). For those who do not enjoy the ritual cliquishness that accompanies TM, read Herbert Benson's 'The Relaxation Response' (1977).
*   Direct body work to encourage relaxation: massage. The basics can be learnt quickly on a course. If there is a Personal Growth centre near you, make contact as they might run courses. Read Downing (1972). You will need to keep an open mind regarding some of the sweeping generalizations made on behalf of some of these techniques.

5. AM I KEEPING TO A REGULAR SCHEDULE? If your internal world is in crisis, keep your external world in order. Keeping irregular hours, eating at strange times, going to lots of new places, meeting new people; all these can be disorientating.

6. DO I KNOW MY 'PERSONAL ANCHOR POINTS'? Toffler (1970) described this concept as one antidote to 'future shock'. When all around us things are changing we need an

anchor point to hold on to. For some people it is their home, for others a relationship, children, a job, a daily routine, a favourite place or a hobby. Anchor points are plentiful, and it is vital to have at least one. In the midst of instability a stable base offers confirmation of identity, disengagement from the problem, and maybe even relaxation.

7. DO I GIVE MYSELF 'TREATS' WHEN UNDER STRESS? Thi list of tips has been packed with work. But play is vital too. If you are feeling low, or under stress, how about simply giving yourself a treat? It might even be a reward for accomplishing a difficult test or situation, but it does not have to be.

Draw up a list of treats. Try to become an expert on self-indulgence: a theatre trip, a massage, a book, see friends, make love, have a disgustingly 'bad for you' meal, take a holiday, or pamper yourself.

The only warning about treats is: do not spend so much time treating yourself that you use these as a diversion from coping directly with the transition.

8. DO I HAVE OTHER PEOPLE WHO WILL TAKE CARE OF ME? It is all right to be taken care of sometimes. Allow a friend, lover or colleague to look after you. If they do not offer, be proactive, ask them. Be brave enough to accept help from others. Recall what you feel when others close to you ask for help. There are pay-offs for helpers as well as those who receive help.

9. CAN I SURVIVE? Of course you can. You may doubt it at the moment. Perhaps it will help to remind yourself that what you are feeling now is normal for someone having experienced what you are experiencing. It is also necessary before you can move on to the next stage of finding out more about you and what this transition can do FOR you instead of TO you.

Do not worry about feelings of suicide. Sometimes survival does not seem like such a good idea. If these feelings really seem to be getting out of hand see a counsellor, ring a Samaritan, or consult a doctor; you will probably get more librium than counselling, but that can take off the pressure until you have regrouped your resources.

The feeling will pass. Talk to people, keep a regular routine, treat yourself; at the end of each day recall one good experience, then you can match it with a bad one, then another good experience followed by a bad one, etc., or contract with a friend to call you at certain times.

10. DO I KNOW WHEN MY LOW POINTS ARE LIKELY TO BE? These can usually be predicted quite easily; after a phone call to your children (in the case of a divorced

parent), seeing your ex-spouse with a new partner, just
seeing your ex-spouse, discovering a personal belonging of
your dead spouse, seeing an old workmate (redundancy,
retirement), and so on.

Keep a diary or a journal. This will help you to
clarify your thoughts and feelings as well as to identify
times, places and people to avoid. If you are experiencing
the loss of a love it is usually advisable to fill your
Sundays, bank holidays and Saturday nights!

Let go of the past

1. DO I EASILY LET GO OF OLD SITUATIONS? Sometimes
people cannot let go because they try too hard to hold on.
It is permissible to grieve. Grief shows that you are
alive. Think about what you are missing, feel it. Ask
people if you can talk to them about it. They will often
be too embarrassed to mention it or worry that it will
'upset' you. Cry, rage, scream, recognize the loss, do not
deny the pain. Wounds hurt when you dress them, but you
know that is the first stage of the wound getting better.
It is permissible to feel anger too.

2. DO I CONTINUALLY FEEL THAT THIS SHOULD NOT
HAPPEN TO ME? Then you are guilty of making yourself
unhappy by hitting yourself over the head with 'shoulds'
and 'oughts'. You need to look again at the section on
supportive self-talk.

3. DO I KNOW HOW TO VENT MY ANGER CONSTRUCT-
IVELY? Allow yourself to feel the anger. If it is kept
inside it will only hurt you. Feel angry at the person who
left you, at the person who took something from you, at
the world that let you down or at friends who cannot be
trusted. Hit a pillow, scream aloud (in a closed car this
is very effective; just like an echo chamber) or play a
hectic sport. Do not hurt anyone, including yourself.

Anger is only a feeling. It cannot hurt anyone. Only
behaviour hurts. Once the anger is cleared away, you are
then freer to begin to evaluate, make plans and decide.

Set goals and make action plans

1. DO I KNOW HOW TO SET GOALS? Some people fail to
manage their transitions effectively because they have not
identified a desirable outcome. 'If you don't know where
you're going, you'll probably end up somewhere else'
(Campbell, 1974).

It is essential to identify what you want to achieve
in terms which are as behaviourally specific as possible,
such as 'I want a new job worth £12,000 per annum where I
have overall responsibility for financial operations of a
medium-scale department.' 'In six months I want to be able
to go out on my own, to visit friends by myself, and to

151

have developed one new interest' (this was an objective of a recent widow in one of my workshops).

2. DO I KNOW WHAT MY GOALS ARE FOR THIS TRANSITION AND FOR MY LIFE GENERALLY? This requires the specific skill of knowing how to set, define, and refine objectives.

3. DO I KNOW HOW TO MAKE AND IMPLEMENT ACTION PLANS? Once the objectives are clear the action steps follow next. There are a variety of resources available with guidelines on making effective action plans. Carkhuff's two books (1974a, b) are useful. An action plan needs to be behaviourally specific: 'I will make an appointment to see the solicitor tomorrow morning'. It needs to be in terms of 'what I will do now', not in terms of 'what I will do sometime', or 'what we will do eventually'. An action plan should read like a computer programme, with each step so clearly defined that someone else would know how to carry it out.

4. DO I KNOW HOW TO SET PRIORITIES? Having a variety of goals is one thing, having the time to achieve them all is another. Skills of time management are required along with a systematic way of measuring the desirability of one goal with another.

5. DO I KNOW HOW TO MAKE EFFECTIVE DECISIONS? Katz (1968) has talked about the importance, not so much of making wise decisions but of making decisions wisely. There are a variety of teaching programmes now available to help people become more proficient at making choices (Hopson and Hough, 1973; Watts and Elsom, 1975).

6. DO I KNOW HOW TO GENERATE ALTERNATIVES, BECAUSE THERE IS ALWAYS AN ALTERNATIVE? Often people do not make as good a decision as they might have simply because they have not generated enough alternatives. The techniques of 'brainstorming', 'morphological forced connections' and 'synectics' (all described in Adams, 1974) are ways of doing this. The key quite often, however, is the belief that no matter how hopeless the situation, how constrained one feels, there is always an alternative, no matter how unpalatable it may initially appear, and that you can choose. This is the central concept in the model of the 'self empowered person' described by Hopson and Scally (1980b).

Look for the gains you have made
If gains are not immediately apparent, review the section again under 'Know yourself'. Have you had to cope with something with which you have not had to cope before? If so, this will have shed light on a new facet of your

personality. What is it? Do you like it? Can you use it to any advantage in the future?

1. DO THEY KNOW WHAT THEY WANT FROM THE NEW SITUATION? If not, you must help define what they want; getting them to be as specific as possible. They may not be used to thinking in terms of objectives. You will have to teach them. Write down options on a blackboard, flip chart, or a note-book. Help them to evaluate the costs and benefits of different alternatives. Give them homework on this to be discussed at a future session.

2. DO THEY TEND TO BE PROACTIVE IN NEW SITUATIONS OR TO SIT BACK AND WAIT FOR THINGS TO HAPPEN? If they appear to be proactive, check out that it really is proactivity and not just acting to minimize anxiety, for instance jumping into something to alleviate ambiguity. If they are reactive you will need to point out that this will minimize chances of getting what they want and you will need to give them a task which is small enough for them to complete successfully (e.g. doing some homework) in order to develop confidence in their ability to make things happen. Give them a suitable book to read (see the section on self-help books) which is simultaneously instructive and a task to be completed.

3. DO THEY HAVE OTHER PEOPLE THEY CAN RELY ON FOR HELP? Get them to specify who and what they can do for them. If they are deficient in help, steer them towards an appropriate self-help group.

4. HAS ANYTHING LIKE THIS HAPPENED BEFORE? Look for links with previous experiences. Help them to discover what they did then which helped, and what in retrospect they would now choose to do differently.

5. HOW WELL CAN THEY LOOK AFTER THEMSELVES? Are they physically fit and eating sensibly? If not, advise them of the importance of this. Similarly, help them to discover the 'anchor points' in their life and persuade them to keep to a regular schedule. Encourage them to give themselves a treat from time to time. Help identify when the low points are likely to be and to plan to minimize the impact of these: for example, always have something planned for Sunday when you are newly divorced.

6. CAN THEY LET GO OF THE PAST? If not, encourage them to experience grief and anger as a way of discharging it and accepting that these feelings are normal and accept-able. They only become a problem if we never let go.

7. CAN THEY SET GOALS AND MAKE ACTION PLANS?

153

Persuade them to begin thinking about specific goals as outlined under point 1. Help define priorities, generate alternatives, and weigh them up.

8. CAN THEY SEE POSSIBLE GAINS FROM THEIR NEW SITUATION? Gently pressure them to begin to look for gains. The timing of this is vital. If they have not sufficiently let go of the past your intervention can appear heartless. Empathy is essential, but also you are trying to get them to see that however much they may not have chosen for an event to happen, that there will be something to gain.

Is it possible to train people to cope more effect- ively with transitions?

This has had to be empirically tested. Our general hypo- thesis is that people experiencing transitions will have similar tasks to cope with, namely, managing strain and dealing with cognitive tasks presented by the transition. We are assuming that to a considerable extent people's reactions to being in transition are learnt as opposed to being inherited. To the extent that individuals' reactions are learnt, we should be able to develop preventive, educative and re-educative strategies to help them manage their affairs and relationships more effectively at lower psychological costs, and derive greater benefits from the opportunity values embedded in every major transition.

This means that training programmes could be generated to help develop more effective coping styles for a number of people either (i) experiencing different transitional events, or who are anticipating transitional events, or (ii) as general training for any presently unknown future transitions.

We have already conducted a variety of transitions workshops in the UK, the USA and Scandinavia with popula- tions including managers, trade unionists, counsellors, organization development specialists, social workers, case workers, teachers and youth workers. These have been pri- marily designed for participants who in turn will have to deal with individuals in transition. We believe that it is only possible to do such work when one has a clear under- standing not just of a theoretical orientation, a collect- ion of coping skills and teaching techniques, but also of one's own transitional experiences, skills and deficits, joys, confusion and sadness.

The final question is always 'why'? Why spend the energy, use the time, deplete the resources, all of which could be directed to something else?

We can only give our answer. A transition simul- taneously carries the seeds of our yesterdays, the hopes and fears of our futures, and the pressing sensations of the present which is our confirmation of being alive. There is danger and opportunity, ecstasy and despair, development and stagnation, but above all there is movement. Nothing and no one stays the same. Nature abhors vacuums and stability. A stable state is merely a stopping point on a journey from one place to another. Stop too long and your journey is ended. Stay and enjoy but with the realization that more is to come. You may not be able to stop the journey, but you can fly the plane.

References

Adams, J.L. (1974)
Conceptual Blockbusting. San Francisco: Freeman.
Adams, J.D., Hayes, J. and Hopson, B. (1976)
Transition: Understanding and managing personal change.
London: Martin Robertson.
Aspy, D.N. and Roebuck, F.N. (1977)
Kids Don't Learn From People They Don't Like. Amherst,
Mass.: Human Resource Development Press.
Benson, H. (1977)
The Relaxation Response. London: Fountain Well Press.
Breckon, W. (1976)
You Are What You Eat. London: BBC Publications.
Campbell, D. (1974)
If You Don't Know Where You're Going You'll Probably
End Up Somewhere Else. Hoddesdon, Herts.: Argus
Publications.
Carkhuff, R.R. (1974a)
The Art of Problem Solving. Amherst, Mass.: Human
Resource Development Press.
Carkhuff, R.R. (1974b)
How To Help Yourself. Amherst, Mass.: Human
Resource Development Press.
Carruthers, M. and Murray, A. (1977)
F/40: Fitness on forty minutes a week. London: Futura.
Cooper, K. (1977)
The New Aerobics. New York: Bantam.
Downing, G. (1972)
The Massage Book. New York: Random House.
Ellis, A. and Harper, R. (1975)
A New Guide to Rational Living. Hollywood, Ca:
Wilshire Books.
Forbes, R. (1979)
Life Stress. New York: Doubleday.
Health Education Council (1976)
Look After Yourself. London: Health Education Council.
Holmes, T.H. and Rahe, R.H. (1967)
The social readjustment rating scale. Journal of
Psychosomatic Research, 11, 213-218.
Hopson, B. and Hough, P. (1973)
Exercises in Personal and Career Development.
Cambridge: Hobsons Press.
Hopson, B. and Scally, M. (1980a)
How to cope with and gain from life transitions. In B.
Hopson and M. Scally, Lifeskills Teaching Programmes
No. 1. Leeds: Lifeskills Associates.

Hopson, B. and Scally, M. (1980b)
Lifeskills Teaching: Education for self-empowerment.
London: McGraw-Hill.
Howe, L.W. and Howe, M.M. (1975)
Personalizing Education: Values clarification and
beyond. New York: Hart.
Johnson. D.W. (1972)
Reaching Out. Englewood Cliffs, NJ: Prentice-Hall.
Katz, M.R. (1968)
Can computers make guidance decisions for students?
College Board Review, No. 72.
Kirschenbaum, H. (1977)
Advanced Value Clarification. La Jolla, Ca: University
Associates.
Krantzler, M. (1973)
Creative Divorce. New York: M. Evans.
Lamott, K. (1975)
Escape from Stress. New York: Berkley.
Mahoney, M.J. and Mahoney, J. (1976)
Permanent Weight Control. New York: W.W. Norton.
Maslow, A. (1968)
Towards a Psychology of Being (2nd edn). New York: Va
Nostrand.
Parkes, C. M. (1972)
Bereavement: Studies of grief in adult life. London:
Tavistock.
Royal Canadian Air Force (1978)
Physical Fitness. Harmondsworth: Penguin.
Russel, P. (1977)
The Transcendental Meditation Technique. London:
Routledge & Kegan Paul.
Sharpe, R. and Lewis, D. (1977)
Thrive on Stress. London: Souvenir Press.
Simon, S. (1974)
Meeting Yourself Halfway. Hoddesdon, Herts.: Argus
Publications.
Simon, S., Howe, L.W. and Kirschenbaum, H. (1972)
Value Clarification. New York: Hart.
Toffler, A. (1970)
Future Shock. London: Bodley Head.
Watts, A.G. and Elsom, D. (1975)
Deciding. Cambridge: Hobsons Press.

Questions

1. Why is an understanding of the psychological processes of level 1 transitions important to your profession?
2. What are the major types of transition and how are they related?
3. How would you set about rating the impact of life events on people?
4. Critically evaluate the Hopson-Adams model of transitions.
5. What effects do transitions have on people?

6. What are the coping tasks relevant to all
   transitions?
7. Describe the coping skills which are relevant to
   transitions.
8. Which will be the most important influence in ensuring
   a successful transition and why? Is it the coping
   skills of the mover or the structure and practices of
   the organization, institution or social norms?
9. Describe a life transition in terms of the stages the
   person might go through and what he could do to
   maximize the chances of coping with it effectively and
   gaining from the experience.
10. How effectively can we train people to improve their
    transition coping skills?

Adams, J.D., Hayes, J. and Hopson, B. (1976) Transition:
Understanding and managing personal change. London: Martin
Robertson.
   This is the first attempt to provide a conceptual
   framework to describe the psychological sequence of a
   transition. It is primarily a theoretical book, although
   some guidelines for the practitioner are available.

Hopson, B. and Scally, M. (1980) How to cope with and
gain from life transitions. In B. Hopson and M. Scally,
Lifeskills Teaching Programmes No. 1. Leeds: Lifeskills
Associates.
   This is for a classroom teacher of young people and
   consists of a series of carefully described group
   exercises to teach young people about transitions and
   how to cope more effectively with them.

Parkes, C. M. (1975) Bereavement: Studies of grief in adult
life. Harmondsworth: Penguin.
   This book is about more than bereavement, although it is
   discussed at great length. Parkes generalizes from
   bereavement to other aspects of separation and loss in
   people's lives.

11

The behavioural casework approach
Martin Herbert

Social workers and probation officers are often
inadequately prepared to deal with the conduct and
delinquent disorders so frequently manifested by their
child and adolescent clientele. These problems provide
cogent reasons for the growing interest in the self-
directed aspects of behaviour modification, especially as
it applies to out-of-control and poorly-self-controlled
youngsters and adults. The goal of behavioural casework
is to help an individual eventually to control his or her
own behaviour and achieve self-selected goals. The aim,
with other more passive, depressive and alienated clients,
is to convert learned helplessness into learned
resourcefulness (see chapter 16).

A behavioural assessment of conduct disorders is
likely to encompass a broad spectrum of problems; the
diagnostic category includes seriously antisocial acts as
well as moderately troublesome behaviours. They range from
legally defined delinquent acts (dealt with only briefly
here because of the magnitude of that topic) to a variety
of nondelinquent behaviours, including the more or less
involuntary forms of what are referred to as coercive or
oppositional problems: commanding, screaming, crying,
pestering, tantrums and negativism.

Remedies

The debate about the nature and origins of behaviour is
not simply an academic preoccupation of psychologists. As
Tutt (1984) illustrates, its outcome may have a profound
effect on social policy, and also the type of intervention
which is likely to prove most effective. Theories about
the nature of conduct problems, criminality and delinquency likewise affect attitudes toward law and order
issues. Moral or social education - in the home and school
- and the provision of counselling services and youth
recreational facilities, have been tried as measures to
prevent children 'at risk' from becoming delinquent, or to
retrieve them from a criminal career. It is notoriously
difficult to identify from the many children who might be
deemed to be vulnerable, from such vague 'predictors' as
broken or disharmonious homes, unsatisfactory parents,

poverty and the like, the relatively few who become
seriously delinquent.

These strategies of prevention were predicated on an
assumption of the major contribution of motivational and
personality factors and the influence of long-term
parental and child-rearing variables in the production of
delinquent tendencies.

Assessment

There has been, of late, a shift in emphasis which takes
into account the fact that behaviour is, to a large
extent, situationally determined (see Tutt's review, op.
cit.). Thus the questions which are generated by the
situational model in relation to a specific delinquent act
might include:

* When did the offence occur?
* Where?
* Who with?
* What led up to it?
* What was being planned (if anything)?
* What actually happened?
* Was it intended?
* If not, why did it happen? (ibid.)

In addition to the analysis of such 'antecedent'
events (see chapters 2 and 3, and Herbert, 1981, on the
ABC assessment) it is necessary to 'tease out' the
consequential events:

* What consequences flowed from this (and similar, if any,
  events)?
* Were they favourable (i.e. representing a 'payoff' for
  the offender)?

As a result of these kinds of formulation, several
theorists recommend projects to reduce delinquent
behaviour by modifying the actions and attitudes of the
youngsters themselves or their parents and teachers, in
behavioural and educational programmes. At the most basic
level there are three preliminary questions to be
answered:

* Does the client know what to do (e.g. the required
  prosocial actions)?
* Does he or she know how to do it?
* Does she or he know when to do it?

Now the client may know the appropriate behaviour or
skill and when to produce it; but still he or she doesn't
perform it. So we have four more questions:

* How can I get the client to do what we have agreed it is
  advantageous/desirable to do?

159

* Now that she or he does it, how can I encourage my client to continue doing it?
* How can I get the client to stop doing what we have agreed it is disadvantageous/undesirable to do (i.e. the antisocial action)?
* Now that he or she has stopped doing it, how can I encourage my client to desist from doing it?

Intervention

Psychology provides an effective technology for changing actions and attitudes:

* Behaviour can be effectively strengthened;
* Behaviour can be effectively weakened.

Such behaviour change is often accompanied or followed by attitude change (e.g. insight).

A treatment programme may include various combination of antecedent and outcome procedures, as well as both environmental and self-control methods. There is no generalized formula or simple recipe approach to the choice of treatment procedures such as X methods for Y problems. The planning of a therapeutic intervention is based upon highly individual and flexible considerations.

One criterion for selecting procedures is based upon whether the problem is conceptualized as representing a deficit or excess of behaviour. Broadly speaking, the therapeutic task with deficit problems is:

* to increase the strength of a particular behaviour pattern (response increment procedures);
* to aid in the acquisition of new behaviour patterns (response acquisition procedures).

With excess behaviours the therapeutic task is to reduce their strength (response decrement procedures) or eliminate them.

Response increment procedures

Contingency management

Contingency management is the generic title given to methods that involve the manipulation of reinforcement. Positive and negative reinforcement are distinctive procedures that serve to maintain, strengthen, or increase the likelihood that a behaviour will be emitted. The general principle of reinforcement - that responses which have contingent reinforcing consequences are likely to occur more frequently in the future - is fundamental to many procedures for the acquisition of behaviour. Reinforcement is defined solely by its effect on behaviour. If the behaviour increases in frequency, it is being reinforced; if it does not, it is not being reinforced.

160

Positive reinforcement as a method of change is indicated when:

* a new behaviour is to be incorporated in the client's repertoire;
* the strength of an already acquired behaviour pattern is to be increased;
* by increasing the strength of a particular behaviour the effect will be to cause an undesirable incompatible response to diminish in strength.

Parents often make use of a mixture of negative and positive reinforcers on the 'stick and carrot' prinicple. Contingency management procedures have been used to treat hyperactivity and aggression and to deal with problems concerning responsiveness to verbal direction, negativism, bizarre behaviour and truancy. Reinforcement techniques have been demonstrated to be helpful in altering behaviour in the classroom and in home settings (see Herbert, 1978, 1981, for a review of the evidence).

CONTRACTS: reinforcement contingencies can be made explicit in the form of behavioural contracts (or agreements) between the individuals who wish for some behaviour change (e.g. parents, teachers, social workers) and those whose behaviour is to be changed (children, students, clients). A contract is signed by both parties to the negotiated agreement indicating that they accept the terms. The contract specifies the relationship between the behaviours desired by (say) the parent who has requested a change in the child's behaviour and the consequences of such a change, i.e. the reinforcers desired by the child or adolescent. (See Sheldon, 1982, for a detailed account of this valuable social work method.)

TOKEN ECONOMIES: positive reinforcement can be applied as a group-management procedure or, as it is called, a token economy programme. The token economy is, in a sense, a work-payment incentive system. The participants receive tokens when they manifest appropriate behaviour and, at some time later, they exchange the tokens for a variety of potent back-up reinforcers - items and activities. These have a prearranged exchange rate. The system parallels the way money is used in society and the economy at large.

SELF-REINFORCEMENT: in the burgeoning literature on self-reinforcement, studies have repeatedly established that self-administered reinforcement is effective in maintaining various kinds of behaviour.

There has been a preoccupation in the literature - over the past years - with consequent events. This has

161

been most marked in special education, in the case of the development of token economy systems. The major drawback of this focus on outcomes is to do with generalization, which is often disappointing and limited. The analysis of antecedent and setting events (stimulus control) offers another (though not necessarily a separate) approach.

Stimulus control

Stimulus control is another generic term, but this time it has to do with the extent to which the value of an antecedent stimulus determines the probability of occurrence of a conditioned response. A frequent complaint from parents is that their child 'won't listen' or 'knows what to do but just won't do it!'. These are examples of faulty stimulus control. The child has a behaviour in his or her repertoire but will not perform it at the appropriate time, i.e. when the would-be directing stimulus is presented. The social worker assists the parent to reinstate stimulus control. The fundamental rule for correcting faulty stimulus control, as for establishing initial stimulus control, is to get the behaviour (or some approximation to it) performed while the child is attending to the stimulus which is to control it.

There are several ways to reinstate the discriminative stimulus. When a young child is to be taught to act in a particular way under one set of circumstances but not another (in other words, to develop new behaviour), she or he is helped to identify the cues that differentiate the circumstances. This involves clear signals as to what is expected of the child and it presupposes unambiguous rules. To achieve stimulus control the appropriate behavioural response is repeatedly reinforced in the presence of the S^D, but never in inappropriate circumstances (S^Δ). This process is called differential reinforcement, and is part of an important approach called discrimination training.

Response aquisition procedures

Shaping

The process of shaping makes possible the building of a new response, viz. by making reinforcements contingent upon successive approximations of the final behaviour. The social worker does this by working out the successive steps the child must, and can, make, so as to approximate more and more closely to the desired final outcome. This last element, called 'shaping', or the principle of 'successive approximation', is an important one in behaviour modification; it involves taking mini-steps towards the final goal. The parent (say) - guided by the social worker - starts by reinforcing very small changes in behaviour which are in the right directions, even if somewhat far removed from the final desired outcome. No reinforcement is given for behaviour in the 'wrong'

direction. Gradually the criteria of the individual's
approximation to the desired goal are made more rigorous.

Modelling - observational learning
In order to teach a child a new pattern of behaviour the
child is given the opportunity to observe a person
performing the desired behaviour and the consequences of
these actions. The application of modelling can be used
effectively in at least three situations:

* acquiring new or alternative patterns of behaviour
  from the model, which the child has never manifested
  before (e.g. social skills, self-control;
* the increase or decrease of responses already in the
  child's repertoire through the demonstration by a high
  prestige model of appropriate behaviour (e.g. the
  disinhibition of a shy withdrawn child's speech and
  social interactions, or the inhibition of learned fears
  or the suppression of impulsive, antisocial behaviour);
* the increase in behaviours which the observing child
  has already learned and for which there are no existing
  inhibitions or constraints.

Response decrement procedures

When a particular behaviour occurs with excessive
frequency, intensity, or magnitude, or where a response is
emitted under conditions a child's environment considers
inappropriate, the social work task is to bring the
behaviour within a range that is more socially acceptable.
Unlike the child with a behaviour deficit, who has to
learn a response that is not in his or her repertoire, the
child with excess behaviour has to learn to modify
existing actions and activities.

Skills training
Many children, because of tragic and depriving life
experiences, lack some of the crucial skills required to
cope with life in a satisfactory manner. Consequently,
they may behave problematically in response to a variety
of stresses, frustrations and humiliations. If such
children can be helped to become more competent, then they
may have less recourse to problem behaviour.

Intellectual, academic and behavioural deficiencies
are commonly found in adolescent offenders. Treatment of
these deficits requires comprehensive social and clinical
casework and (prior to that) a thorough assessment that
specifies the youngster's particular strengths and
weaknesses in a variety of problem areas (see Ollendick
and Cerny, 1981).

Reducing aversive stimuli
Problem behaviour may be instigated in the child by a
large variety of aversive stimuli: by bullying and by
teasing of a painful, threatening, or humiliating nature,

163

and by deprivation of the proper nurturance, rights, and opportunities that are his or her due. Reduction of such aversive stimuli may be accompanied by a reduction in the undesired behaviour - a proposal easier to make on paper than to meet in practice. The bleak reality of the lives of many delinquent youths makes the possibilities for the reduction of stress and temptation very limited. A helpful technique involves the defusing of aversive stimuli by diminishing their power to arouse anger in the child. This may be achieved by desensitization procedures, by cognitive restructuring (providing a different interpretation/perception of the situation), or humour.

Desensitization and relaxation

Relaxation is thought to be incompatible with emotional behaviours such as fright, anger, or frustration. It may be possible to teach a child how to relax when he or she becomes frustrated, agitated, or angered.

Promotion of alternative behaviour

Reinforcement, which is so crucial to the acquisition of behaviour, is also useful in eliminating unwanted responses. For example, the caseworker can strengthen (by reinforcement) alternative acts that are incompatible with, or cannot be performed at the same time as, the maladaptive (say aggressive) response. Indeed, there are very few occasions where it is desirable only to eliminate given behaviour without at the same time training the child in some alternative prosocial act. Principles of operant conditioning are applied to strengthen socially acceptable alternatives.

EXTINCTION: this is the term used to describe the relatively permanent unlearning of a behaviour (the elimination of a behaviour from a person's repertoire). It also applies to a procedure by which reinforcement that has previously followed an operant behaviour (say, a tantrum) is discontinued. For example, to stop a child from acting in such a persistently disruptive attention-seeking manner, conditions are arranged so that he or she receives no attention (if this is assessed to be the reinforcer) following the undesirable act. It is thought essential that the behaviour should occur in order for extinction to take place, for only then are the internal motivating factors truly weakened. Always ask yourself why a child needs to behave 'badly' in order to obtain (say) attention. Can it not get attention in any other appropriate ways? Never 'take away' a child's problem behaviour without checking out its raison d'etre and always put something in its place (see Herbert, 1981, 1985).

TIME-OUT FROM POSITIVE REINFORCEMENT (TO): TO provides another means of reducing specified actions by the withdrawal of reinforcement. TO is a period of time during which the child is prevented from emitting the problematic behaviour (say, screaming) in the situation in which he or she has been positively reinforced in the past. The child is temporarily removed, contingent upon the performance of the maladaptive act, from an activity or from a place so that it finds itself in a situation in which reinforcement is no longer available.

RESPONSE-COST (RC): parents often withhold approval and privileges when their children are 'naughty'. This is an informal use of RC which essentially refers to the withdrawal of specified amounts of reinforcement from the child contingent upon his or her displaying unwanted behaviours which have been specified in advance. In effect the child pays a penalty for violating the rules; the withdrawal of reinforcers constitutes the 'cost' of the maladaptive action.

OVERCORRECTION: with overcorrection we have a method combining positive reinforcement and penalties, which is used to discourage inappropriate or disruptive behaviour. Two types of overcorrection have been described. The first, Restitutional Overcorrection, requires the youth to correct the consequences of misbehaviour. The person who has engaged in the inappropriate behaviour not only remedies the situation he or she has caused, but also 'overcorrects' it to a better-than-normal situation. He or she makes restitution by performing some work as a penalty for maladaptive behaviour; he or she is required to res- tore the disrupted situation to a better state than existed before the disruption. The second component of overcorrection is an extensive rehearsal of the correct forms of appropriate behaviour. This is called Positive Practice Overcorrection and it requires the individual to practise correct behaviours contingent upon episodes of misbehaviour. For example, with aggression, the aggressor is required to comfort the victim.

SELF-CONTROL OF ANTECEDENT CONDITIONS: these procedures involve the manipulation of those eliciting, reinforcing, or discriminative stimuli in the youngster's symbolic processes which influence his or her maladaptive behaviour.
    The adolescent girl with a weight and eating problem might make a rule never to eat anywhere but at her place at the table and then at specified times, and to remove herself from food stimuli whenever possible, by avoiding the kitchen and by asking her siblings not to eat cakes and sweets in front of her.

SELF-CONTROL OF OUTCOME CONDITIONS: during the intervention youngsters can be taught to rearrange contingencies that influence behaviour in such a way that they experience long-range benefits, even though they may have to give up some satisfactions or tolerate some discomforts at first. This involves, first, a precise analysis of the behaviour to be controlled and, as with any other behavioural analysis, its antecedent and consequent conditions. Second, it is necessary to identify behaviours which enhance appropriate actions as well as behaviours which interfere with the undesired inappropriate responses. The third stage involves identifying positive and negative reinforcers which control these patterns of behaviour.

There is evidence, as we have seen, that children may be able to modify or maintain their own behaviour by administering rewards or punishments to themselves in a contingent manner.

SELF-INSTRUCTION: this provides another antecedent control procedure. 'Self-talk' is a particular preoccupation of everyone when under pressure. We can talk ourselves into a panic, but also (more constructively) through, and out of, a crisis. Impulsive clients can be trained to talk to themselves about 'thinking first' and 'acting afterwards', aggressive clients to tell themselves to 'stay cool' and anxious clients to instruct themselves that they are calm.

Training parents

Patterson and his colleagues at the Oregon Research Institute have been a prolific source of ideas and data on the subject of (inter alia) children's conduct disorders, notably aggression and stealing. They have developed a treatment package that involves training parents in child management skills (Patterson et al., 1975). It is difficult to summarize such an extensive contribution, but it is worth reporting the team's results with 27 conduct disordered boys referred to them and accepted for treatment from January 1968 to June 1972. Training the families took an average of 31.5 hours of professional time. The treatment programme (parents read a semi-programmed text followed by a multiple choice test; staff teach parents to pinpoint problem areas and collect appropriate data on them; parents join a parent training group to learn appropriate change techniques; home visits occur where necessary) lasted on average from three to four months. Most parents opted to work on reducing their children's noncompliance to requests, but overall a further 13 behaviours in the conduct disorder syndrome were also pinpointed for treatment.

With regard to criterion measures such as the targeted deviant behaviours of the boys, an average 60 per cent reduction from baseline level to termination was achieved. In 75 per cent of cases, reductions exceeded 30 per cent from baseline levels. In six cases the rate of problematic behaviour deteriorated. On another criterion - total deviant scores - the 27 boys showed a reduction from higher than normal overall rate (scores computed for normal boys over 14 'problem areas') to within normal limits. According to parental daily reports there was a significant drop in the level of reported problems during follow-up (data were obtained here on 14 families only). About two-thirds of the families reported marked reductions in the problems for which they were originally referred.

Follow-up data were obtained monthly for the first six months after termination of treatment, and every two months after that until a year after termination. Booster treatment programmes during follow-up took an average of 1.9 hours of professional time. It was soon discovered that improvements at home did not generalize to school, so a separate but parallel package was prepared to use in classroom settings. Patterson found that a substantial proportion of families (approximately one third in his sample) required much more in the way of intervention than child management skills: the parents needed help with social problems, negotiation skills, depression, and resolving marital conflict.

The apparent connection between family functioning and delinquency is one good reason for working with families whenever possible. Also, in order to counter peer influence where it is deviant, it is necessary to establish some community-based sources of control and reinforcement for socially appropriate behaviour. The family remains one of the most obvious candidates for this role given the amount of time the adolescent spends there.

Alexander and Parsons (1973) describe behavioural family therapy with delinquent adolescents. During the project families were referred to the Family Clinic at the University of Utah. The adolescents' offences included absconding, being ungovernable, chronic truanting, shoplifting, drug possession, and so on. Families were randomly assigned (as near as possible) to either the treatment programme comparison groups, or a no-treatment control condition. The treatment group (46 families) involved a short-term family intervention programme. The goal was to modify the interactions of deviant families so that they would approximate those patterns characteristic of 'normal' or 'adjusted' families. Therapists emphasized the removal of the circumstances (interactions) that elicited the behavioural offence, substituting for them a process of contingency contracting. Therapists modelled and prompted, and reinforced all the members of the family where they manifested (1) clear communications, and (2) clear presentation of 'demands' and alternative solutions, leading to (3) negotiation to the point of compromise. The behavioural group showed a recidivism rate (six to 18 months following termination of treatment) of 26 per cent compared to 50 per cent, 47 per cent and 73 per cent, respectively, for the no-treatment, family groups (comparison) programme and the eclectic psychodynamic family programmes respectively.

Residential settings
Not infrequently, children and adolescents with conduct disorders are removed from their homes and are ostensibly exposed to treatment or rehabilitation programmes in a variety of residential settings. The success rates of individual approved schools in England differ consid- erably; nevertheless, overall rates of success - based on a three-year period free from reconviction - reach no higher than 30 per cent to 35 per cent (Her Majesty's Stationery Office, 1972). One explanation for the failure of institutional programmes is a model of human deviance that places the main source of behavioural variance within the individual. The primary thrust of therapy is in changing the individual; the hope is that a change in behaviour in the institutional setting represents a funda- mental change (e.g. in personality, maturity, character, or self-discipline) and will therefore accompany the individual upon return to the community - no matter what its temptations, deprivations, or other disadvantages.

Much of the delinquent's behaviour is maintained by his or her social network. In institutions, behaviour that is deviant (anti-social) is far more often reinforced by peers than it is prescribed by members of staff. On the other hand acceptable (pro-social) actions are punished by peers more often than they are rewarded by staff. On top of all this youngsters' antisocial actions are reinforced more immediately by the peer group than socially accept- able actions are rewarded by the staff group (see Buehler et al., 1966; Kazdin, 1972). Small wonder institutions fail so often in their task of rehabilitation, and worse, seem to provide for many youths a 'higher education' in criminality (Herbert, 1978).

A variety of residential projects have emerged in recent years that adopt a less sanguine view of the permanence and internalization of change. Many make use of behaviour management principles, and a growing number emphasize the need for integrated programming with the subject's family and local community in order to enhance the likelihood of success. One of the best-known schemes, Achievement Place - a community-based, family-style group home for six to eight predelinquent or delinquent boys under the direction of teaching parents - has enjoyed positive results (Wolf, Phillips and Fixsen, 1975). Behavioural methods are used. The boys can remain largely in their usual community, and through carefully phasing their return home, the improvements in social and academic

168

skills and in self-control appear not only more frequent
but also more enduring than in traditional regimes. Wolf
and his colleagues have described the results for the
first 41 boys to be admitted (average age 13.8) - mainly
from very deprived social backgrounds, all with serious
conduct disorders. There are many ways to evaluate such a
programme. To take one criterion, reconviction rates and
later institutinalization of the first 18 boys in the
experiment: three were placed in other institutional care
in the two years following treatment - compared with nine
of the 19 local reformatory boys in the contrast group.
Court contacts decreased among Achievement Place boys
during the treatment, but increased among the boys at the
reformatory.

Several evaluative reports are available, not only for
the original Achievement Place but also for some of the
many replications of the scheme in the United States and
elsewhere. The model of teaching parents and a family-
style (but nevertheless controlled) environment has proved
to be an ever-evolving idea. It is refreshing to find
detailed accounts of procedures that allow for repli-
cation, and indeed to see - in that most difficult of
settings for research - painstaking efforts made to
measure and specify change.

Despite such promising findings with conduct
disorders, a realistic assessment of the over-all results
of behavioural work with juvenile delinquents must concede
their still somewhat tentative nature. It is true that
behaviour modification programmes employed to enhance a
variety of prosocial activities and to reduce several
classes of antisocial actions in juvenile delinquents have
been found generally effective (Ollendick et al., 1980).
However, the major gap in our knowledge has to do with
prognosis. A majority of the experimental studies fail to
report any subsequent follow-up of their subjects.

Person variables such as locus of control cannot be
disregarded. By locus of control is meant the individual's
sense of being in charge or in control (by and large) of
his or her life. Such a person is called an 'internal'.
The concepts of internal and external represent the
extremes of a continuum. People range somewhere between
these extremes of orientation. 'Externals' locate the
control of their destinies outside themselves and tend to
be fatalistic, pessimistic and passive. Jesness and De
Risi (1973) demonstrated that juvenile delinquents who
have a capacity for insight and responsibility and who are
internally oriented with regard to locus of control
respond most favourably to behavioural programmes.

Ollendick et al. (1980) used a fixed token economy
and a flexible behavioural contracting system in a
treatment programme for 90 delinquent adolescents.
Although the overall program resulted in a relatively low
recidivism rate (38 per cent), the findings relating to

locus of control are particularly significant. Internally oriented youths committed fewer offences during the institutional programme and manifested lower recidivism rates a year after discharge; externally oriented youths derived less benefit from the programme and evidenced higher rates of reconviction. The authors state that 'such findings tend to affirm the basic principles underlying the social learning approach to treatment; namely, that behaviour is learned and maintained through a reciprocal interaction between the person and his environment' (p.261).

References

Alexander, J.F. and Parsons, B.V. (1973)
Short-term behavioural intervention with delinquent families. Journal of Abnormal Psychology, 81, 219-225.

Buchler, R.E., Patterson, G.R. and Furniss, J.M. (1966)
The reinforcement of behaviour in institutional settings. Behaviour Research and Therapy, 4, 461-476.

Herbert, M. (1978)
Conduct Disorders of Childhood and Adolescence. Chichester: John Wiley & Sons Ltd.

Herbert, M. (1981)
Behavioural Treatment of Problem Children: A practice manual. London: Academic Press.

Jesness, C.F. and De Risi, W.J. (1973)
Some variations in techniques of contingency managemen in a school for delinquents. In J.S. Stumphauzer (ed), Behaviour Therapy with Delinquents. Springfield, Ill.: Charles C. Thomas.

Kazdin, A.E. (1972)
Response cost: The removal of conditioned reinforcers for therapeutic change. Behaviour Therapy, 3, 533-546.

Ollendick, T.H. and Cerny, J.A. (1981)
Clinical Behaviour Therapy With Children. New York: Plenum Press.

Ollendick, T.H., Elliott, W. and Matson, J.L. (1980)
Locus of control as related to effectiveness in a behaviour modification programme for juvenile delinquents. Journal of Behaviour Therapy and Experimental Psychiatry, 11, 259-262.

Patterson, G.R., Reid, J.B., Jones, J.J. and Conger, R.E. (1975)
A Social Learning Approach to Family Intervention. Oregon: Castalia.

Tutt, N. (1984)
Contemporary Approaches to the Understanding, Assessment and Treatment of Delinquency. In J. Nicholson and H. Beloff (eds), Psychology Survey 5. Leicester: The British Psychological Society.

Wolf, M.M., Phillips, E.L., and Fixsen, D.L. (1975)
Achievement Place Phase II: Final Report. Lawrence: Department of Human Development, University of Kansa

Further
reading

Herbert, M. (1985)
    Understanding Your Children. Oxford: Basil Blackwell.
Sheldon, B. (1982)
    Behaviour Modification. London: Tavistock.
Walker, S. (1976)
    Learning and Reinforcement. London: Methuen.

12

Counselling and helping
Barrie Hopson

Counselling today

From a situation in the mid-1960s when 'counselling' was seen by many in education as a transatlantic transplant which hopefully would never 'take', we have today reached the position of being on board a band-wagon; 'counsellors' are everywhere: beauty counsellors, tax counsellors, investment counsellors, even carpet counsellors. There are 'counsellors' in schools, industry, hospitals, the social services. There is marriage counselling, divorce counselling, parent counselling, bereavement counselling, abortion counselling, retirement counselling, redundancy counselling, career counselling, psychosexual counselling, pastoral counselling, student counselling and even disciplinary counselling! Whatever the original purpose for coining the word 'counselling', the coinage has by now certainly been debased. One of the unfortunate consequences of the debasing has been that the word has become mysterious; we cannot always be sure just what 'counselling' involves. One of the results of the mystification of language is that we rely on others to tell us what it is: that is, we assume that we, the uninitiated, cannot know and understand what it is really about. That can be a first step to denying ourselves skills and knowledge we already possess or that we may have the potential to acquire.

It is vital that we 'de-mystify' counselling, and to do that we must look at the concept within the broader context of ways in which people help other people, and we must analyse it in relation to objectives. 'Counselling' is often subscribed to as being 'a good thing', but we must ask the question, 'good for what?'

Ways of helping

'Counselling' is only one form of helping. It is decidedly not the answer to all human difficulties, though it can be extremely productive and significant for some people, sometimes. Counselling is one way of working to help people overcome problems, clarify or achieve personal goals. We can distinguish between six types of helping strategies (Scally and Hopson, 1979).

172

* Giving advice: offering somebody your opinion of what would be the best course of action based on your view of their situation.
* Giving information: giving a person the information he needs in a particular situation (e.g. about legal rights, the whereabouts of particular agencies, etc.). Lacking information can make one powerless; providing it can be enormously helpful.
* Direct action: doing something on behalf of somebody else or acting to provide for another's immediate needs; for example, providing a meal, lending money, stopping a fight, intervening in a crisis.
* Teaching: helping someone to acquire knowledge and skills; passing on facts and skills which improve somebody's situation.
* Systems change: working to influence and improve systems which are causing difficulty for people; that is, working on organizational development rather than with individuals.
* Counselling: helping someone to explore a problem, clarify conflicting issues and discover alternative ways of dealing with it, so that they can decide what to do about it; that is, helping people to help themselves.

There is no ranking intended in this list. What we do say is that these strategies make up a helper's 'tool-bag'. Each one is a 'piece of equipment' which may be useful in particular helping contexts. What helpers are doing is choosing from their resources whichever approach best fits the situation at the time.

There are some interesting similarities and differences between the strategies. Giving advice, information, direct action, teaching and possibly systems change recognize that the best answers, outcomes, or solutions rely on the expertise of the helper. The 'expert' offers what is felt to be most useful to the one seeking help. Counselling, on the other hand, emphasizes that the person with the difficulty is the one with the resources needed to deal with it. The counsellor provides the relationship which enables the clients to search for their own answers. The 'expert' does not hand out solutions. This does not deny the special skills of the helper, but does imply that having 'expertise' does not make a person an 'expert'. We all have expertise. In counselling, the counsellor is using personal expertise to help to get the clients in touch with their own expertise. Counselling is the only helping strategy which makes no assumption that the person's needs are known.

Teaching, systems change, and counselling are only likely to be effective if the 'helper' has relationship-making skills. Giving advice, information and direct action are likely to be more effective if he has them.

Systems change is different in that it emphasizes work with groups, structures, rules and organizations.

The counsellor possibly uses most of the other strategies at some time or other, when they seem more appropriate than counselling. The other strategies would have an element of counselling in them if the 'helper' had the necessary skills. For example, a new student having difficulties making friends at school could involve a counsellor, in addition to using his counselling skills, teaching some relationship-building skills to the student, getting the staff to look at induction provision, making some suggestions to the student, or even taking him to a lunchtime disco session in the school club.

Who are the helpers?

Strictly speaking we are all potential helpers and people to be helped, but in this context it may be useful to distinguish between three groups.

Professional helpers

These are people whose full-time occupation is geared towards helping others in a variety of ways. They have usually, but not always, received specialist training. Social workers, doctors, teachers, school counsellors, nurses, careers officers and health visitors are a few examples. They define their own function in terms of one or more of the helping strategies.

Paraprofessional helpers

These people have a clearly defined helping role but it does not constitute the major part of their job specification or represent the dominant part of their lives, such as marriage guidance counsellors, priests, part-time youth workers, personnel officers and some managers. Probably they have received some short in-service training, often on-the-job.

Helpers in general

People who may not have any specially defined helping role but who, because of their occupational or social position or because of their own commitment, find themselves in situations where they can offer help to others, such as shop stewards, school caretakers, undertakers, social security clerks or solicitors. This group is unlikely to have received special training in helping skills. In addition to these groupings there are a variety of unstructured settings within which helping occurs: the family, friendships, and in the community (Brammer, 1973).

What makes people good helpers?

In some ways it is easier to begin with the qualities that quite clearly do not make for good helping. Loughary and Ripley (1979) people their helpers' rogue's gallery with

174

four types of would-be helpers:

* the 'You think YOU'VE got a problem! Let me tell you about mine!' type;
* the 'Let me tell you what to do' type;
* the 'I understand because I once had the same problem myself' person;
* the 'I'll take charge and deal with it' type.

The first three approaches have been clearly identified as being counter-productive (Carkhuff and Berenson, 1976) while the fourth one certainly deals with people's problems but prevents them ever learning skills or concepts to enable them to work through the problem on their own the next time it occurs. The only possible appropriate place for this person is in a crisis intervention. However, even this intervention would need to be followed up with additional counselling help if the needy person were to avoid such crises.

Rogers (1958) came out with clearly testable hypotheses of what constitutes effective helping. He said that helpers must be open and that they should be able to demonstrate UNCONDITIONED POSITIVE REGARD: acceptance of clients as worth while regardless of who they are or what they say or do; CONGRUENCE: helpers should use their feelings, their verbal and non-verbal behaviour should be open to clients and be consistent; GENUINENESS: they should be honest, sincere and without facades; EMPATHIC: they should be able to let the client know that they understand their frame of reference and can see the world as they see it, whilst remaining separate from it. These qualities must be not only possessed but conveyed: that is, the client must experience them.

Truax and Carkhuff (1967) put these hypotheses to the test and found considerable empirical support for what they identified as the 'core facilitative conditions' of effective helping relationships - empathy, respect and positive regard, genuineness, and concreteness - the ability to be specific and immediate to client statements. They differed from Rogers in that whereas he claimed that the facilitative conditions were necessary and sufficient, they only claimed that they were necessary. Carkhuff has gone on to try to demonstrate (Carkhuff and Berenson, 1976) that they are clearly not sufficient, and that the helper needs to be skilled in teaching a variety of life and coping skills to clients. The other important finding from Truax and Carkhuff was that helpers who do not possess those qualities are not merely ineffective, for they can contribute to people becoming worse than they were prior to helping.

The evidence tends to suggest that the quality of the interpersonal relationship between helper and client is more important than any specific philosophy of helping adhered to by the helper. This has been demonstrated to be the case in counselling, psychotherapy and also teaching (Aspy and Roebuck, 1977). A recent review of the many research studies on this topic would suggest, as one might expect, that things are not quite that simple (Parloff, Waskow, and Wolfe, 1978), but after a reappraisal of the early work of Truax and Carkhuff and a large number of more recent studies, the authors conclude that a relationship between empathy, respect and genuineness with helper effectiveness has been established. They also shed light on a number of other factors which have been discussed periodically as being essential for effective therapists (their focus was therapy, not helping):

* personal psychotherapy has not been demonstrated to be a prerequisite for an effective therapist;
* sex and race are not related to effectiveness;
* the value of therapist experience is highly questionable; that is, people are not necessarily better therapists because they are more experienced;
* therapists with emotional problems of their own are likely to be less effective;
* there is some support for the suggestion that helpers are more effective when working with clients who hold values similar to their own.

What they do point out is the importance of the match between helper and client. No one is an effective helper with everyone, although we as yet know little as to how to match helpers with clients to gain the greatest benefits.

Helping and human relationships

Carl Rogers states very clearly that psychotherapy is not a 'special kind of relationship, different in kind from all others which occur in everyday life' (1957). A similar approach has been taken by those theorists looking at the broader concept of helping. Brammer (1973) states that 'helping relationships have much in common with friendships, family interactions, and pastoral contacts. They are all aimed at fulfilling basic human needs, and when reduced to their basic components, look much alike'. This is the approach of Egan (1975) in his training programmes for effective interpersonal relating, of Carkhuff and Berenson (1976) who talk of counselling as 'a way of life', of Illich (1977) who is concerned with the de-skilling of the population by increasing armies of specialists, and of Scally and Hopson (1979) who emphasize that counselling 'is merely a set of beliefs, values and behaviours to be found in the community at large'. Considerable stress is placed later in this chapter on the trend towards demystifying helping and counselling.

Models of helping

Any person attempting to help another must have some model
in his or her head, however ill-formed, of the process
which is about to be undertaken. There will be goals,
however hazy, ranging from helping the person to feel
better through to helping the person to work through an
issue independently. It is essential for helpers to become
more aware of the value-roots of their behaviours and the
ideological underpinning of their proffered support.

> The helper builds his theory through three overlapping
> stages. First he reflects on his own experience. He
> becomes aware of his values, needs, communication
> style, and their impact on others. He reads widely on
> the experience of other practitioners who have tried
> to make sense out of their observations by writing
> down their ideas into a systematic theory ... Finally
> the helper forges the first two items together into a
> unique theory of his own (Brammer, 1973).

Fortunately, in recent years a number of theorists and
researchers have begun to define models of helping. This
can only assist all helpers to define their own internal
models which will then enable them in turn to evaluate
their personal, philosophical and empirical bases.

CARKHUFF AND ASSOCIATES: Carkhuff took Rogers'
ideas on psychotherapy and expanded on them to helping in
general. He has a three-stage model through which the
client is helped to (i) explore, (ii) understand and (iii)
act. He defines the skills needed by the helper at each
stage of the process (Carkhuff, 1974), and has also
developed a system for selecting and training prospective
helpers to do this. Since the skills he outlines are
basically the same skills which anyone needs to live
effectively, he suggests that the best way of helping
people is to teach them directly and systematically in
life, work, learning and relationship-building skills. He
states clearly that 'the essential task of helping is to
bridge the gap between the helpee's skills level and the
helper's skills level' (Carkhuff and Berenson, 1976). For
Carkhuff, helping equals teaching, but teaching people the
skills to ensure that they can take more control over
their own lives.

BRAMMER (1973) has produced an integrated, eclectic
developmental model similar to Carkhuff's. He has expanded
Carkhuff's three stages into the eight stages of entry,
classification, structure, relationship, exploration, con-
solidation, planning and termination. He has also identified seven clusters of skills to promote 'understanding of
self and others'. His list of 46 specific skills is somewhat daunting to a beginner but a rich source of stimulation for the more experienced helper.

IVEY AND ASSOCIATES (1971) have developed a highly

systematic model for training helpers under the label
'microcounselling'. Each skill is broken up into its
constituent parts and taught via closed-circuit
television, modelling and practice.

HACKNEY AND NYE (1973) have described a helping
model which they call a 'discrimination' model. It is goal-
centred and action-centred and it stresses skills
training.

KAGAN AND ASSOCIATES (1967) have also developed a
microskills approach to counsellor training which is
widely used in the USA. It is called Interpersonal Process
Recall which involves an enquiry session in which helper
and client explore the experience they have had together
in the presence of a mediator.

EGAN (1975) has developed perhaps the next most influential model of helping in the USA after Carkhuff's and
has been highly influenced by Carkhuff's work. The model
begins with a pre-helping phase involving attending
skills, to be followed by Stage I: responding and self-
exploration; Stage II: integrative understanding and
dynamic self-understanding; and Stage III: facilitating
action and acting. The first goal labelled at each stage
is the helper's goal and the second goal is that of the
client.

LOUGHARY AND RIPLEY (1979) approach helping from
different viewpoint, which, unlike the previous theorists,
is not simply on the continuum beginning with Rogers and
Carkhuff. They have used a demystifying approach aimed at
the general population with no training other than what
can be gleaned from their book. Their model is shown in
figure 1.

Figure 1

Model of helping (from Loughary and Ripley, 1979)

Assisting

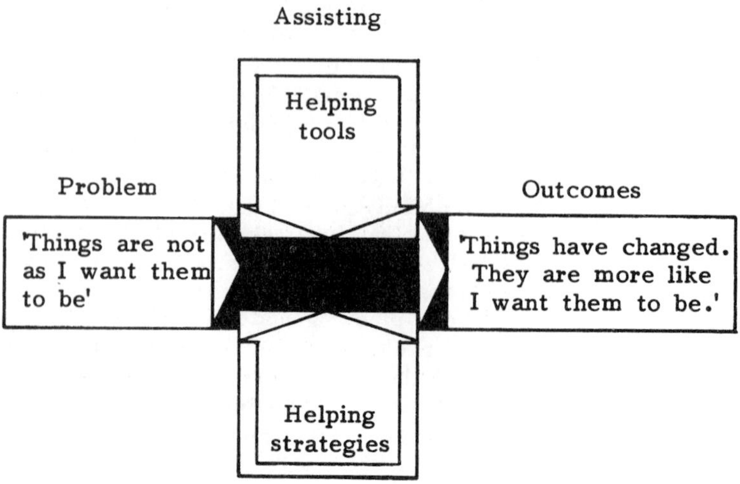

The helping tools include information, ideas, and skills (such as listening and reflecting dealings). The strategies are the plans for using the tools and the first step is always translating the problem into desired outcomes. Their four positive outcomes of helping are: changes in feeling states, increased understanding, decisions, and implementing decisions. Their approach does move away from the counselling-dominated approach of the other models.

HOPSON AND SCALLY: we reproduce our own model in some detail here, partly because it is the model we know best and it has worked very effectively for us and for the 3,000 teachers and youth workers who have been through our counselling skills training courses (Scally and Hopson, 1979), but also because it attempts to look at all the aspects of helping defined at the beginning of this chapter.

Figure 2 outlines three goal areas for helpers, central to their own personal development. It also defines specific helping outcomes. Helpers can only help people to the levels of their own skills and awareness (Aspy and Roebuck, 1977). They need to clarify their own social, economic and cultural values and need to be able to recognize and separate their own needs and problems from those of their clients. Helpers see in others reflections of themselves. To know oneself is to ensure a clarity of distinction between images: to know where one stops and the other begins. We become less helpful as the images blur. To ensure that does not happen, we need constantly to monitor our own development. Self-awareness is not a stage to be reached and then it is over. It is a process which can never stop because we are always changing. By monitoring these changes we simultaneously retain some control of their direction.

From a greater awareness of who we are, our strengths, hindrances, values, needs and prejudices, we can be clearer about skills we wish to develop. The broader the range of skills we acquire, the larger the population group that we can help.

As helpers involved in the act of helping we learn through the process of praxis. We reflect and we act. As we interact with others, we in turn are affected by them and are in some way different from before the interaction. As we attempt to help individuals and influence systems we will learn, change, and develop from the process of interaction, just as those individuals and systems will be affected by us.

Having access to support should be a central concern for anyone regularly involved in helping. Helpers so often are not as skilled as they might be at saying 'no' and looking after themselves.

Figure 2

Goals of helping

SELF-EMPOWERED
INDIVIDUALS

possessing
awareness
self   others   the world

GOALS

commitments outcomes

VALUES

SKILLS
(see figure 3)

INFORMATION
self   others   the world

PERSONAL
DEVELOPMENT
OF THE HELPER

Increasing self-
awareness and
level and range of
skills

Monitoring own
welfare and
development

Using skills to
assist development
of others

Giving and getting
support

Interacting with,
learning from,
changing and
being changed by
individuals and
systems

HEALTHY SYSTEMS
(MICRO, MACRO)

Exist to serve the
development of
individuals

Value and promote
behaviours which
convey respect,
genuineness and
empathy

Encourage
members to
work co-
operatively
towards shared
identifiable
goals

Are open to
internal and
external
influences for
change

Re-evaluate
periodically
goals, methods
and effectiveness

Are dynamic
not static

Feature the
giving and
receiving of
support by
members

Focus on
individual's
strengths

And build on them
(continued ...)

HEALTHY SYSTEMS (MICRO, MACRO) (... continued)	SPECIFIC OUTCOMES
Use problem solving strategies rather than scapegoating, blaming or focussing on faults	Increase understanding
	Changes in feeling states (discharge or exploration)
Use methods which are consistent with goals	Able to make a decision
Encourage power-sharing and enable individuals to pursue their own direction as a contribution to shared goals	Able to implement a decision
	Confirms a decision
	Gets support
Monitor their own performance in a continuing cycle of reflection/action	Adjusts to a situation which is not going to change
Allow people access to those whose decisions have a bearing on their lives	Examines alternatives
Have effective and sensitive lines of communication	Receives direct action/ practical help
	Increases skills, develops new ones
Explore differences openly and use compromise, negotiation and contracting to achieve a maximum of win/win outcomes for all	Receives information
	Reflects on acts
Are always open to alternatives	

181

We would maintain that the ultimate goals of helping are to enable people to become self-empowered and to make systems healthier places in which to live, work and play.

Self-empowerment

There are five dimensions of self-empowerment (Hopson and Scally, 1980a).

* Awareness: without an awareness of ourselves and others we are subject to the slings and arrows of our upbringing, daily events, social changes and crises. Without awareness we can only react, like the pinball in the machine that bounces from one thing to another without having ever provided the energy for its own passage.

* Goals: given awareness we have the potential for taking charge of ourselves and our lives. We take charge by exploring our values, developing commitments, and by specifying goals with outcomes. We learn to live by the question: 'what do I want now?' We reflect and then act.

* Values: we subscribe to the definition of values put forward by Raths, Harmin and Simon (1964): a value is a belief which has been chosen freely from alternatives after weighing the consequences of each alternative; it is prized and cherished, shared publicly and acted upon repeatedly and consistently. The self-empowered person, by our definition, has values which include recognizing the worth of self and others, of being proactive, working for healthy systems, at home, in employment, in the community and at leisure; helping other people to become more self-empowered.

* Life skills: values are good as far as they go, but it is only by developing skills that we can translate them into action. We may believe that we are responsible for our own destiny, but we require the skills to achieve what we wish for ourselves. In a school setting, for example, we require the skills of goal setting and action-planning, time management, reading, writing and numeracy, study skills, problem-solving skills and how to work in groups. Figure 3 reproduces the list of life skills that we have identified at the Counselling and Career Development Unit (Hopson and Scally, 1980b) as being crucial to personal survival and growth.

* Information: information is the raw material for awareness of self and the surrounding world. It is the fuel for shaping our goals. Information equals power. Without it we are helpless, which is of course why so many people and systems attempt to keep information to themselves. We must realize that information is essential (a concept), that we need to know how to get appropriate information, and from where (a skill).

ME AND YOU

Skills I need to relate to you
- communicate effectively
- make, keep and end a relationship
- give and get help
- manage conflict
- give and receive feedback

ME AND OTHERS

Skills I need to relate to others
- be assertive
- influence people and systems
- work in groups
- express feelings constructively
- build strengths in others

ME

Skills I need to manage and grow
- read and write
- achieve basic numeracy
- how to find information and resources
- think and solve problems constructively
- identify my creative potential and develop it
- manage time effectively
- make the most of the present
- discover my interests
- discover my values and beliefs
- set and achieve goals
- take stock of my life
- discover what makes me do the things I do
- be positive about myself
- cope and gain from life transistions
- make effective decisions
- be proactive
- manage negative emotions
- cope with stress
- achieve and maintain physical well being
- manage my sexuality

ME AND SPECIFIC SITUATIONS

Skills I need for my education
- discover the educational options open to me
- how to choose a course
- how to study

Skills I need at work
- discover the job options open to me
- how to find a job
- how to keep a job
- how to change jobs
- how to cope with unemployment
- achieve a balance between my job and the rest of my life
- how to retire and enjoy it

Skills I need at home
- choose a style of living
- maintain a home
- live with other people

Skills I need at leisure
- choose between leisure options
- maximize my leisure opportunities
- use my leisure to increase income

Skills I need in the community
- be a skilled consumer
- develop and use political awareness
- use public facilities

Figure 3

Lifeskills: taking charge of yourself and your life

Healthy systems

Too often counsellors and other helpers have pretended to be value free. Most people now recognize that fiction. Not only is it impossible but it can be dangerous. If we honestly believe that we are capable of being value free, we halt the search for the ways in which our value systems are influencing our behaviour with our clients. If we are encouraging our clients to develop goals, how can we pretend that we do not have them too? Expressing these goals can be the beginning of a contract to work with a client for, like it or not, we each have a concept, however shadowy, for the fully functioning healthy person to which our actions and helping are directed.

As with clients, so too with systems. If we are working towards helping people to become 'better', in whatever way we choose to define that, let us be clear about what changes we are working towards in the systems we try to influence. Figure 2 lists our characteristics of healthy systems. Each of us has our own criteria so let us discover them and bring them into the open. Owning our values is one way of demonstrating our genuineness.

What is counselling?

Having identified six common ways of helping people, counselling will now be focussed on more intensively, which immediately gets us into the quagmire of definition.

Anyone reviewing the literature to define counselling will quickly suffer from data-overload. Books, articles, even manifestoes, have been written on the question.

In training courses run from the Counselling and Career Development Unit we tend to opt for the parsimonious definition of 'helping people explore problems so that they can decide what to do about them'.

The demystification of counselling

There is nothing inherently mysterious about counselling. It is merely a set of beliefs, values and behaviours to be found in the community at large. The beliefs include one that says individuals benefit and grow from a particular form of relationship and contact. The values recognize the worth and the significance of each individual and regard personal autonomy and self-direction as desirable. The behaviours cover a combination of listening, conveying warmth, asking open questions, encouraging specificity, concreteness and focusing, balancing support and confrontation, and offering strategies which help to clarify objectives and identify action plans. This terminology is more complex than the process needs to be. The words describe what is essentially a 'non-mystical' way in which some people are able to help other people to help themselves (see figure 4).

Training courses can sometimes encourage the mystification. They talk of 'counselling skills' and may, by implication, suggest that such skills are somehow separate from other human activities, are to be conferred upon those who attend courses, and are probably innovatory. In fact, what 'counselling' has done is to crystallize what we know about how warm, trusting relationships develop between people. It recognizes that:

* relationships develop if one has and conveys respect for another, if one is genuine oneself, if one attempts to see things from the other's point of view (empathizes), and if one endeavours not to pass judgement. Those who operate in this way we describe as having 'relationship-building skills';
* if the relationship is established, an individual will be prepared to talk through and explore thoughts and feelings. What one can do and say which helps that to happen we classify as exploring and clarifying skills (see figure 4);
* through this process individuals become clear about difficulties or uncertainties, and can explore options and alternatives, in terms of what they might do to change what they are not happy about;
* given support, individuals are likely to be prepared to, and are capable of, dealing with difficulties or problems they may face more effectively. They can be helped by somebody who can offer objective setting and action planning skills.

Counselling skills are what people use to help people to help themselves. They are not skills that are exclusive to one group or one activity. It is clear that the behaviours, which we bundle together and identify as skills, are liberally scattered about us in the community. Counselling ideology identifies which behaviours are consistent with its values and its goals, and teaches these as one category of helping skills.

What may happen, unfortunately, is that the promotion of counselling as a separate training responsibility can increase the mystification. An outcome can be that instead of simply now being people who, compared to the majority, are extra-sensitive listeners, are particularly good at making relationships, and are more effective at helping others to solve problems, they have become 'counsellors' and licensed to help. A licence becomes a danger if:

* those who have it see themselves as qualitatively different from the rest of the population;
* it symbolizes to the non-licensed that they are incapable, or inferior, or calls into question valuable work they may be doing, but are 'unqualified' to do.

It is important to recognize that labelling people can have unfortunate side-effects. Let us remember that

Figure 4

The counselling process

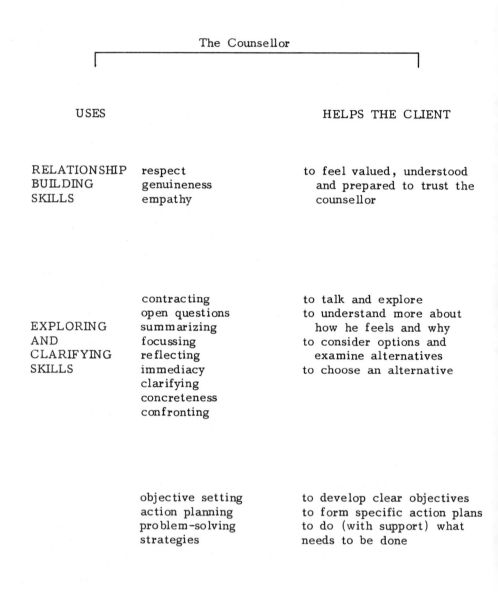

The Counsellor

USES   HELPS THE CLIENT

RELATIONSHIP   respect   to feel valued, understood
BUILDING   genuineness   and prepared to trust the
SKILLS   empathy   counsellor

                contracting   to talk and explore
                open questions   to understand more about
EXPLORING   summarizing   how he feels and why
AND   focussing   to consider options and
CLARIFYING   reflecting   examine alternatives
SKILLS   immediacy   to choose an alternative
                clarifying
                concreteness
                confronting

                objective setting   to develop clear objectives
                action planning   to form specific action plans
                problem-solving   to do (with support) what
                strategies   needs to be done

COUNSELLING IS HELPING PEOPLE TO HELP THEMSELVES

whatever the nomenclature - counsellor, client or whatever - at a particular time or place, they are just people. All, at some time or other, will be able to give help, at other times will need to seek or receive help. Some are naturally better fitted to help others; some by training can improve their helping skills. All, through increased awareness and skill development, can become more effective helpers than they are now.

Counselling is not only practised by counsellors. It is a widespread activity in the community and appears in several guises. Its constituent skills are described variously as 'talking it over', 'having a friendly chat', 'being a good friend' or simply 'sharing' with somebody. These processes almost certainly include some or all of the skills summarized in figure 4. Often, of course, there are notable exceptions: for instance, we do not listen well; we cannot resist giving our advice, or trying to solve problems for our friends; we find it difficult to drop our facades and roles. Counselling skills training can help reduce our unhelpful behaviours and begin to develop these skills in ourselves, making us more effective counsellors, as well as simply being a good friend. In almost any work involving contact with other people, we would estimate there is a potential counselling component. There is a need for the particular inter-personal skills categorized here as counselling skills to be understood and used by people at large, but parti-cularly by all people who have the welfare of others as part of their occupational roles. Specialist 'counsellors' have an important part to play, but it is not to replace the valuable work that is done by many who would not claim the title. Having said that, people sometimes think they are counselling, but in fact are doing things very far removed: disciplining, persuading people to conform to a system, and so on.

Types of counselling

Developmental versus crisis counselling

Counselling can operate either as a RESPONSE to a situation or as a STIMULUS to help a client develop and grow. In the past, counselling has often been concerned with helping someone with a problem during or after the onset of a crisis point: a widow unable to cope with her grief, the boy leaving school desperate because he has no idea what job to choose, the pregnant woman with no wish to be pregnant. This is a legitimate function of counsel-ling, but if this is all that counselling is, it can only ever be concerned with making the best of the situation in which one finds oneself. How much more ambitious to help people anticipate future problems, to educate them to recognize the cues of oncoming crisis, and to provide them with skills to take charge of it at the outset instead of running behind in an attempt to catch up! This is counsel-

187

ling as a stimulus to growth: developmental as opposed to crisis counselling. All successful counselling entails growth, but the distinction between the two approaches is that the crisis approach generates growth under pressure, and since this is often limited only to the presenting problem, the client's behavioural and conceptual repertoire may remain little affected by the experience. There will always be a need for crisis counselling in a wide variety of settings, but the exciting prospect of developmental counselling for growth and change has only recently begun to be tackled.

Individual counselling

As counselling was rooted in psychotherapy it is hardly surprising that the primary focus has been on the one-to-one relationship. There are a number of essential elements in the process. Clients are to be helped to reach decisions by themselves. This is achieved by establishing a relationship of trust whereby individual clients feel that the counsellor cares about them, is able to empathize with their problems, and is authentic and genuine in relating to them. Counsellors will enter the relationship as persons in their own right, disclosing relevant information about themselves as appropriate, reacting honestly to clients' statements and questions, but at no time imposing their own opinions on the clients. Their task is to facilitate clients' own abilities and strengths in such a way that clients experience the satisfaction of having defined and solved the problem for themselves. If a client lacks information on special issues, is incapable of generating alternative strategies, or cannot make decisions in a programmatic way, then the counsellor has a function as an educator whose skills are offered to the client. In this way the client is never manipulated. The counsellor is negotiating a contract to use some skills which are possessed by the counsellor, and which can be passed on to the client if the client wishes to make use of them.

Individual counselling has the advantages over group counselling of providing a safer setting for some people to lower their defences, of developing a strong and trusting relationship with the counsellor, and of allowing the client maximum personal contact with the counsellor.

Group counselling

Group counselling involves one or more counsellors operating with a number of clients in a group session. The group size varies from four to sixteen, with eight to ten being the most usual number. The basic objectives of group and individual counselling are similar. Both seek to help the clients achieve self-direction, integration, self-responsibility, self-acceptance, and an understanding of their motivations and patterns of behaviour. In both cases

the counsellor needs the skills and attitudes outlined
earlier, and both require a confidential relationship.
There are, however, some important differences (Hopson,
1977).

* The group counsellor needs an understanding of group
  dynamics: communication, decision making, role-playing,
  sources of power, and perceptual processes in groups.
* The group situation can provide immediate opportunities
  to try out ways of relating to individuals, and is an
  excellent way of providing the experience of intimacy
  with others. The physical proximity of the clients to
  one another can be emotionally satisfying and supportive. Clients give a first-hand opportunity to test
  others' perception of themselves.
* Clients not only receive help themselves; they also help
  other clients. In this way helping skills are generated
  by a larger group of people than is possible in
  individual counselling.
* Clients often discover that other people have similar
  problems, which can at the least be comforting.
* Clients learn to make effective use of other people, not
  just professionals, as helping agents. They can set up a
  mutual support group which is less demanding on the
  counsellor and likely to be a boost to their self-esteem
  when they discover they can manage to an increasing
  extent without him.

There are many different kinds of group counselling. Some
careers services in higher education offer counsellor-led
groups as groundwork preparation for career choices; these
small groups give older adolescents an opportunity to
discuss the inter-relations between their conscious values
and preferred life styles and their crystallizing sense of
identity. Other groups are provided in schools where young
people can discuss with each other and an adult counsellor
those relationships with parents and friends which are so
important in adolescence. Training groups are held for
teaching decision-making skills and assertive skills.
There are also groups in which experiences are pooled and
mutual help given for the married, for parents, for those
bringing up families alone and for those who share a
special problem such as having a handicapped child. All
these types of groups are usually led by someone who has
had training and experience in facilitating them. The word
'facilitating' is used advisedly, for the leader's job is
not to conduct a seminar or tutorial, but to establish an
atmosphere in which members of the group can explore the
feelings around a particular stage of development or
condition or critical choice.
    Another type of group is not so specifically focused
on an area of common concern but is set up as a sort of
laboratory to learn about the underlying dynamics of how

189

people in groups function, whatever the group's focus and purpose may be. These are often referred to as sensitivity training groups (e.g. Cooper and Mangham, 1971; Smith, 1975). Yet a third category of group has more therapeutic goals, being intended to be successive or complementary to, or sometimes in place of, individual psychotherapy. This type of group will not usually have a place in work settings, whereas the other two do have useful applications there. Obvious uses for this type of group occur in induction procedures, in preparation for retirement, in relation to job change arising from promotion, or in relation to redundancy. The second type of group is employed in training for supervisory or management posts, though one hears less about their use in trade unions.

Schools of counselling

Differences in theories of personality, learning and perception are reflected in counselling theory. It is useful to distinguish between five major schools.

1. PSYCHOANALYTIC APPROACHES were historically the first. Psychoanalysis is a personality theory, a philosophical system, and a method of psychotherapy. Concentrating on the past history of a patient, understanding the internal dynamics of the psyche, and the relationship between the client and the therapist are all key concerns for psychoanalysis. Key figures include Freud, Jung, Adler, Sullivan, Horney, Fromm and Erikson.

2. CLIENT-CENTRED APPROACHES are based upon the work of Rogers, originally as a non-directive therapy developed as a reaction against psychoanalysis. Founded on a subjective view of human experiencing, it places more faith in and gives more responsibility to the client in problem-solving. The techniques of client-centred counselling have become the basis for most counselling skills training, following the empirical evaluations by Truax and Carkhuff (1967).

3. BEHAVIOURAL APPROACHES arise from attempts to apply the principles of learning to the resolution of specific behavioural disorders. Results are subject to continual experimentation and refinement. Key figures include Wolpe, Eysenck, Lazarus and Krumboltz.

4. COGNITIVE APPROACHES include 'rational-emotive therapy' (Ellis), 'Transactional analysis' (Berne) and 'reality therapy' (Glasser), along with Meichenbaum's work on cognitive rehearsal and inoculation. All have in common the belief that people's problems are created by how they conceptualize their worlds: change the concepts and feelings will change too.

5. AFFECTIVE APPROACHES include 'Gestalt therapy'
(Perls), 'primal therapy' (Janov), 're-evaluation counselling' (Jackins), and 'bioenergetics' (Lowen). These have
in common the belief that pain and distress accumulate and
have to be discharged in some way before the person can
become whole or think clearly again.

There are many other approaches and orientations. The
existential-humanistic school is exemplified by May,
Maslow, Frankl and Jourard. Encounter approaches have been
developed by Schutz, Bindrim and Ichazo, 'psychosynthesis'
by Assagioli, 'morita therapy' by Morita, and 'eclectic
psychotherapy' by Thorne. In the United Kingdom the biggest influence on counsellor training has been from the
client-centred school. Behavioural approaches are becoming
more common and, to a lesser extent, transactional
analysis, Gestalt therapy and re-evaluation counselling.

**Where does
counselling
take place?**

Until recently counselling was assumed to take place in
the confines of a counsellor's office. This is changing
rapidly. It is now increasingly accepted that effective
counselling, as defined in this chapter, can take place on
the shop floor, in the school corridor, even on a bus. The
process is not made any easier by difficult surroundings,
but when people need help, the helpers are not always in a
position to choose from where they would like to admin-
ister it. Initial contacts are often made in these kinds
of environment, and more intensive counselling can always
be scheduled for a later date in a more amenable setting.

**What are the
goals of
counselling?**

Counselling is a process through which a person attains a
higher stage of personal competence. It is always about
change. Katz (1969) has said that counselling is concerned
not with helping people to make wise decisions but with
helping them to make decisions wisely. It has as its goal
self-empowerment: that is, the individual's ability to
move through the following stages.

* 'I am not happy with things at the moment'
* 'What I would prefer is ...'
* 'What I need to do to achieve that is ...'
* 'I have changed what I can, and have come to terms, for
  the moment, with what I cannot achieve'.

Counselling has as an ultimate goal the eventual redundancy of the helper, and the activity should discourage
dependency and subjection. It promotes situations in which
the person's views and feelings are heard, respected and
not judged. It builds personal strength, confidence and
invites initiative and growth. It develops the individual
and encourages control of self and situations. Counselling

191

obviously works for the formation of more capable and effective individuals, through working with people singly or in groups.

In its goals it stands alongside other approaches concerned with personal and human development. All can see how desirable would be the stage when more competent, 'healthier' individuals would live more positively and more humanly. Counselling may share its goals in terms of what it wants for individuals; where it does differ from other approaches is in its method of achieving that. It concentrates on the individual - alone or in a group - and on one form of helping. Some other approaches would work for the same goals but would advocate different methods of achieving them. It is important to explore the inter-relatedness of counselling and other forms of helping as a way of asking, 'If we are clear about what we want for people, are we being as effective as we could be in achieving it?'

Counselling outcomes

This chapter has defined the ultimate outcome of counselling as 'helping people to help themselves'. A natural question to follow might be, 'to help themselves to do what?' There follows a list of counselling outcomes most frequently asked for by clients:

* increased understanding of oneself or a situation;
* achieving a change in the way one is feeling;
* being able to make a decision;
* confirming a decision;
* getting support for a decision;
* being able to change a situation;
* adjusting to a situation that is not going to change;
* the discharge of feelings;
* examining options and choosing one (Scally and Hopson, 1979).

Clients sometimes want other outcomes which are not those of counselling but stem from one or more of the other forms of helping: information, new skills, or practical help.

All of these outcomes have in common the concept of change. All counselling is about change. Given any issue or problem a person always has four possible strategies to deal with it:

* change the situation;
* change oneself to adapt to the situation;
* exit from it;
* develop ways of living with it.

192

**s counselling
he best way
f helping
eople?**

In the quest for more autonomous, more self-competent, self-employed individuals the helper is faced with the question 'If that is my goal, am I working in the most effective way towards achieving it?' As much as one believes in the potential of counselling, there are times when one must ask whether spending time with individuals is the best investment of one's helping time and effort.

Many counsellors say that time spent in this way is incredibly valuable; it emphasizes the importance of each individual, and hence they justify time given to one-to-one counselling. At the other end of the spectrum there are those who charge 'counsellors' with:

* being concerned solely with 'casualties', people in crisis and in difficulty, and not getting involved with organizational questions;
* allowing systems, organizations and structures to continue to operate 'unhealthily', by 'treating' these 'casualties' so effectively.

To reject these charges out-of-hand would be to fail to recognize the elements of truth they contain. One respects tremendously the importance that counselling places on the individual, and this is not an attempt to challenge that. What it may be relevant to establish is that counselling should not be seen as a substitute for 'healthy' systems, which operate in ways which respect individuality, where relationships are genuine and positive, where communication is open and problem-solving and participation are worked at (see figure 2). 'Healthy' systems can be as important to the welfare of the individual as can one-to-one counselling. It is unfortunate therefore that 'administrators' can see personal welfare as being the province of 'counselling types', and the latter are sometimes reluctant to 'contaminate' their work by getting involved in administrational or organizational matters. These attitudes can be very detrimental to all involved systems. The viewpoint presented here is that part of a helper's repertoire of skills in the 'tool-bag' alongside counselling skills should be willingness, and the ability, to work for systems change. Some counsellors obviously do this already in more spontaneous ways; for example, if one finds oneself counselling truants, it may become apparent that some absconding is invited by timetable anomalies (French for remedial groups on Friday afternoons?). The dilemma here is whether one spends time with a series of individual truants or persuades the designers of timetables to establish a more aware approach.

One realizes sometimes also that one may, in counselling, be using one's skills in such a way that individuals accept outcomes which possibly should not be accepted. For example, unemployment specialists in careers services sometimes see themselves as being used by 'the system' to help

193

black youths come to terms with being disadvantaged. Such specialists ask whether this is their role or whether they should in fact be involved politically and actively in working for social and economic change.

Resistance to the idea of becoming more involved in 'systems' and 'power structures' may not simply be based upon a reluctance to take on extra, unattractive work. Some will genuinely feel that this approach is 'political' and therefore somehow tainted and dubious. It is interesting that in the USA during the last five years there has been a significant shift in opinion towards counsellors becoming more ready to accept the need to be involved in influencing systems:

> Their work brings them face to face with the victim of poverty; or racism, sexism, and stigmatization; of political, economic and social systems that allow individuals to feel powerless and helpless; of governing structures that cut off communication and deny the need for responsiveness; of social norms that stifle individuality; of communities that let their members live in isolation from one another. In the face of these realities human service workers have no choice but to blame those victims or to see ways to change the environment (Lewis and Lewis, 1977).

In this country, perhaps a deeper analysis is needed of the 'contexts' in which we work as helpers.

Can counselling be apolitical? It is very interesting that in his recent book, Carl Rogers (Rogers, 1978) reviewing his own present position vis-à-vis counselling, indicates the revolutionary impact of much of his work as perceived by him in retrospect. Perhaps identifiable as the 'arch-individualist', Rogers signals now that he had not seen the full social impact of the values and the methodology he pioneered. He writes eloquently of his realization that much of his life and work has in fact been political, though previously he had not seen it in those terms. Counselling invites self-empowerment; it invites the individual to become aware and to take more control; it asks 'How would you like things to be?' and 'How will you make them like that?' That process is a very powerful one and has consequences that are likely to involve changing 'status quos'. Clearly processes that are about change, power, and control are 'political' (although not necessarily party political).

From this viewpoint counsellors are involved in politics already. As much as one may like there to be, there can really be no neutral ground. Opting out or not working for change is by definition maintaining the status quo. If the 'status quo' means an organization, systems or relationships which are insensitive, uncaring, manipu-

lative, unjust, divisive, autocratic, or function in any
way which damages the potential of the people who are part
of them, then one cannot really turn one's back on the
task of working for change. 'One is either part of the
solution or part of the problem!' We have argued (Scally
and Hopson, 1979) that counsellors have much to offer by
balancing their one-to-one work with more direct and more
skilled involvement in making systems more positive,
growthful places in which to live and work.

**To counsel
or to teach?**
Counselling is a process through which a person attains a
higher level of personal competence. Recently, attacks
have been made on the counselling approach by such widely
differing adversaries as Illich (1973) and Carkhuff (Carkhuff and Berenson, 1976). They, and others, question what
effect the existence of counsellors and therapists has had
on human development as a whole. They maintain that,
however benevolent the counselling relationship is felt to
be by those involved, there are forces at work overall
which are suspect. They suggest:

*   that helpers largely answer their own needs, and
    consciously or unconsciously perpetuate dependency or
    inadequacy in clients;
*   helping can be 'disabling' rather than 'enabling'
    because it often encourages dependency.

For counsellors to begin to answer such charges requires a
self-analysis of their own objectives, methods and
motives. They could begin by asking:

*   how much of their counselling is done at the 'crisis' or
    'problem' stage in their clients' lives?
*   how much investment are they putting into 'prevention'
    rather than 'cure'?

To help somebody in crisis is an obvious task. It is, however, only one counselling option. If 'prevention' is
better than 'cure' then maybe that is where the emphasis
ought to be. Perhaps never before has there been more
reason for individuals to feel 'in crisis'. Toffler (1970)
has identified some likely personal and social consequences of living at a time of incredibly rapid change.
Many, like Stonier (1979), are forecasting unparalleled
technological developments over the next 30 years which
will change our lives, especially our work patterns,
dramatically. There are so many complex forces at work
that it is not surprising that many people are feeling
more anxious, unsure, pessimistic, unable to cope,
depersonalized, and helpless. Helpers are at risk as much
as any, but are likely to be faced with ever-increasing
demands on their time and skills. Again, this requires a

195

reassessment of approaches and priorities, which could suggest a greater concentration on the development of personal competence in our systems. We need to develop more 'skilled' (which is not the same as 'informed') individuals and thereby avert more personal difficulties and crisis. One view is that this, the developmental, educational, teaching approach, needs to involve more of those who now spend much time in one-to-one counselling; not to replace that work but to give balance to it.

Personal competence and self-empowerment, which are the 'goals' of counselling, can be understood in many ways. A recent movement has been to see competence as being achievable through skill development. 'Life skills' are becoming as large a band-wagon as counselling has become.

There is a series of Lifeskills Teaching Programmes (Hopson and Scally, 1980b) which covers a range of more generic personal skills: for example, 'How to be assertive rather than aggressive', 'How to make, maintain and end relationships', 'How to manage time effectively', 'How to be positive about oneself', 'How to make effective transitions', etc. (figure 3). The programmes attempt to break down the generalization of 'competence' into 'learnable' units, with the overall invitation that, by acquiring these skills, one can 'take charge of oneself and one's life'. The programme devisers have the advantage, working in a training unit, of being able to work directly with teachers and youth workers on the skills this way. Aspy and Roebuck (1977) have identified that the most effective teachers are those who have, and demonstrate, a high respect for others, who are genuine, and display a high degree of empathy with their students. Many professional counsellors therefore should have the basic qualities required in teaching, and could make appreciable contributions by being involved in programmes in the community which encourage 'coping' and 'growth' skills. More personally skilled individuals could reduce the dependence, inadequacy and crises which are individually and collectively wasteful, and take up so much counselling time.

Towards a 'complete helper'

The argument here is for the development of more complete helpers, more 'all-rounders', with a range of skills and 'tool-bags' full of more varied helping equipment. It is possible to work to increase the level of skill in each particular helping technique and go for 'broader' rather than 'higher' skill development. This diagram (figure 5) could map out for individual helpers how they may want to plan their own development.

On a graph such as this an effective teacher may be placed typically along the line marked 'x'. A full-time counsellor working in a school or workplace may typically be indicated by the line marked 'o'. An organization-change consultant may typically be somewhere along the dotted line.

How much one wants to be involved in helping, at whatever level and in whatever form, obviously depends upon many factors. How much one sees helping as part of the roles one fills; how much helping is part of the job one does; how much one wants to be involved as a part-time activity; how much helping is consistent with one's values, politics and personality; all will have a bearing on where an individual may wish to be placed on the graph. One person may decide to specialize in a particular approach and develop sophisticated skills in that field. Another may go for a broader approach by developing skills from across the range. Yet another may at particular times develop new specialisms as a response to particular situations or as part of a personal career development.

Figure 5

Helpers' skills levels and possible approaches to increasing them

(What skills do I have and in which directions can I develop?)

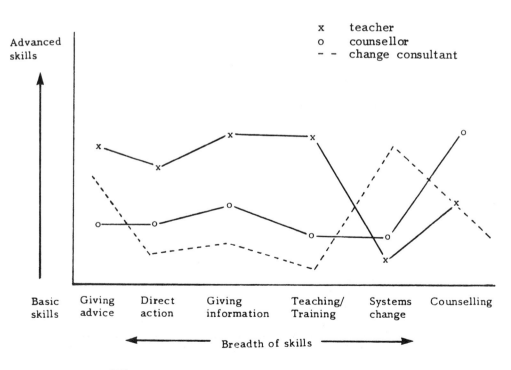

x   teacher
o   counsellor
- - change consultant

Advanced skills

Basic skills

| Giving advice | Direct action | Giving information | Teaching/ Training | Systems change | Counselling |

Breadth of skills

What is advocated here is that basic helping skills can be regarded as essential life skills. These skills can be made available to, and developed very fully in, professional helpers and in those for whom helping is part of their job specification in the workshop, in hospitals, in the social service agencies or in education. They can also be taught to young people in schools and at work.

Counselling in the UK

It is interesting that 'counselling' was a term rarely used in Britain until the mid-1960s. According to Vaughan's analysis (1976):

> three factors gradually tended to focus more attention on this area. One was the emergence throughout this century of a wider band of 'helping' professions, such as the Youth Employment Service, the social work services, and psychotherapy, as well as other 'caring' organizations, such as marriage guidance, and more recently such bodies as the Samaritans and Help the Aged. A second was the development of empirical psychology and sociology, which began to offer specific techniques for the analysis of personal difficulties; and a third was the rapid spread from about the mid-1960s onwards of the concept of counselling as a specific profession derived almost wholly from North America, where it had undergone a long evolution throughout the century from about 1910. Thus today we have a situation comparable in some ways to that of the development of primary education in Britain before the 1870 Act. A new area of specialization seems to be emerging.

It is just because a new area of specialization is developing that people already engaged in, or about to involve themselves in, counselling need to think carefully of where and how they wish to invest their time and resources. Counselling clearly is an important way of helping people, but it is not the only way.

References

Aspy, D.N. and Roebuck, F.N. (1977)
Kids Don't Learn from People They Don't Like. Amherst, Mass.: Human Resource Development Press.
Blocher, D. (1966)
Developmental Counseling (2nd edn). New York: Ronald Press.
Bonnex, J.T. (1965)
Cells and Societies. Princeton University, NJ: Princeton University Press.
Boy, A.V. and Pine, G.J. (1968)
The Counselor in the Schools. New York: Houghton Mifflin.

Brammer, L.M. (1973)
   The Helping Relationship. Englewood Cliffs, N.J.:
   Prentice-Hall.
Burnet, F.M. (1971)
   Self-recognition in colonial marine forms and
   flowering plants. Nature, 232, 230-235.
Carkhuff, R.R. (1969)
   Helping and Human Relations. New York: Holt Rinehart
Carkhuff, R.R. (1974)
   The Art of Helping. Amherst, Mass.: Human Resource
   Development Press.
Carkhuff, R.R. and Berenson, B.G. (1976) Teaching As
   Treatment. Amherst, Mass.: Human Resource
   Development Press.
Coombs, A., Avila, D. and Purkey, W. (1971)
   Helping Relationships: Basic concepts for the helping
   profession. Boston: Allyn & Bacon.
Cooper, C.L. and Mangham, I.L. (eds) (1971)
   T-Groups: A survey of research. Chichester: Wiley.
Corey, G. (1977)
   Theory and Practice of Counselling and Psychotherapy.
   Monterey, Ca: Brooks/Cole.
Corsini, R. (ed.) (1977)
   Current Psychotherapies (2nd edn). Itasca,
   Ill.:Peacock Publications.
Egan, G. (1975)
   The Skilled Helper. Monterey, Ca: Brooks/Cole.
Eibl-Eibesfeldt, I. (1971)
   Love and Hate. London: Methuen.
Hackney, H.L. and Nye, S. (1973)
   Counseling Strategies and Objectives. Englewood
   Cliffs, NJ: Prentice-Hall.
Hoffman, A.M. (1976)
   Paraprofessional effectiveness. Personnel and Guidance
   Journal, 54, 494-497.
Hopson, B. (1977)
   Techniques and methods of counselling. In A.G. Watts
   (ed.), Counselling at Work. London: Bedford Square
   Press.
Hopson, B. and Scally, M. (1980a)
   Lifeskills Teaching: Education for self-empowerment.
   Maidenhead: McGraw-Hill.
Hopson, B. and Scally, M. (1980b)
   Lifeskills Teaching Programmes No. 1. Leeds:
   Lifeskills Associates.
Illich, I. (1973)
   Tools of Conviviality. London: Calder & Boyars.
**Illich, I., Zola, I.K., McKnight, J., Kaplan, J. and
   Sharken, H.** (1977)
   The Disabling Professions. London: Marion Boyars.
Ivey, A.E. (1971)
   Microcounseling: Innovations in interviewing training.
   Springfield, Ill.: Thomas.

Jackins, H. (1965) The Human Side of Human Beings.
Seattle: Rational Island Publications.

Kagan, N., Krathwohl, D.R. et al. (1967)
Studies in Human Interaction: Interpersonal process
recall stimulated by videotape. East Lansing, Mich.:
Educational Publication Services, College of
Education, Michigan State University.

Katz, M.R. (1969)
Can computers make guidance decisions for students?
College Board Review, New York, No. 72.

Kennedy, E. (1977)
On Becoming a counsellor: A basic guide for non-
professional counsellors. Dublin: Gill & Macmillan.

Lewis, J. and Lewis, M. (1977)
Community Counseling: A human services approach. New
York: Wiley.

Loughary, J.W. and Ripley, T.M. (1979)
Helping Others Help Themselves. New York: McGraw-
Hill.

Maslow, A. (1968)
Toward a Psychology of Being (2nd edn). New York: Van
Nostrand.

Mowrer, O.H. (1950)
Learning Theory and Personality Dynamics. New York:
Ronald Press.

Newell, P.C. (1977)
How cells communicate. Endeavour, 1, 63–68.

Parloff, M.B., Waskow, I.E. and Wolfe, B. (1978)
Research on therapist variables in relation to process
and outcome. In S.L. Garfield and A.E. Bergin (eds),
Handbook of Psychotherapy and Behavior Change: An
empirical analysis (2nd edn). New York: Wiley.

**Pietrofesa, J.L., Hoffman, A., Splete, H.H. and Pinto,
D.V.** (1978)
Counselling; Theory, research and practice. Chicago:
Rand McNally.

Proctor, B. (1979)
The Counselling Shop. London: Deutsch.

Raths, L., Harmin, M. and Simon, S. (1964)
Values and Teaching. Columbus, Ohio: Merrill.

Rogers, C.R. (1957)
The necessary and sufficient conditions of therapeutic
personality change. Journal of Consulting Psychology,
21, 95–103.

Rogers, C.R. (1958)
The characteristics of a helping relationship.
Personnel and Guidance Journal, 37, 6–16.

Rogers, C.R. (1978)
Carl Rogers on Personal Power. London: Constable.

Scally, M. and Hopson, B. (1979)
A Model of Helping and Counselling: Indications for
training. Leeds: Counselling and Careers Development
Unit, Leeds University.

Sinick, D. (1979)
  Joys of Counseling. Mincie, Indiana: Accelerated
  Development Inc.
Smith, P.B. (1975)
  Controlled studies of the outcome of sensitivity
  training. Psychological Bulletin, 82, 597-622.
Stonier, T. (1979)
  On the Future of Employment. N.U.T. guide to careers
  work. London: National Union of Teachers.
Toffler, A. (1970)
  Future Shock. London: Bodley Head.
Truax, C.B. and Carkhuff, R.R. (1967)
  Toward Effective Counselling and Psychotherapy:
  Training and practice. Chicago: Aldine.
Tyler, L. (1961)
  The Work of the Counselor. New York: Appleton-
  Century-Crofts.
Vaughan, T. (ed.) (1976)
  Concepts of Counselling. London: Bedford Square
  Press.

Questions

1. Distinguish counselling from other forms of helping.
2. How can counselling and helping be 'demystified'?
3. How large a part do you think counselling does and should play in your work?
4. Distinguish between counselling and counselling skills.
5. Who are 'the helpers'?
6. What makes people effective helpers?
7. Compare and contrast two different models of helping.
8. What in your opinion are the legitimate goals of helping and why?
9. How useful a concept is 'self-empowerment' in the context of helping?
10. What are the advantages and disadvantages of individual and group counselling techniques?

Annotated reading

Corey, G. (1977) Theory and Practice of Counseling and
Psychotherapy. Monterey, Ca: Brooks/Cole.
  This contains an excellent review of all the schools
  of counselling described in the chapter. There is an
  accompanying workbook designed for students and tutor
  which gives self-inventories to aid students in
  identifying their own attitudes and beliefs, overviews
  of each major theory of counselling, questions for
  discussion and evaluation, case studies, exercises
  designed to sharpen specific counselling skills, out-
  of-class projects, group exercises, examples of client
  problems, an overview comparision of all models,
  ethical issues and problems to consider, and issues
  basic to the therapist's personal development.

Corsini, R. (ed.) (1977) Current Psychotherapies (2nd edn).
Itasca, Ill.: Peacock Publications.
An excellent introduction to the main schools of
psychotherapy by leading practitioners who have been
bullied to stick to the same format. Covers psychoanalysis, Adlerian, client-centred, analytical,
rational-emotive therapy, transactional analysis,
Gestalt, behavioural, reality, encounter, experiential
and eclectic. Contributors include Carl Rogers, Albert
Ellis, William Glasser, Alan Goldstein, Will Schutz
and Rudolf Dreikurs.

Vaughan, T.D. (ed.) (1975) Concepts of Counselling. British
Association for Counselling, London: Bedford Square Press.
A guide to the plethora of definitions of counselling.
Uneven, illuminating, with some useful descriptions of
developments in the UK.

13

Social behaviour
Michael Argyle

Introduction: social behaviour as a skill

We start by presenting the social skill model of social behaviour, and an account of sequences of social interaction. This model is relevant to our later discussion of social skills and how these can be trained. The chapter then goes on to discuss the elements of social behaviour, both verbal and non-verbal, and emphasizes the importance and different functions of non-verbal signals. The receivers of these signals have to decode them, and do so in terms of emotions and impressions of personality; we discuss some of the processes and some of the main errors of person perception. Senders can manipulate the impressions they create by means of 'self-presentation'. The processes of social behaviour, and the skills involved, are quite different in different social situations, and we discuss recent attempts to analyse these situations in terms of their main features, such as rules and goals.

We move on to a number of specific social skills. Research on the processes leading to friendship and love makes it possible to train and advise people who have difficulty with these relationships. Research on persuasion shows how people can be trained to be more assertive. And research on small social groups and leadership of these groups makes it possible to give an account of the most successful skills for handling social groups.

Social competence is defined in terms of the successful attainment of goals, and it can be assessed by a variety of techniques such as self-rating and observation of role-played performance. The most successful method of improving social skills is role-playing, combined with modelling, coaching, videotape-recorder (VTR) playback, and 'homework'. Results of follow-up studies with a variety of populations show that this form of social skills training (SST) is very successful.

Harré and Secord (1972) have argued persuasively that much human social behaviour is the result of conscious planning, often in words, with full regard for the complex meanings of behaviour and the rules of the situations. This is an important correction to earlier social psychological views, which often failed to recognize the complexity of individual planning and the different meanings which may be given to stimuli, for example in laboratory experiments. However, it must be recognized that much social behaviour is not planned in this way: the smaller elements of behaviour and longer automatic sequences are outside conscious awareness, though it is possible to attend, for example, to patterns of gaze, shifts of orientation, or the latent meanings of utterances. The social skills model, in emphasizing the hierarchical structure of social performance, can incorporate both kinds of behaviour.

The social skills model also emphasizes feedback processes. A person driving a car sees at once when it is going in the wrong direction, and takes corrective action with the steering wheel. Social interactors do likewise; if another person is talking too much they interrupt, ask closed questions or no questions, and look less interested in what is being said. Feedback requires perception, looking at and listening to the other person. Skilled performance requires the ability to take the appropriate corrective action referred to as 'translation' in the model: not everyone knows that open-ended questions make people talk more and closed questions make them talk less. And it depends on a number of two-step sequences of social behaviour whereby certain social acts have reliable effects on another. Let us look at social behaviour as a skilled performance similar to motor skills like driving a car (see figure 1).

Figure 1

The motor skill model (from Argyle, 1969)

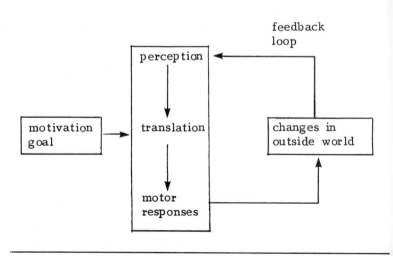

In each case the performer is pursuing certain goals, makes continuous response to feedback, and emits hierarchically-organized motor responses. This model has been heuristically very useful in drawing attention to the importance of feedback, and hence to gaze; it also suggests a number of different ways in which social performances can fail, and suggests the training procedures that may be effective, through analogy with motor skills training (Argyle and Kendon, 1967; Argyle, 1969).

The model emphasizes the motivation, goals and plans of interactors. It is postulated that every interactor is trying to achieve some goal, whether or not there is awareness of that. These goals may be, for example, to be liked by another person, to obtain or convey information, to modify the other's emotional state, and so on. Such goals may be linked to more basic motivational systems. Goals have sub-goals; for example, doctors must diagnose patients before they can be treated. Patterns of response are directed towards goals and sub-goals, and have a hierarchical structure: large units of behaviour are composed of smaller ones, and at the lowest levels these are habitual and automatic.

The role of reinforcement
This is one of the key processes in social skills sequences. When interactor A does what B wants him to do, B is pleased and sends immediate and spontaneous reinforcements: smile, gaze, approving noises, and so on, and modifies A's behaviour, probably by operant conditioning; for example, modifying the content of subsequent utterances. At the same time A is modifying B's behaviour in exactly the same way. These effects appear to be mainly outside the focus of conscious attention, and take place very rapidly. It follows that anyone who gives strong rewards and punishments in the course of interaction will be able to modify the behaviour of others in the desired direction. In addition, the stronger the rewards that A issues, the more strongly other people will be attracted to A.

The role of gaze in social skills
The social skills model suggests that the monitoring of another's reactions is an essential part of social performance. The other's verbal signals are mainly heard, but non-verbal signals are mainly seen; the exceptions being the non-verbal aspects of speech and touch. It was this implication of the social skills model which directed us towards the study of gaze in social interaction. In dyadic interaction each person looks about 50 per cent of the time, mutual gaze occupies 25 per cent of the time, looking while listening is about twice the level of looking while talking, glances are about three seconds, and mutual glances about one second, with wide variations

due to distance, sex combination, and personality (Argyle and Cook, 1976). However, there are several important differences between social behaviour and motor skills.

* Rules: the moves which interactors may make are governed by rules; they must respond properly to what has gone before. Similarly, rules govern the other's responses and can be used to influence behaviour; for example, questions lead to answers.
* Taking the role of the other: it is important to perceive accurately the reactions of others. It is also necessary to perceive the perceptions of others; that is, to take account of their points of view. This appears to be a cognitive ability which develops with age (Flavell, 1968), but which may fail to develop properly. Those who are able to do this have been found to be more effective at a number of social tasks, and more altruistic. Meldman (1967) found that psychiatric patients are more egocentric (i.e. talked about themselves more than controls), and it has been our experience that socially unskilled patients have great difficulty in taking the role of the other.
* The independent initiative of the other sequences of interaction: social situations inevitably contain at least one other person, who will be pursuing personal goals and using social skills. How can we analyse the resulting sequences of behaviour? For a sequence to constitute an acceptable piece of social behaviour, the moves must fit together in order. Social psychologists have by no means discovered all the principles or 'grammar' underlying these sequences, but some of the principles are known, and can explain common form of interaction failure.

Verbal and non-verbal communication

Verbal communication

There are several different kinds of verbal utterance.

* Egocentric speech: this is directed to the self, is found in infants and has the effect of directing behaviour.
* Orders, instructions: these are used to influence the behaviour of others; they can be gently persuasive or authoritarian.
* Questions: these are intended to elicit verbal information; they can be open-ended or closed, personal or impersonal.
* Information: may be given in response to a question, or as part of a lecture or during problem-solving discussion.

(The last three points are the basic classes of utterance.)

Figure 2

The Bales categories (from Bales, 1950)

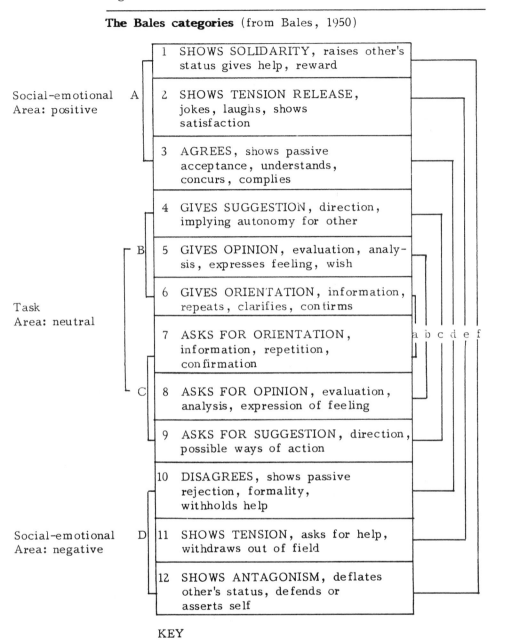

Social-emotional A Area: positive	1	SHOWS SOLIDARITY, raises other's status gives help, reward
	2	SHOWS TENSION RELEASE, jokes, laughs, shows satisfaction
	3	AGREES, shows passive acceptance, understands, concurs, complies
Task Area: neutral B	4	GIVES SUGGESTION, direction, implying autonomy for other
	5	GIVES OPINION, evaluation, analysis, expresses feeling, wish
	6	GIVES ORIENTATION, information, repeats, clarifies, confirms
C	7	ASKS FOR ORIENTATION, information, repetition, confirmation
	8	ASKS FOR OPINION, evaluation, analysis, expression of feeling
	9	ASKS FOR SUGGESTION, direction, possible ways of action
Social-emotional D Area: negative	10	DISAGREES, shows passive rejection, formality, withholds help
	11	SHOWS TENSION, asks for help, withdraws out of field
	12	SHOWS ANTAGONISM, deflates other's status, defends or asserts self

a b c d e f

KEY

A positive reactions	a problems of communication
B attempted answers	b problems of evaluation
C questions	c problems of control
D negative reactions	d problems of decision
	e problems of tension reduction
	f problems of reintegration

* Informal speech: consists of casual chat, jokes, gossip, and contains little information, but helps to establish and sustain social relationships.
* Expression of emotions and interpersonal attitudes: this is a special kind of information; however, this information is usually conveyed, and is conveyed more effectively, non-verbally.
* Performative utterances: these include 'illocutions' where saying the utterance performs something (voting, judging, naming, etc.), and 'perlocutions', where a goal is intended but may not be achieved (persuading, intimidating, etc.).
* Social routines: these include standard sequences like thanking, apologizing, greeting, etc.
* Latent messages: in these, the more important meaning is made subordinate ('As I was saying to the Prime Minister ...').

There are many category schemes for reducing utterances to a limited number of classes of social acts. One of the best known is that of Bales (1950), who introduced the 12 classes shown in figure 2.

Non-verbal signals accompanying speech

Non-verbal signals play an important part in speech and conversation. They have three main roles:

* completing and elaborating on verbal utterances: utterances are accompanied by vocal emphasis, gestures and facial expressions, which add to the meaning and indicate whether it is a question, intended to be serious or funny, and so on;
* managing synchronizing: this is achieved by head-nods, gaze-shifts, and other signals. For example, to keep the floor a speaker does not look up at the end of an utterance, keeps a hand in mid-gesture, and increases the volume of his speech if the other interrupts;
* sending feedback signals: listeners keep up a con-tinuous, and mainly unwitting, commentary on the speaker's utterances, showing by mouth and eyebrow positions whether they agree, understand, are surprised, and so on (Argyle, 1975).

Other functions of non-verbal communication (NVC)

NVC consists of facial expression, tone of voice, gaze, gestures, postures, physical proximity and appearance. We have already described how NVC is linked with speech; it also functions in several other ways, especially in the communication of emotions and attitudes to other people.

A sender is in a certain state, or possesses some information; this is encoded into a message which is then decoded by a receiver.

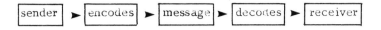

Encoding research is done by putting subjects into some state and studying the non-verbal messages which are emitted. For example Mehrabian (1972), in a role-playing experiment, asked subjects to address a hat-stand, imagining it to be a person. Male subjects who liked the hat-stand looked at it more, did not have hands on hips and stood closer.

Non-verbal signals are often 'unconscious': that is, they are outside the focus of attention. A few signals are unconsciously sent and received, like dilated pupils, signifying sexual attraction, but there are a number of other possibilities as shown in table 1.

Table 1

Awareness of non-verbal signals

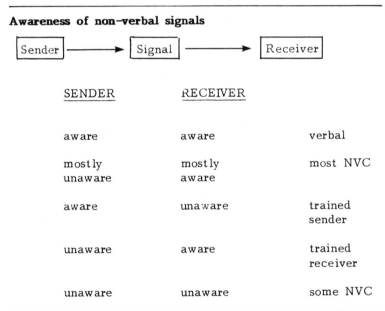

SENDER	RECEIVER	
aware	aware	verbal
mostly unaware	mostly aware	most NVC
aware	unaware	trained sender
unaware	aware	trained receiver
unaware	unaware	some NVC

Strictly speaking pupil dilation is not communication at all, but only a physiological response. 'Communication' is usually taken to imply some intention to affect another; one criterion of successful communication is that it makes a difference whether the other person is present and in a position to receive the signal; another is that the signal is repeated, varied or amplified if it has no effect. These criteria are independent of conscious intention to communicate, which is often absent.

* Interpersonal attitudes: interactors indicate how much

they like or dislike one another, and whether they think they are more or less important, mainly non-verbally. We have compared verbal and non-verbal signals and found that non-verbal cues like facial expression and tone of voice have far more impact than verbal ones (Argyle et al., 1970).

* Emotional states: anger, depression, anxiety, joy, surprise, fear and disgust/contempt, are also communicated more clearly by non-verbal signals, such as facial expression, tone of voice, posture, gestures and gaze. Interactors may try to conceal their true emotions, but these are often revealed by 'leakage' via cues which are difficult to control.

Person perception

In order to respond effectively to the behaviour of others it is necessary to perceive them correctly. The social skills model emphasizes the importance of perception and feedback; to drive a car one must watch the traffic outside and the instruments inside. Such perception involves selecting certain cues, and being able to interpret them correctly. There is evidence of poor person perception in mental patients and other socially unskilled individuals, while professional social skills performers need to be sensitive to special aspects of other people and their behaviour. For selection interviewers and clinical psychologists the appraisal of others is a central part of the job.

We form impressions of other people all the time, mainly in order to predict their future behaviour, and so that we can deal with them effectively. We categorize others in terms of our favourite cognitive constructs, of which the most widely used are:

* extraversion, sociability;
* agreeableness, likeability;
* emotional stability;
* intelligence;
* assertiveness.

There are, however, wide individual differences in the constructs used, and 'complex' people use a larger number of such dimensions. We have found that the constructs used vary greatly with the situation: for example, work-related constructs are not used in purely social situations. We also found that the constructs used vary with the target group, such as children versus psychologists (Argyle et al., in press

A number of widespread errors are made in forming impressions of others which should be particularly avoided by those whose job it is to assess people:

* assuming that a person's behaviour is mainly a product

of personality, whereas it may be more a function of situation he is in: at a noisy party, in church, etc.;

* assuming that his behaviour is due to him rather than his role; for example, as a hospital nurse, as a patient or as a visitor;

* attaching too much importance to physical cues, like beards, clothes, and physical attractiveness;

* being affected by stereotypes about the characteristics of members of certain races, social classes, etc.

During social interaction it is also necessary to perceive the emotional states of others: for example, to tell if they are depressed or angry. There are wide individual differences in the ability to judge emotions correctly (Davitz, 1964). As we have seen, emotions are mainly conveyed by non-verbal signals, especially by facial expression and tone of voice. The interpretation of emotions is also based on perception of the situation the other person is in. Lalljee at Oxford found that smiles are not necessarily decoded as happy, whereas unhappy faces are usually regarded as authentic.

Similar considerations apply to the perception of interpersonal attitudes, for instance who likes whom, which is also mainly based on non-verbal signals, such as proximity, gaze and facial expression. Again use is made of context to decode these signals: a glance at a stranger may be interpreted as a threat, an appeal for help or a friendly invitation. There are some interesting errors due to pressures towards cognitive consistency: if A likes B, he thinks that B likes him more than B on average actually does: if A likes both B and C, he assumes that they both like each other more than, on average, they do.

It is necessary to perceive the on-going flow of interaction in order to know what is happening and to participate in it effectively. People seem to agree on the main episodes and sub-episodes of an encounter, but they may produce rather different accounts of why those present behaved as they did. One source of variation, and indeed error, is that people attribute the causes of others' behaviour to their personality ('He fell over because he is clumsy'), but their own behaviour to the situation ('I fell over because it was slippery'), whereas both factors operate in each case (Jones and Nisbett, 1972). Interpretations also depend on the ideas and knowledge an individual possesses: just as an expert on cars could understand better why a car was behaving in a peculiar way, so also can an expert on social behaviour understand why patterns of social behaviour occur.

Situations, their rules and other features

We know that people behave very differently in different situations; in order to predict behaviour, or to advise people on social skills in specific situations, it is necessary to analyse the situations in question. This can be done in terms of a number of fundamental features.

Goals
In all situations there are certain goals which are
commonly obtainable. It is often fairly obvious what these
are, but socially inadequate people may simply not know
what parties are for, for example, or may think that the
purpose of a selection interview is vocational guidance.

We have studied the main goals in a number of common
situations, by asking samples of people to rate the importance of various goals, and then carrying out factor analysis. The main goals are usually:

* social acceptance, etc.;
* food, drink and other bodily needs;
* task goals specific to the situation.

We have also studied the relations between goals, within
and between persons, in terms of conflict and instru-
mentality. This makes it possible to study the 'goal
structure' of situations. An example is given in figure 3,
showing that the only conflict between nurses and patients
is between the nurses' concern for the bodily well-being
of the patients and of themselves (Argyle, Furnham and
Graham, in press).

Rules
All situations have rules about what may or may not be
done in them. Socially inexperienced people are often
ignorant or mistaken about the rules. It would obviously
be impossible to play a game without knowing the rules and
the same applies to social situations.

We have studied the rules of a number of everyday situations. There appear to be several universal rules; to be
polite, friendly, and not embarrass people. There are also
rules which are specific to situations, or groups of situations, and these can be interpreted as functional, since
they enable situational goals to be met. For example, when
seeing the doctor one should be clean and tell the truth;
when going to a party one should dress smartly and keep to
cheerful topics of conversation.

Special skills
Many social situations require special social skills, as
in the case of various kinds of public speaking and interviewing, but also such everyday situations as dates and
parties. A person with little experience of a particular
situation may find that he lacks the special skills needed
for it (cf. Argyle et al., in press).

Repertoire of elements
Every situation defines certain moves as relevant. For
example, at a seminar it is relevant to show slides, make

long speeches, draw on the blackboard, etc. If moves
appropriate to a cricket match or a Scottish ball were
made, they would be ignored or regarded as totally
bizarre. We have found 65-90 main elements used in several
situations, like going to the doctor. We have also found
that the semiotic structure varies between situations: we
found that questions about work and about private life
were sharply contrasted in an office situation, but not on
a date.

Roles
Every situation has a limited number of roles: for
example, a classroom has the roles of teacher, pupil,
janitor, and school inspector. These roles carry different
degrees of power, and the occupant has goals peculiar to
that role.

Cognitive structure
We found that the members of a research group classified
each other in terms of the concepts extraverted and enjoy-
able companion for social occasions, but in terms of
dominant, creative and supportive for seminars. There are
also concepts related to the task, such as 'amendment',
'straw vote' and 'nem con', for committee meetings.

Figure 3

The goal structure for nurse and patient

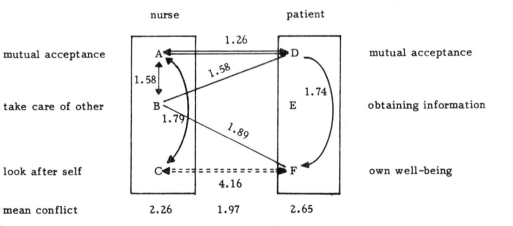

Environmental setting and pieces

Most situations involve special environmental settings and props. Cricket needs bat, ball, stumps, etc.; a seminar requires a blackboard, slide projector and lecture notes.

How do persons fit into situations, conceived in this way? To begin with, there are certain pervasive aspects of persons, corresponding to the 20 per cent or so of person variance found in P x S (personality and situation) studies. This consists of scores on general dimensions like intelligence, extraversion, neuroticism and so on. In addition, persons have dispositions to behave in certain ways in classes of situations; this corresponds to the 50 per cent or so of the P x S variance in relation to dimensions of situations like formal-informal, and friendly-hostile. Third, there are more specific reactions to particular situations; for example, behaviour in social psychology seminars depends partly on knowledge of social psychology, and attitudes to different schools of thought in it. Taken together these three factors may predict performance in, and also avoidance of, certain situations - because of lack of skill, anxiety, etc. - and this will be the main expectation in such cases.

Friendship

This is one of the most important social relationships: failure in it is a source of great distress, and so it is one of the main areas of social skills training. The conditions under which people come to like one another have been the object of extensive research, and are now well understood.

There are several stages of friendship: (i) coming into contact with the other, through proximity at work or elsewhere; (ii) increasing attachment as a result of reinforcement and discovery of similarity; (iii) increasing self-disclosure and commitment; and, sometimes, (iv) dissolution of the relationship. Friendship is the dominant relationship for adolescents and the unmarried; friends engage in characteristic activities, such as talking, eating, drinking, joint leisure, but not, usually, working.

Frequency of interaction

The more two people meet, the more polarized their attitudes to one another become, but usually they like one another more. Frequent interaction can come about from living in adjacent rooms or houses, working in the same office, belonging to the same club, and so on. So interaction leads to liking, and liking leads to more interaction. Only certain kinds of interaction lead to liking. In particular, people should be of similar status. Belonging to a co-operative group, especially under crisis conditions, is particularly effective, as Sherif's robbers' cave experiment (Sherif et al., 1961) and research on inter-racial attitudes have shown.

Reinforcement

The next general principle governing liking is the extent
to which one person satisfies the needs of another. This
was shown in a study by Jennings of 400 girls in a
reformatory (1950). She found that the popular girls
helped and protected others, encouraged, cheered them up,
made them feel accepted and wanted, controlled their own
moods so as not to inflict anxiety or depression on
others, were able to establish rapport quickly, won the
confidence of a wide variety of other personalities, and
were concerned with the feelings and needs of others. The
unpopular girls on the other hand were dominating,
aggressive, boastful, demanded attention, and tried to get
others to do things for them. This pattern has been
generally interpreted in terms of the popular girls
providing rewards and minimizing costs, while the
unpopular girls tried to get rewards for themselves, and
incurred costs for others. It is not necessary for the
other person to be the actual source of rewards: Lott and
Lott (1960) found that children who were given model cars
by the experimenter liked the other children in the
experiment more, and several studies have shown that
people are liked more in a pleasant environmental
setting.

Being liked is a powerful reward, so if A likes B, B
will usually like A. This is particularly important for
those who have a great need to be liked, such as
individuals with low self-esteem. It is signalled, as
discussed above, primarily by non-verbal signals.

Similarity

People like others who are similar to themselves, in
certain respects. They like those with similar attitudes,
beliefs and values, who have a similar regional and social
class background, who have similar jobs or leisure
interests, but they need not have similar personalities.
Again there is a cyclical process, since similarity leads
to liking and liking leads to similarity, but effects of
similarity on liking have been shown experimentally.

Physical attractiveness

Physical attractiveness (p.a.) is an important source of
both same-sex and opposite sex liking, especially in the
early stages. Walster et al. (1966) arranged a 'computer
dance' at which couples were paired at random: the best
prediction of how much each person liked their partner was
the latter's p.a. as rated by the experimenter. Part of
the explanation lies in the 'p.a. stereotype'. Dion et al.
(1972) found that attractive people were believed to have
desirable characteristics of many other kinds. However,
people do not seek out the most attractive friends and

mates, but compromise by seeking those similar to themselves in attractiveness.

Self-disclosure

This is a signal for intimacy, like bodily contact, because it indicates trust in the other. Self-disclosure can be measured on a scale (1-5) with items like:

> What are your favourite forms of erotic play and sexual lovemaking? (scale value 2.56)

> What are the circumstances under which you become depressed and when your feelings are hurt? (3.51)

> What are your hobbies, how do you best like to spend your spare time? (4.98) (Jourard, 1971).

As people get to know each other better, self-disclosure slowly increases, and is reciprocated, up to a limit.

Commitment

This is a state of mind, an intention to stay in a relationship, and abandon others. This involves a degree of dependence on the other person and trusting them not to leave the relationship. The less committed has the more power.

Social skills training

The most common complaint of those who seek social skills training is difficulty in making friends. Some of them say they have never had a friend in their lives. What advice can we offer, on the basis of research on friendship?

* As we showed earlier, social relations are negotiated mainly by non-verbal signals. Clients for social skills training who cannot make friends are usually found to be very inexpressive, in face and voice.
* Rewardingness is most important. The same clients usually appear to be very unrewarding, and are not really interested in other people.
* Frequent interaction with those of similar interests and attitudes can be found in clubs for professional or leisure activities, in political or religious groups.
* Physical attractiveness is easier to change than is social behaviour.
* Certain social skills may need to be acquired, such as inviting others to suitable social events, and engaging in self-disclosure at the right speed.

The meaning and assessment of social competence   By social competence we mean the ability, the possession of the necessary skills, to produce the desired effects on other people in social situations. These desired effects may be to persuade the others to buy, to learn, to recover

216

from neurosis, to like or admire the actor, and so on.
These results are not necessarily in the public interest:
skills may be used for social or antisocial purposes. And
there is no evidence that social competence is a general
factor: a person may be better at one task than another,
for example, parties or committees. Social skills training
for students and other more or less normal populations has
been directed to the skills of dating, making friends and
being assertive. SST for mental patients has been aimed at
correcting failures of social competence, and also at
relieving subjective distress, such as social anxiety.

To find out who needs training, and in what areas, a
detailed descriptive assessment is needed. We want to
know, for example, which situations individual trainees
find difficult (formal situations, conflicts, meeting
strangers, etc.), and which situations they are inadequate
in, even though they do not report them as difficult. And
we want to find out what individuals are doing wrong:
failure to produce the right non-verbal signals, low
rewardingness, lack of certain social skills, and so on.

Social competence is easier to define and agree upon
in the case of professional social skills: an effective
therapist cures more patients, an effective teacher
teaches better, an effective salesperson sells more. When
we look more closely, it is not quite so simple: examination marks may be one index of a teacher's effectiveness, but usually more is meant than just this.
Salespersons should not simply sell a lot of goods, they
should make the customers feel they would like to go to
that shop again. So a combination of different skills is
required and an overall assessment of effectiveness may
involve the combination of a number of different measures
or ratings. The range of competence is quite large: the
best salesmen and saleswomen regularly sell four times as
much as some others behind the same counter; some super-
visors of working groups produce twice as much output as
others, or have 20-25 per cent of the labour turnover and
absenteeism rates (Argyle, 1972).

For everyday social skills it is more difficult to
give the criteria of success; lack of competence is easier
to spot: failure to make friends, or opposite sex friends,
quarrelling and failing to sustain co-operative relationships, finding a number of situations difficult or a
source of anxiety, and so on.

Methods of social skills training

Role-playing with coaching
This is now the most widely-used method of SST. There are
four stages:

* instruction;
* role-playing with other trainees or other role partners
  for 5-8 minutes;

*   feedback and coaching, in the form of oral comments from the trainer;
*   repeated role-playing.

A typical laboratory set-up is shown in figure 4. This also shows the use of an ear-microphone for instruction while role-playing is taking place. In the case of patients, mere practice does no good: there must be coaching as well.

Figure 4
___

A social skills training laboratory

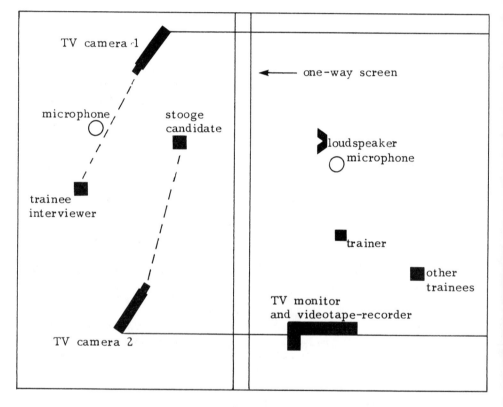

For an individual or group of patients or other trainees a series of topics, skills or situations is chosen, and introduced by means of short scenarios. Role partners are used, who can be briefed to present carefully graded degrees of difficulty.

It is usual for trainers to be generally encouraging, and also rewarding for specific aspects of behaviour, of such reinforcement. It is common to combine role-playing with modelling and video-playback, both of which

are discussed below. Follow-up studies have found that
role-playing combined with coaching is successful with
many kinds of mental patients, and that it is one of the
most successful forms of SST for these groups.

Role-playing usually starts with 'modelling', in which
a film is shown or a demonstration given of how to perform
the skill being taught. The feedback session usually
includes videotape-playback and most studies have found
that this is advantageous (Bailey and Sowder, 1970). While
it often makes trainees self-conscious at first, this
wears off after the second session. Skills acquired in the
laboratory or class must be transferred to the outside
world. This is usually achieved by 'homework': trainees
are encouraged to try out the new skills several times
before the next session. Most trainers take people in
groups which provides a source of role partners, but
patients may need individual sessions as well for individual problems.

Other methods of training

TRAINING ON THE JOB: this is a widely used traditional
method. Some people improve through experience but others
do not, and some learn the wrong things. The situation can
be improved if there is a trainer who regularly sees the
trainee in action, and is able to hold feedback sessions
at which errors are pointed out and better skills
suggested. In practice this method does not appear to work
very well, for example with trainee teachers (see Argyle,
1969).
GROUP METHODS: these, especially T-groups (T standing
for training), are intended to enhance sensitivity and
social skills. Follow-up studies have consistently found
that 30-40 per cent of trainees are improved by group
methods, but up to 10 per cent are worse, sometimes
needing psychological assistance (e.g. Lieberman, Yalom
and Miles, 1973). It has been argued that group methods
are useful for those who are resistant to being trained.
EDUCATIONAL METHODS: these, such as lectures and
films, can increase knowledge, but to master social skills
it is necessary to try them out, as is the case with motor
skills. Educational methods can be a useful supplement to
role-playing methods.

Areas of application of SST

NEUROTIC PATIENTS: role-playing and the more specialized
methods described above have been found to be slightly
more effective than psychotherapy, desensitization, or
other alternative treatments, but not much (Trower, Bryant
and Argyle, 1978). Only one study so far has found really
substantial differences: Maxwell (1976), in a study of
adults reporting social difficulties and seeking treatment
for them, in New Zealand, insisted on homework between
training sessions. However, SST does produce more improve-

ment in social skills and reduction of social anxiety. A few patients can be cured by SST alone, but most have other problems as well, and may require other forms of treatment in addition.

PSYCHOTIC PATIENTS: these have been treated in the USA by assertiveness training and other forms of roleplaying. Follow-up studies have shown greater improvement in social behaviour than from alternative treatments. The most striking results have been obtained with intensive clinical studies of one to four patients, using a 'multiple baseline' design: one symptom is worked on at a time over a total of 20-30 sessions. It is not clear from these follow-up studies to what extent the general condition of patients has been improved, or how well they have been able to function outside the hospital (Hersen and Bellack, 1976). It has been argued by one practitioner that SST is more suitable than psychotherapy for working-class patients in view of their poor verbal skills (Goldstein, 1973).

Other therapeutic uses of SST

ALCOHOLICS have been given SST to improve their assertiveness, for example in refusing drinks, and to enable them to deal better with situations which they find stressful and make them drink. Similar treatment has been given to drug addicts. In both cases treatment has been fairly successful, though the effects have not always been long-lasting; SST is often included in more comprehensive packages.

DELINQUENTS AND PRISONERS have often been given SST with some success, especially in the case of aggressive and sex offenders. SST can also increase their degree of internal control.

TEACHERS, MANAGERS, DOCTORS, etc.: SST is increasingly being included in the training of those whose work involves dealing with people. The most extensive application so far has been in the training of teachers by 'micro-teaching'. They are instructed in one of the component skills of teaching, such as the use of different kinds of question, explanation or the use of examples; they then teach five or six children for 10-15 minutes, followed by a feedback session and 're-teaching'. Follow-up studies show that this is far more effective than a similar amount of teaching practice, and it is much more effective in eradicating bad habits (Brown, 1975). In addition to role-playing, more elaborate forms of simulation are used, for example to train people for administrative positions. Training on the job is a valuable addition or alternative, provided that trainers really do their job.

NORMAL ADULTS: students have received a certain amount of SST, especially in North American universities, and follow-up studies have shown that they can be successfully

trained in assertiveness (Rich and Schroeder, 1976),
dating behaviour (Curran, 1977), and to reduce anxiety at
performing in public (Paul, 1966). Although many normal
adults apart from students have social behaviour difficulties, very little training is available unless they
seek psychiatric help. It would be very desirable for SST
to be more widely available, for example in community
centres.
SCHOOLCHILDREN: a number of attempts have been made
to introduce SST into schools, though there are no follow-
up studies on its effectiveness. However, there have been
a number of successful follow-up studies of training
schemes for children who are withdrawn and unpopular or
aggressive, using the usual role-playing methods (Rinn and
Markle, 1979).

Conclusion

In this chapter we have tried to give an account of those
aspects of social psychology which are most relevant to
the work of teachers, social workers and others, both in
understanding the behaviour of their clients and also in
helping them with their own performance. We have used
various models of social behaviour, such as the social
skills model and the model of social behaviour as a game.
Some of the phenomena described cannot be fully accounted
for in terms of these models: for example, the design of
sequences of interaction. A number of practical implications have been described; in particular, discussion of
the skills which have been demonstrated to be the most
effective in a number of situations, and the methods of
SST which have been found to have most impact. It should
be emphasized that much of this research is quite new and
it is expected that a great deal more will be found out on
these topics in the years to come.

References

Argyle, M. (1969)
Social Interaction. London: Methuen.
Argyle, M. (1972)
The Social Psychology of Work. London: Allen Lane and
Penguin Books.
Argyle, M. (1975)
Bodily Communication. London: Methuen.
Argyle, M. and Cook, M. (1976)
Gaze and Mutual Gaze. London: Cambridge University
Press.
Argyle, M., Furnham, A. and Graham, J.A. (1981)
Social situations. London: Cambridge University Press.
Argyle, M. and Kendon, A. (1967)
The experimental analysis of social performance. In L.
Berkowitz (ed.), Advances in Experimental Social
Psychology, Volume 3. New York: Academic Press.

Argyle, M., Salter V., Nicholson, H., Williams, M. and Burgess, P. (1970)
The communication of inferior and superior attitudes by verbal and non-verbal signals. British Journal of Social and Clinical Psychology, 9, 221-231.

Bailey, K.G. and Sowder, W.T. (1970)
Audiotape and videotape self-confrontation in psychotherapy. Psychological Bulletin, 74, 127-137.

Bales, R.F. (1950)
Interaction Process Analysis. Cambridge, Mass.: Addison-Wesley.

Brown, G.A. (1975)
Microteaching. London: Methuen.

Curran, J.P. (1977)
Skills training as an approach to the treatment of heterosexual-social anxiety. Psychological Bulletin, 84, 140-157.

Davitz, J.R. (1964)
The Communication of Emotional Meaning. New York: McGraw-Hill.

Dion, K., Berscheid, E. and Walster, E. (1972)
What is beautiful is good. Journal of Personality and Social Psychology, 24, 285-290.

Flavell, J.H. (1968)
The Development of Role-taking and Communication Skills in Children. New York: Wiley.

Goldstein, A.J. (1973)
Structured Learning Therapy: Toward a psychotherapy for the poor. New York: Academic Press.

Harré, R. and Secord, P. (1972)
The Explanation of Social Behaviour. Oxford: Blackwell.

Hersen, M. and Bellack, A.S. (1976)
Social skills training for chronic psychiatric patients: rationale, research findings, and future directions. Comprehensive Psychiatry, 17, 559-580.

Jennings, H.H. (1950)
Leadership and Isolation. New York: Longmans Green.

Jones, E.E. and Nisbett, R.E. (1972)
The actor and the observer: divergent perceptions of the causes of behavior. In E.E. Jones, D. Kanouse, H. Kelley, R.E. Nisbett, S. Valins and B. Weiner (eds), Attribution: Perceiving the causes of behavior. Morristown, NJ: General Learning Press.

Jourard, S.M. (1971)
Self Disclosure. New York: Wiley Interscience.

Lieberman, M.A., Yalom, I.D. and Miles, M.R. (1973)
Encounter Groups: First facts. New York: Basic Books.

Lott, A.J. and Lott, B.E. (1960)
The formation of positive attitudes towards group members. Journal of Abnormal and Social Psychology, 61, 297-300.

Maxwell, G.M. (1976)
An evolution of social skills training. (Unpublished,

University of Otago, Dunedin, New Zealand.)

Mehrabian, A. (1972)
Nonverbal Communication. New York: Aldine-Atherton.

Meldman, M.J. (1967)
Verbal behavior analysis of self-hyperattentionism.
Diseases of the Nervous System, 28, 469-473.

Paul, G.L. (1966)
Insight v. Desensitization in Psychotherapy. Stanford,
Ca: Stanford University Press.

Rich, A.R. and Schroeder, H.E. (1976)
Research issues in assertiveness training. Psychological
Bulletin, 83, 1081-1096.

Rinn, R.C. and Markle, A. (1979)
Modification of social skill deficits in children. In
A.S. Bellack and M. Hersen (eds), Research and Prac-
tice in Social Skills Training. New York: Plenum.

**Sherif, M., Harvey, O.J., White, B.J., Hood, W.R.
and Sherif, C.** (1961)
Intergroup Conflict and Cooperation: The Robbers' Cave
experiment. Norman, Okla: The University of Oklahoma
Book Exchange.

Trower, P., Bryant, B. and Argyle, M. (1978)
Social Skills and Mental Health. London: Methuen.

Walster, E., Aronson, E., Abrahams, D. and Rottmann, L.
(1966)
Importance of physical attractiveness in dating
behavior. Journal of Personality and Social Psychology,
5, 508-516.

Questions

1. Is it useful to look at social behaviour as a kind of skill?
2. What do bad conversationalists do wrong?
3. What information is conveyed by non-verbal communication?
4. How is the perception of other people different from the perception of other physical objects?
5. What information about a social situation would a newcomer to it need to know?
6. Do we like other people primarily because they are rewarding?
7. Why do some people have difficulty in making friends?
8. What criticisms have been made of experiments in social psychology? What other methods are available?
9. Does social behaviour take the same form in other cultures?
10. Are there fundamental differences between social behaviour in families, work-groups and groups of friends?

Annotated reading

Argyle, M. (1978) The Psychology of Interpersonal Behaviour (3rd edn). Harmondsworth: Penguin.

Covers the field of the chapter, and related topics at Penguin level.

Argyle, M. and Trower, P. (1979). Person to Person. London: Harper & Row.
A more popular account of the area covered by the chapter, with numerous coloured illustrations.

Argyle, M. (1975). Bodily Communication. London: Methuen
Covers the field of non-verbal communication in more detail, with some illustrations.

Berscheid, E. and Walster, E.H. (1978). Interpersonal Attraction (2nd edn). Reading, Mass.: Addison-Wesley.
A very readable account of research in this area.

Bower, S.A. and Bower, G.H. (1976). Asserting Yourself. Reading, Mass.: Addison-Wesley.
An interesting and practical book about assertiveness, with examples and exercises.

Cook, M. (1979). Perceiving Others. London: Methuen.
A clear account of basic processes in person perception.

Goffman, E. (1956). The Presentation of Self in Everyday Life. Edinburgh: Edinburgh University Press.
A famous and highly entertaining account of self-presentation.

Trower, P., Bryant, B. and Argyle, M. (1978). Social Skills and Mental Health. London: Methuen.
An account of social skills training with neurotics, with full details of procedures.

14

Institutional climates
Jim Orford

A person's behaviour is influenced by the surrounding
environment, as well as by attributes which the person
brings to that environment, such as personality, abilities
and attitudes; behaviour is a function of person and
environment. Many people either live or work in institutions of one kind or another. For such people, the
institution constitutes an important part of their
environment. For some people it constitutes almost their
total environment. Those who work in an institutional
setting cannot fail to notice how the institution influences its members, either for good or ill. Many will have
felt frustrated by the values which the institution seems
to embody, or by the practices which are prevalent within
it, feeling that members could be helped more if things
were otherwise, or even that members are being harmed by
the institution. The great importance of these matters has
begun to be recognized in psychology and there is a
growing psychological literature on the organization of
institutions and how to change them. The study of institutions holds wider lessons for social psychology too. An
institution is a social psychological laboratory. The
experiments which take place there are naturally occurring
experiments in the psychology of social interaction,
social roles, intergroup attitudes, conflict and cohesive-
ness. The study of institutions is of vital significance
for both theoretical and applied psychology.

Much of the literature on the subject concerns health
care or social service institutions such as mental
hospitals and hostels or homes for children, the elderly,
or the disabled. Although many of the examples upon which
this chapter draws are taken from such institutions, the
chapter attempts to build up a general picture of institutional life which is equally as relevant, for example, to
educational institutions such as schools and colleges, and
to penal institutions such as prisons and detention
centres. These different institutions have a great deal in
common. Each is a collection of people, gathered together
in a special building or group of buildings. These people
are not normally linked by family ties, but are there

because of the special 'needs' (for education, care, treatment, rehabilitation, or punishment) of inmates, users, or 'clients' (pupils, residents, patients, members). It is the responsibility of another group of people, the staff, to provide for the clients' needs. This they are in a position to do on account of their special training, skills, or occupation (as teacher, prison officer, warden, doctor or nurse). Usually the institution has been set up by, and is part of, a larger organization which is responsible for managing the institution. Penal institutions in Britain are governed by the complex machinery of the Home Office; hospitals by the Department of Health and its network of Regional, Area and District Authorities, each with a complex system of members, officers and management teams; local authority schools and homes by committees and sub-committees of elected and co-opted representatives, the Authority's officers and the institution's committee of governors or managers; and institutions run by voluntary bodies by their trustees and management committees. Institutions are almost always influenced by people, often a large number of them, who have control over the institution but who are not involved in day-to-day work with the institution's clients. It is more than purely academic to consider some of these defining features of human service institutions. They immediately suggest ways in which an institution differs from a person's own home, and hence they indicate where some problems with institutions are to be expected. The small family home provides the clearest contrast to the large residential institution. People are not gathered together in the former on account of their special needs or their special qualifications, there is no demarcation between staff and clients, and the influence of outside organizations is minimal. It is no wonder that a great deal of thought and effort has been devoted to the goal of making institutions as normal and home-like as possible. Many other comparisons and contrasts between organizations and groups could be made, and there is no absolute definition of an institution.

Ideal types: the total institution and the therapuetic community

It is important to be clear what is meant by a 'total institution' and by the term 'therapeutic community'. They are important ideas which have had much influence but as terms they are liable to be used loosely, and hence may obscure rather than reveal the true facts about institutional climates. In a much-read and often-quoted collection of essays, Goffman (1961) noted that it is normal in modern society for people to conduct different aspects of their life, for example sleeping, playing and working, in different places, with different people, and under different authorities. Total institutions, in contrast, are places where these barriers between different spheres of life are broken down. All aspects of life are conducted in the same place and, most importantly, under the same single authority. It is quite likely that activities are tightly scheduled by those in authority in accordance with an overall plan. He noted that many penal and caring institutions were total institutions in this sense. So were a number of places, with which this chapter is less concerned, such as army barracks, ships and monasteries. On the other hand, certain places with which we are concerned, such as day schools and day hospitals or centres, would not qualify as total institutions.

It is also important to recognize the variety of climates which exist even within total institutions. Tizard, Sinclair and Clarke (1975) point out the danger of generalizing from studies of single institutions, such as Goffman's study of an American mental hospital. Used loosely, the expression 'total institution' can give rise to a misleading stereotype. There is now ample evidence, some of which is considered later in this chapter, that institutions vary greatly, and furthermore that individual institutions can be changed.

Nevertheless, the harm that institutions may do has increasingly been recognized. Barton (1959) has gone so far as to say that the symptoms of institutionalization are so well marked that they constitute a disease entity which he called 'institutional neurosis'. He has written:

> Institutional Neurosis is a disease characterized by apathy, lack of initiative, loss of interest ..., submissiveness, and sometimes no expression of feelings of resentment at harsh and unfair orders. There is also lack of interest in the future ..., a deterioration in personal habits ..., a loss of individuality, and a resigned acceptance that things will go on as they are.

The concept of the 'therapeutic community' is an important one because it represents one type of ideal contrasting markedly with the most inhumane or least therapeutic institutional climates. The model therapeutic community was the Henderson Unit at the Belmont Hospital in Surrey. The unit, described by Maxwell Jones (1952) and studied by Rapoport (1960), was principally aimed at helping young adult psychiatric patients, many of whom had problems of repeated antisocial conduct and who were difficult to accommodate elsewhere. Amongst the ideals of the therapeutic community are an emphasis on ACTIVE REHABIL-ITATION as opposed to custodialism; DEMOCRATIZATION, namely that decision making about the unit's affairs should be shared amongst staff and patients alike; PER-MISSIVENESS, that is, that distressing or deviant behaviour should be tolerated rather than repressed in the interests of institutional conformity; COMMUNALISM, that is, that the climate should be informal without the development of highly specialized roles, and that relationships should be close but never exclusive; and REALITY CONFRONTATION, that is, that patients should be continually given interpretations of their behaviour as other members of the unit see it. It is important to appreciate that the Henderson model is a very specific one. Structurally it was a total institution and although its climate was undoubtedly in contrast to that of many large impersonal institutions, in some ways it was rather formal, with a detailed programme of therapeutic and administrative groups, work assignments and other activities. Units are often self-styled 'therapeutic communities', but they are rarely aiming to recreate the type of therapeutic community unit described by Jones and Rapoport.

Structural features of institutions

There are many separate features of institutions which contribute to climate and a number of these are considered in turn.

Size

There is considerable evidence that people prefer, and are more active socially in, small units of organization. One explanation for these findings is based on the idea of 'manning'. Where there are relatively few patients, pupils or residents, there are relatively many tasks and activities for them to undertake. There is much scope for involvement in activity; the setting may be said to be relatively undermanned. In contrast, settings with relatively many individuals may be over-manned, with relatively less opportunity for involvement for all.

This is perhaps why efforts are often made to break up an institution into smaller, more manageable, groups such as classes, houses or year groups in schools, and wards and small units within hospitals. Unfortunately, the overall institution may continue to exercise a strong influence on the smaller units that comprise it. One recent study (reported in Canter and Canter, 1979) found that staff working in institutions for handicapped children adopted more institution-orientated as opposed to child-orientated practices in looking after the children when their unit was part of a larger overall institution. The size of the unit itself was unimportant. Individual units within institutions are rarely fully autonomous but continue to be dependent on the larger institution in many ways. This notion of autonomy is an important one to which this chapter returns.

Location

Location is of both symbolic and concrete significance. The isolated mental hospital symbolizes community attitudes to the mentally ill, for example. Other features of institutions may symbolize a similar relationship between institution and community. Prisons are often located in cities but their isolation is ensured by their high walls and impenetrable, fortress-like entrances; they are in the community, but not of it. It is important to consider what factors are operating to promote closeness of contact between an institution and its local community, and what factors are operating to inhibit it. It is interesting to speculate, for example, on whether a prominent sign announcing that a house is a home for the elderly eases visiting by members of the community or makes it more difficult? Certainly many small residential caring units such as hostels and halfway houses pride themselves on carrying no such institutional signboard.

Ease of access to community facilities may be crucial for those who must remain in an institution for a long time. A lack of interest in, or desire to return to, life outside are considered by Barton and others to be amongst the main features of institutionalization, and he lists loss of contact with the outside world, loss of personal friends, and loss of prospects outside as three of its main causes.

The issue of location illustrates an important point about the psychology of social organizations. The point is that no single variable is independent of others, and consequently it is almost impossible to impute causal significance to single features of institutions. In this case, it is very unlikely that the location of an insti-tution is independent of the philosophy or ideology under which it operates, or the attitudes of staff who work in it. A rehabilitation philosophy is likely to be associated with close community contacts, either because the institution was located close to the community in the first place, or because means had been found to overcome an unsatisfactory location.

Internal design

Large rooms with high ceilings, glossy interior wall paint in drab colours, no change of decor from one area to another, lack of personalization by the use of pictures, photographs and ornaments, lack of privacy, even sometimes extending to a bathroom and toilet, absence of individual-ized sleeping accommodation, few personal possessions or places to keep them, and generally an absence of opportunity to express individuality; these are amongst the internal design features of an institution which contribute to an institutional as opposed to homely atmosphere.

Once again, however, it is important to avoid over-simple ideas of cause and effect. Two examples from Canter and Canter's book (1979) on the influence of design in institutions illustrate this point. One example concerns the first several years' operation of a purpose-built unit for disturbed children. A number of features, such as outside play facilities, were designed by the architect with the express purpose of reducing institutional climate. Others, such as doors for bedrooms, were strongly advocated by the director and were eventually installed. Observation of the day-to-day life of the unit, however, led to the view that the overwhelming ideology of the unit, which placed emphasis on the children's disturbance and on the need for staff control and surveillance, undermined the use of these design features. Play facilities were rarely spontaneously used, bedroom doors were hardly ever closed, and rooms which were designed for personal use were used as seclusion rooms for punishment. The second example concerns a purpose-built forensic unit where it was possible to show, by a process of behaviour mapping (a procedure whereby a map of WHO does WHAT and WHERE is produced by observing samples of behaviour i different places at different times), the use to which different spaces were put and the meanings that became attached to them. Certain areas were clearly designated as staff offices, and others as patient lounges. As a result, segregation of staff and patients was the rule rather than the exception.

One small-scale feature of physical layout which is relatively easily manipulated is that of SEATING ARRANGEMENT. The terms 'sociopetal' (meaning encouraging interpersonal relationships) and 'sociofugal' (discouraging relationships) have been used to describe possible seating arrangements in institutions. Seats in the lounge areas of old people's homes and other institutions are often arranged around the edge of the room or in some other sociofugal pattern, such as in rows facing a television set. Sociopetal patterns, on the other hand, have been found to lead to more interaction, more multi-person interaction, and more personal conversations. Once again, it is important to appreciate other, more human, aspects of the environment. It is often found, when attempts have been made to rearrange furniture in a more sociopetal fashion, that there is a tendency for the seating to revert to its former arrangement. It is as if the institution has a will of its own and is in some way resistant to change. Exploring how this reversion to type comes about, and making a diagnosis of what is to blame, may provide vital insights into the nature of the institution.

It is worth speculating on the function which may be served by furniture arrangement in different types of institution. For example, why is the seating arrangement of pupils in a primary school often very different from, and usually more sociopetal in design than, that to be found in a secondary school? Is this difference accidental, or does it say something about the expected relationship between teacher and pupils, and perhaps thereby about the whole underlying philosophy of education?

Rules, regul-
ations and
routines

Studies of institutional practices

Considerable progress has been made in describing the variety which exists within health and social care residential institutions. Similar variety exists within educational establishments, and within penal settings.

Studies have compared hostels and hospitals for mentally handicapped children, and have found the latter to be much more institutional in their handling of the children: routine is more rigid, children are more likely to be treated en bloc, treatment is less personalized, and social distance between staff and children is greater. Wide variation is found in the degree of 'ward restrictiveness' in adult mental hospitals. Similar variation exists in halfway houses for ex-psychiatric patients. On average, hostels are less institutional than mental hospitals, the former having between one-half and two-thirds the number of 'restrictive practices' found in the average hospital ward in one study. However, considerable variation is found in both types of facility and there is an overlap between them. Some of the hostels, whilst being small in size, and designed to provide a link between the large institution and the community, nevertheless retain a number of institutional practices. In one instance a hostel had more institutional practices than the hospital rehabilitation ward from which most of its residents came.

A key idea linking these studies is that of clients' DECISION MAKING freedom. Table 1 provides an indication of some of the major areas of decision making considered in such studies. The list could be expanded greatly to include a large range of day-to-day activities over which most people are able to exercise personal choice. Whether an institution allows this exercise of choice to continue for its clients or whether these decision-making freedoms are curtailed is crucial in determining whether an institution creates a therapeutic climate or institutionalization.

Staff autonomy

Reference has already been made, when considering the size of an institution, to the importance of a unit's autonomy within the larger institution. Decision-making freedom may be limited not only for clients but also for those staff who have the closest dealings with them. The advantages of the informality which can occur in a truly independent small unit are illustrated by an incident which occurred at Woodley House, an American halfway house for the mentally ill. It concerned a dispute between pro- and anti-television factions in the house. The former decided to convert part of the basement of the house for their use, leaving the living room to the others. A staff member took them in her car to buy paint and other materials and later the same day the newly-decorated television room was in use. Such an incident could not easily occur in that way in a larger and more formal institution. There are a number of reasons for this, one being that the staff member at Woodley House was not limited to a prescribed professional role, and there were no other members of staff upon whose role territory she was trespassing.

It is this variable of staff autonomy which Tizard et al. (1975) considered to be one of the strongest influences upon the quality of staff-client interaction in an institutional setting. The firmest evidence for this hypothesis is contained in a chapter of their book written by Barbara Tizard. It concerns residential nurseries run by voluntary societies. She observed 13 such units, all of which had been modernized in recent years to provide 'family group' care. Mixed-age groups of six children each had their own suite of rooms and their own nurse and assistant nurse to care for them. Despite this effort at 'de-institutionalizing', marked differences existed in the degree to which nurses were truly independent agents. Nurseries were divided by the research team into three classes on the basis of the amount of unit autonomy. The first group, it was felt, was in effect run centrally by the matron:

> Decisions were made on an entirely routine basis or else referred to the matron. Each day was strictly time-tabled, the matron would make frequent inspections of each group, and freedom of the nurse and child was very limited. The children were moved through the day 'en bloc' ... The nurse had little more autonomy than the children, e.g. she would have to ask permission to take the children for a walk or to turn on the television set. As in hospital each grade of staff wore a special uniform, and had separate living quarters, and the nurse's behaviour when off duty was governed by quite strict rules.

At the other extreme was a group of nurseries which more closely approximated a normal family setting:

> The staff were responsible for shopping, cooking, making excursions with the children and arranging their own day. The children could move freely about the house and garden and the staff rarely referred a decision to the matron. The nurse-in-charge did not wear uniform, and her off-duty time was not subject to rules. Her role, in fact, approximated more closely to that of a foster-mother. Since she could plan her own

day and was not under constant surveillance she could treat the children more flexibly.

A third group of nurseries was intermediate in terms of independence. As predicted, the more autonomous staff were observed to spend more time talking to children, and more time playing, reading and giving information to them. Furthermore, children in units with more autonomous staff had higher scores on a test of verbal comprehension. The difficulty of teasing out what is important in complex social situations, such as those that exist in institutions, is illustrated by Barbara Tizard's findings. Autonomy was correlated with having a relatively favourable staff-to-child ratio and hence we cannot be certain that autonomy is the crucial variable.

Nevertheless, an effect of staff hierarchy was noticed which could explain the apparent importance of autonomy. When two staff were present at once, one was always 'in charge'. This had an inhibiting effect on a nurse's behaviour towards children: she would function in a 'notably restricted way, talking much less and using less "informative talk" than the nurse in charge'. This might explain differences between autonomous and less independent units,

---

Table 1

A range of decisions which may be allowed or restricted in institutions and which are illustrative of those considered in studies of institutional practices

What time to get up and go to bed
What to wear
What to eat for breakfast and other meals
Planning future meals
Whether to make a drink or snack
Whether to visit the local shops
Whether to go to work
Whether to go to the pictures
How to spend own money
When to have a bath
When to have a haircut
Whether to have medicine
Deciding arrangement of own room
Deciding decoration of own room
Whether to smoke
Whether to play the radio or TV
When to invite friends in
Whether to have a sexual relationship with a friend
Planning decoration or repair of the place
Deciding how to care for or control other members
Deciding policy

---

as staff in the latter type of unit would be much more likely to feel that someone else was in charge whether that person was present or not.

Flexible use of space, time and objects

Inflexible routine is one of the major charges brought against the institution by such writers as Barton and Goffman. Institutional life can be 'normalized' as much as possible by allowing flexible use of different areas of buildings and grounds, by varying time schedules, and by allowing flexible use of objects such as kitchen and laundry equipment, televisions, radios and record players. Residential institutions usually deprive adult inmates of the opportunity to take part in 'complete activity cycles'. Instead of taking part in a complete cycle of shopping for food, preparing it, eating, clearing away and washing up after it, residents may simply be required to eat what others have purchased and prepared, rather like guests in a hotel.

Staff attitudes and behaviour

Ideology

The influence of an institution's ideology or philosophy is pervasive, although its significance can be missed altogether by those taken up in the day-to-day activities of the place. Many examples could be given. The philosophy of a progressive school such as Summerhill, with its emphasis on personal development, is distinct from that of a regular secondary school with its emphasis on academic learning. The rehabilitation philosophy of Grendon Underwood prison is distinct from that of most closed penal establishments with their emphasis on custody. Many institutions have mixed and competing ideologies. These frequently give rise to conflict within the institution, the different ideologies often being represented by different cadres of staff. For example, educational and child care philosophies compete within institutions for handicapped children, as do educational and disciplinary philosophies within institutions for young delinquents. Important shifts may take place gradually over time. For example, a general shift from a custodial philosophy to a more therapeutic ideology has occurred in mental hospitals over the last several decades. Quite recently some of those working in British prisons have detected a move in the opposite direction in response to the call for tighter security.

Words such as 'open' to describe penal institutions, 'progressive' to describe educational facilities, and expressions such as 'therapeutic community' to describe an institution for residential care, all serve as public announcements of ideology and intended behaviour. However it has already been noted that terms such as 'therapeutic community' are frequently used loosely, and sufficient is known about the absence of a strong correlation between attitudes and behaviour to make us doubtful that ideal philosophies will always be perfectly borne out in practice.

Staff attitudes

Nevertheless, no one who has worked in an institution for very long can have failed to notice what appear to be marked individual differences in staff attitudes. In the mental hospital setting questionnaires have been devised to detect staff attitudes of 'custodialism' or 'traditionalism'. The matter is by no means simple, however, and attitudes vary along a number of dimensions. For example, one study distinguished between 'restrictive control' and 'protective benevolence'. Staff high on restrictive control tended to be described as 'impatient with others' mistakes' and 'hardboiled and critical', and not 'sensitive and understanding' and 'open and honest with me'. Those high on protective benevolence, on the other hand, were described as 'stays by himself' and 'reserved and cool', and not 'lets patients get to know him' and 'talks about a variety of things'. Staff members high on this attitude scale expressed attitudes that appeared to suggest kindliness towards patients and yet they appear to have been seen by the latter as basically aloof, distant and non-interacting.

A study of hostels for boys on probation also illustrates the complexity of the matter. This study examined the relationship between failure rate, based on the percentage of residents leaving as a result of absconding or being reconvicted, and the attitudes of 16 different wardens. Two components of attitude were identified, each positively associated with success: strictness as opposed to permissiveness; and emotional closeness, which included warmth and willingness to discuss residents' problems with them, versus emotional distance. However, the two components, each separately associated with success, were negatively associated with one another. Hence wardens who displayed more warmth and willingness to discuss problems were also likely to be over-permissive, whilst those who were relatively strict tended to be lacking in emotional closeness. The ideal combination of warmth and firmness was a combination relatively rarely encountered.

Individual staff attitudes can partly be explained in terms of individual differences in general attitudes or personality: members of staff who are more generally authoritarian in personality tend to hold more custodial attitudes. This alone, however, cannot explain differences that are found between different institutions. Although the correspondence is far from complete, it has been found to be the case that where the prevailing policy is custodial, staff subscribe to a custodial view and tend to be generally authoritarian in personality. This raises the fascinating question of how such relative uniformity comes about. It can be presumed that the same three main processes are at work as those that operate to produce consensus and similarity of attitude in any social group or organization. The three processes are (i) selection-in, (ii) selection-out, and (iii) attitude change. Selection of new staff will most likely operate in a way that increases uniformity of attitude, both because certain people are more attracted than others by the prospect of working in a particular institution, and also because certain potential staff members are thought more suitable by those responsible for the selection (selection-in). Staff remain in one place for a variable length of time, and the institution may retain for longer periods those members whose attitudes are in conformity with the prevailing ideology (selection-out).

As social psychological experiments on conformity show so clearly, it is difficult to maintain a non-conformist position in the face of combined opinion, and the third process - attitude change - is likely to be a strong factor.

Staff behaviour and staff-client social distance
Although research leads us to expect none too close a correspondence between attitudes and behaviour, a number of studies in institutions suggest that philosophy and attitudes can be conveyed to residents via staff behaviour. Studies of units for handicapped children, for autistic children, and for the adult mentally ill, suggest that staff behaviour towards clients is more personal, warmer and less rejecting or critical when management practices are more client-orientated and less institution-orientated. Large differences have also been detected in the amount of time which staff members in charge of hoste units spend in face-to-face contact with their residents. Sharing space and activities together, and spending relatively more time in contact with one another, may be the most important factors in reducing social distance.

Social distance between staff and clients was an important concept in Goffman's and Barton's analyses of institutions. Avoidance, or reduced time in contact, is a fairly universal indication of lack of affection and often of prejudiced and stereotyped attitudes. There are numerous means of preserving social distance including designation of separate spaces, such as staff offices. A clearly designated staff office makes staff and client separation easier, but such a space may be used in a variety of different ways. The door may be kept open, or closed, or even locked with a key only available to staff.

Controversy often surrounds the wearing of staff uniform in institutions. There are arguments for and against, but inevitably the uniform creates or reinforces a distinction and may therefore increase social distance.

A movement away from the traditional institutional
organization is very frequently accompanied by the
abandonment of uniforms where these previously existed.
The use of names and titles in addressing different
members of a community is another indication of the
presence or absence of social distance. Forms of address
are known to be good signs of both solidarity and status
within social groups. The reciprocal use of first names is
a sign of relative intimacy, and the reciprocal use of
titles (Mr, Mrs, etc.) a sign of distance. Non-reciprocal
forms of address, on the other hand, are indications of a
status difference, with the person of higher status almost
always using the more familiar form of address (say a
first name or nickname) in addressing the person of lower
status, and the latter using title and surname towards the
former, or even a form of address which clearly indicates
the former's superior status (sir, boss, etc.). If forms
of address change as people get to know one another
better, it is usually the person of higher status who
initiates the use of familiar forms of address first.

Hence an examination of a particular institution in
terms of designated spaces for staff and others, uniforms
and other visual indications of role or rank, and of forms
of address, can give useful clues to status divisions and
social distance within the institution. However, it is of
the utmost importance to keep in mind that social
distance, like all of the social psychological features of
institutions considered here, is a highly complex matter.
It has been suggested, for example, that there are at
least two distinct forms of social distance, namely status
distance and personal distance. If these aspects of social
distance are relatively independent, as has been suggested, it follows that status distance need not necessarily
preclude the formation of a personally close
relationship.

**Instutions
as complex
systems**

The client contribution

Staff may be crucial determinants of climate, particularly
senior staff, but so too are the institution's users or
clients. The climate in an institution is the product of a
bewildering complexity of factors which interact in ways
that are far from straightforward. No simple theory which
attempts to explain what goes on inside an institution in
terms of physical design alone, of the attitudes of senior
staff alone, or of management practices alone, can do
justice to them. It would be as faulty to ignore the personalities, abilities and disabilities of the users as it
would be to ignore the philosophy of the institution or
the design of its buildings. This point is forcefully
brought home in Miller and Gwynne's (1972) account of
homes catering for people with irreversible and severe
physical handicaps where the most likely termination of

residence is death. They contrasted two ideologies which they believed existed in such institutions: the 'warehousing' philosophy, with its emphasis upon physical care and the dependence of residents; and the 'horticultural' philosophy, with its emphasis on the cultivation of residents' interests and abilities. They stress that each has dangers - the one of dependence and institutionalization, the other of unrealistic expectations being set - and that each is a response to the serious nature of the residents' handicaps.

There are a number of studies of social behaviour on the wards of mental hospitals which prove the point that social climate depends upon the mix of patients who are residing there. A clear instance was provided by Fairweather's (1964) study which is described more fully below. Introducing changes of a progressive nature on a hospital ward increased the level of social interaction generally but significant differences between different patient groups still persisted, with non-psychotic patients interacting most, acute psychotic patients an intermediate amount, and chronic psychotic patients the least. The mix of clients is especially crucial where group influence is considered to be one of the principal media of change (whether the change desired be educational, therapeutic or rehabilitative). Even in the relatively permissive climate of the Henderson therapeutic community, those with particularly socially disruptive personalities cannot be tolerated and, if accidentally admitted, may have to be discharged.

Under circumstances where group influence operates, it is particularly important that the client group exerts its main influence in a manner consistent with the overriding philosophy espoused by staff. This is always in danger of going wrong in secondary schools where the 'adolescent subculture' may exert a countervailing force, and in prisons where the 'inmate code' has to be contended with. In Canadian schools and centres for juvenile delinquents a procedure known as the 'Measurement of Treatment Potential' (MTP) has been in use to assess this aspect of climate. Where clients choose as liked fellow clients the same members as those whose behaviour is approved of by staff, then treatment potential is considered to be high. When there is a mismatch between residents' and staff choices, treatment potential is said to be low.

Climate

Many factors contributing to climate have been considered in this chapter and there are many others which it has not been possible to consider. Repeatedly emphasized has been the complex way in which these factors interact to influence the climate of an institutional unit. 'Climate', a word used here to cover any perceptions of, or feelings about, the institution held by those who use it, work in it or observe it, is not the same thing as success, effectiveness, or productivity. However, the latter are notoriously difficult to define, let alone measure, whereas people's perceptions of atmosphere can be collected and their relationships with features of the institution analysed. A massive programme of research along these lines has been conducted by Moos (1974). He has devised a series of questionnaires to tap the perceptions of members of various types of institutions and organizations. The most thoroughly tested of these scales is the Ward Atmosphere Scale (WAS), which assesses perceptions along the ten dimensions shown in table 2. This list was based upon earlier research by others as well as a great deal of preliminary work of Moos' own. He claims that dimensions 1-3 (the relationship dimensions) and 8-10 (the system maintenance and system change dimensions) are equally relevant across a wide range of institutions including schools, universities, hospitals and penal institutions. Dimensions 4-7 (the personal development dimensions), on the other hand, need modification depending upon the setting.

Amongst the many findings from research based upon the WAS and similar scales are the following. First, when staff and patient perceptions are compared in hospital treatment settings, average staff scores are regularly found to be higher on all dimensions except Order and Organization (no difference between staff and patients), and Staff Control (patients scoring higher than staff). Second, when scores are correlated with size of unit and with staff-to-patient ratio, it has been found that Support and Spontaneity are both lower and Staff Control is higher where patient numbers are greater and staff-to-patient ratios are poorer (MTP has also been found to correlate with smallness of size and favourability of staff to pupil ratios). Third, where patients have greater 'adult status' (access to bedrooms, television, unrestricted smoking, less institutional admission procedure, etc.), Spontaneity, Autonomy, Personal Problem Orientation, and Anger and Aggression are all higher and Staff Control is lower. Fourth, all scales correlate positively with ratings of general satisfaction with the ward and with ratings of liking for staff, with the exception of Staff Control which correlates negatively with both.

Changing institutions

A knowledge of the factors discussed in this chapter should enable those involved in policy, planning and management to generate ideas for constructive change, and those in relatively junior positions to try and bring about change in their practice within the prevailing limits of autonomy. However, major changes may require innovations or interventions from outside and it is these that are now discussed in the remainder of this chapter.

Table 2

The 10 dimensions measured by Moos' Ward Atmosphere Scale

Relationship dimensions

1. INVOLVEMENT measures how active and energetic patients are in the day-to-day social functioning of the ward. Attitudes such as pride in the ward, feelings of group spirit, and general enthusiasm are also assessed.

2. SUPPORT measures how helpful and supportive patients are towards other patients, how well the staff understand patient needs and are willing to help and encourage patients, and how encouraging and considerate doctors are towards patients.

3. SPONTANEITY measures the extent to which the environment encourages patients to act openly and to express freely their feelings towards other patients and staff.

Personal development dimensions

4. AUTONOMY assesses how self-sufficient and independent patients are encouraged to be in their personal affairs and in their relationships with staff, and how much responsibility and self-direction patients are encouraged to exercise.

5. PRACTICAL ORIENTATION assesses the extent to which the patient's environment orients him towards preparing himself for release from the hospital and for the future.

6. PERSONAL PROBLEM ORIENTATION measures the extent to which patients are encouraged to be concerned with their feelings and problems and to seek to understand them through openly talking to other patients and staff about themselves and their past.

7. ANGER AND AGGRESSION measures the extent to which a patient is allowed and encouraged to argue with patients and staff, and to become openly angry.

System maintenance and system change dimensions

8. ORDER AND ORGANIZATION measures the importance of order on the ward; also measures organization in terms of patients (do they follow a regular schedule and do they have carefully planned activities?) and staff (do they keep appointments and do they help patients follow schedules?)

9. PROGRAMME CLARITY measures the extent to which the patient knows what to expect in the day-to-day routine of the ward and how explicit the ward rules and procedures are.

10. STAFF CONTROL measures the necessity for the staff to restrict patients: that is, the strictness of rules, schedules and regulations, and measures taken to keep patients under effective control.

240

Innovative programmes

One of the best documented programmes of institutional
change in the mental health care system is the work
reported in a series of publications by Fairweather and
his colleagues. The first report (Fairweather, 1964)
described dramatic differences in patient social behaviour
between an experimental 'small group' ward and a
physically identical 'traditional' ward in a mental
hospital. In the traditional ward, staff members made
final decisions on all important matters. By contrast, on
the small group ward it was the responsibility of a group
of patients to orient new fellow patients to the ward, to
carry out work assignments, to assess patient progress,
and to recommend privileges and even final discharge. The
total experiment lasted for six months, and staff switched
wards halfway through. Social activity was at a much
higher level on the small group ward, and the climate in
the daily ward meeting was quite different with more
silence and staff control on the traditional ward, and
more lively discussion, less staff talk, and many more
patient remarks directed towards fellow patients on the
small group ward. Nursing and other staff evaluated their
experience on the small group ward more highly, and
patients spent significantly fewer days in hospital.

In a further report, Fairweather, et al. (1969)
compared the community adjustment of ex-patients who
moved together as a group from a small group ward in the
hospital to a small hostel unit in the community (the
'lodge'), and others who moved out of the hospital in the
normal way. The results were quite dramatic, with the
lodge group surviving much better in the community in
terms of the prevention of readmission to hospital, the
amount of time in work (much of which was organized by
the ex-patient group as a consortium), and residents'
morale and self-esteem. This is a particularly good
example of the setting-up from scratch of a new small
institution designed to avoid many of the most disagree-
able features of large institutions.

Changes in the philosophies and modes of practice in
institutions mostly take place over a period of years as a
result of the slow diffusion of new ideas. A third report
by Fairweather, et al. (1974) was concerned with this
process.

Having established the value of the lodge programme,
they set out to sell the idea to mental hospitals
throughout the USA. They were concerned to know the
influence of a number of variables upon the diffusion
process, and consequently adopted a rigorous experimental
approach. First, they varied the degree of effort required
on the part of the hospital contacted in order to accept
the initial approach offered. Of 255 hospitals contacted,
one-third were merely offered a brochure describing the
lodge programme (70 per cent accepted but only 5 per cent

finally adopted the lodge programme), one-third were offered a two-hour workshop about the programme (80 per cent accepted and 12 per cent finally adopted), and one-third were offered help with setting up a demonstration small group ward in the hospital for a minimum of 90 days (only 25 per cent accepted but 11 per cent finally adopted the lodge). A second variable was the position in the hospital hierarchy of the person contacted with the initial approach offer. One-fifth of initial contacts were made to hospital superintendents and one-fifth to each of the four professions, psychiatry, psychology, social work and nursing. This variable turned out to be relatively unimportant: contacts were just as likely to result in the adoption of the lodge programme when they were made to people in nursing as to superintendents or those in psychiatry.

Much more important than the status of the person who initiates an idea is, according to Fairweather et al., a high level of involvement across disciplines, professions, and social status levels within the institution. When change did occur there was most likely to exist a multi-disciplinary group which spearheaded the change, led by a person who continuously pushed for change and attempted to keep the group organized and its morale high. The disciplinary group to which this person belonged was of little importance. Nor was change related to financial resources. The need for perseverance is stressed. The need to keep pushing for change despite 'meetings that came to naught, letters that stimulated nothing, telephone calls unreturned, and promises unkept' is a necessary ingredient of institutional change.

Action research

Fairweather's studies concerned the setting-up of new facilities or units. If, on the other hand, constructive change is to be brought about in existing institutions and their units, the total climate of the institution, and particularly the autonomy of the individual staff members, are limiting factors. A number of schemes have been described for providing helpful intervention from outside in the form of a person or team who act as catalysts or change agents. Several of these involve the process known as Action Research. For example, Towell and Harries (1979) have described a number of changes brought about at Fulbourn psychiatric hospital in Cambridgeshire with the help of a specially appointed 'social research adviser'.

The process begins when the interventionist(s) is invited to a particular unit to advise or help. It is stressed that the initiative should come from the unit and not from the interventionist, although it is clearly necessary for the latter to advertise the service being offered, and Moos (1974), for example, has argued that feeding back research data on social climate can itself initiate a change process. After the initial approach there follows a period during which the action researcher gets to know the unit, usually by interviewing as many members as possible individually, by attending unit meetings, and by spending time in the unit observing. Then follow the stages which give 'action research' its name. With the help of the action researcher, members of the unit (usually the staff group collectively) decide upon a piece of research which can be quickly mounted and carried through and which is relevant to the matter in hand. The results of this research are then used to help decide what changes are necessary. The action researcher remains involved during these phases and subsequently as attempts are made to implement changes and to make them permanent.

For example, one of the Fulbourn projects concerned a long-stay ward which had adopted an 'open door', no-staff-uniforms policy and which was designated as suitable for trainee nurses to gain 'rehabilitation experience'. The staff, however, felt 'forgotten' at the back of the hospital, felt that scope for patient improvement was not often realized, and that they were unable to provide the rehabilitation experience intended. The social research adviser helped the staff devise a simple interview schedule which focussed on such matters as how patients passed their time, friendships among patients, and feelings patients had about staff and their work. Each member of staff was responsible for carrying out certain interviews and for writing them up and presenting them to the group. All reports were read by all members of staff and discussed at a special meeting. The group reached a consensus that patients were insular, took little initiative, expected to be led by staff, had no idea of 'self-help', saw little treatment function for the nurses, saw little purposeful nurse-patient interaction, and had only negative feelings, if any, towards fellow patients.

Although there were no immediate or dramatic changes, a slow development over a period of 18 months was reported in the direction of a much increased 'counselling approach to care'. The research interview was incorporated into routine care. This itself involved the setting-up of a special contact between individual nurse and individual patient, a factor which is mentioned in other projects described by Towell and Harries and by many other writers who have described constructive changes in institutions. At first the social research adviser took a leading role in groups in helping to understand the material gathered in interviews. This role was later taken over by the ward doctor and later still by a senior member of the nursing staf At this point the social research adviser withdrew. Later on patients read back interview reports and there were many other signs of reduced staff and patient distance. Over the three-year period during which these changes came about, the number of patients resettled

outside the hospital increased from two in the first year
to eight in the second and eleven in the third.

It is stressed by those who have described 'action
research' and schemes like it, such as 'administrative
consultation' and the type of social systems change faci-
litated by a consultant described by Maxwell Jones (1976),
that staff of a unit must be fully involved and identified
with any change that is attempted. It is relatively easy
to bring about acceptance of change on an attitudinal
level, largely through talking, but to produce a
behavioural commitment to change is something else. Those
who have written of the 'action research' process talk of
the importance of 'ownership' of the research activity.
The aim is to get the unit's members fully involved and to
make them feel the research is theirs.

Resistance to change

We should expect such complex social systems, whose mode
of operation must have been arrived at because it serves
certain needs or produces certain pay-offs for those involved, to be resistant to change. Particularly should we
expect it to be resistant to change when this threatens to
involve change in status and role relationships. Unfortunately, it is just such changes for which we so frequently
search. The themes of decision-making autonomy and social
power have been constant ones throughout this chapter;
they lie at the heart of what is wrong with many of the
worst institutions. Maxwell Jones (1976) believes it is
almost always the required task of the social systems
facilitator to 'flatten' the authority hierarchy, and to
support lower status members in taking the risks involved
in expressing their feelings and opinions, whilst at the
same time supporting higher status members in the belief
that they can change in the direction of relinquishing
some of their authority.

As in most earlier sections of this chapter, examples
of attempts to change institutions or parts of
institutions have been taken from the mental health field.
Nevertheless, the processes and problems involved can be
recognized by those whose main concern is with other types
of institution such as the educational and penal. In
particular, those who have in any way, large or small,
attempted to change such institutions can recognize the
problem of resistance to change. Nothing illustrates
better the need to add to our understanding of how
institutions work. In the process of finding out more on
this topic we learn more of man in a social context, which
is part of the central core of the study of psychology.

References   **Barton, R.** (1959; 3rd edn, 1976)
   Institutional Neurosis. Bristol: Wright.
Canter, D. and Canter, S. (eds) (1979)

Designing for Therapeutic Environments: A review of research. Chichester: Wiley.

Fairweather, G.W. (ed.) (1964)
Social Psychology in Treating Mental Illness. New York: Wiley.

Fairweather, G.W., Sanders, D.H., Cressler, D.L. and Maynard, H. (1969)
Community Life for the Mentally Ill: An alternative to institutional care. Chicago: Aldine.

Fairweather, G.W., Sanders, D.H. and Tornatsky, L.G. (1974)
Creating Change in Mental Health Organizations. New York: Pergamon.

Goffman, E. (1961)
Asylums: Essays on the social situation of mental patients and other inmates. New York: Anchor Books, Doubleday.

Jones, Maxwell (1952)
Social Psychiatry: A study of therapeutic communities. London: Tavistock. (Published as The Therapeutic Community, New York: Basic Books: 1953.)

Jones, Maxwell (1976)
Maturation of the Therapeutic Community: An organic approach to health and mental health. New York: Human Sciences Press.

Miller, E.J. and Gwynne, G.V. (1972)
In Life Apart: A pilot study of residential institutions for the physically handicapped and the young chronic sick. London: Tavistock.

Moos, R.H. (1974)
Evaluating Treatment Environments: A social ecological approach. New York: Wiley.

Rapoport, R.M. (1960)
Community as Doctor: New perspectives on a therapeutic community. London: Tavistock.

Tizard, J., Sinclair, I. and Clarke, R.V.G. (eds) (1975)
Varieties of Residential Experience. London: Routledge & Kegan Paul.

Towell, D. and Harries, C. (1979)
Innovations in Patient Care. London: Croom Helm.

Questions

1. Give two different definitions of 'institution' and give examples of places which fit both definitions, which fit one but not the other, and which fit neither.
2. What do you understand by the term 'total institution'? Why is it thought that they may do harm?
3. What principles are embodied in a proper Therapeutic Community? Is it possible in your view to say when these have been achieved, and when not?
4. What structural features contribute to the climate of an institution, and why?
5. How can the internal design of an institutional unit be

changed to bring about change in the behaviour of those who live or work in it?

6. Discuss the proposition that the most important thing to change in an institution is staff attitudes.

7. Are staff more important than the users or residents in determining the climate of an institution.

8. What formal and informal methods would you use to assess the climate or atmosphere of an institution?

9. What important principles should be kept in mind when trying to change an institution in some way?

10. The only sensible thing to do with institutions is to abolish them altogether. Discuss.

Annotated reading

Barton, R. (1959; 3rd edn, 1976) Institutional Neurosis. Bristol: Wright.

This is now a classic, describing institutionalization as a state analogous to a disease. It is written from a medical perspective but is brief, easy to read, describes the effects of institutionalization within a hospital setting, but forcefully makes the point that the state can arise in any institutional setting.

Fairweather, G.W., Sanders, D.H., Cressler, D.L. and Maynard, H. (1969) Community Life for the Mentally Ill: An alternative to institutional care. Chicago: Aldine.

The main part of this book describes the story of a group of mental hospital patients who left the hospital together and set up home in a 'lodge', living and working productively together. Elsewhere in the book research findings are reported. Those who enjoy reading about research findings may also wish to read Fairweather, G. W. (ed.) (1964), 'Social Psychology in Treating Mental Illness', New York: Wiley.

Goffman, E. (1961) Asylums: Essays on the social situation of mental patients and other inmates. New York: Anchor Books, Doubleday.

Another classic, in which a sociologist describes the events and processes he saw in a large American mental hospital. The book is full of telling sociological insights, but it is important when reading 'Asylums' to have in mind the knowledge that not all institutions, not even all mental hospitals, are alike and there are important differences amongst them.

Jones, Maxwell (1952) Social Psychiatry: A study of therapeutic communities. London: Tavistock. (Published as The Therapeutic Community, New York: Basic Books, 1953.)

Again a classic. The original description of the concept of the Therapeutic Community. Revolutionary in its time and still very well worth reading to understand the basic ideas behind the concept.

King, R.D., Raynes, N.V. and Tizard, J. (1971) Patterns of Residential Care: Sociological studies in institutions for handicapped children. London: Routledge & Kegan Paul.
  This book is detailed and has quite a high research content. It is especially useful for the definitions and criteria for assessing institutional practices. Because of this it has been an influential book upon which later research has been based.

King's Fund (undated). Living in Hospital: The social needs of people in long-term care. London: Research Publications Limited.
  This is an easy to digest pamphlet designed to be read by people who work in institutions. It poses a number of very detailed questions which readers should ask themselves about the environment created in their own institution for those who reside there.

Miller, E.J. and Gwynne, G.V. (1972) A Life Apart: A pilot study of residential institutions for the physically handicapped and the young chronic sick. London: Tavistock.
  This is an account of a study of several homes and hospital units for a very disadvantaged group, most of whom would never leave the institutions in which they were resident. It describes several places in considerable detail and in the course of so doing raises many of the issues with which the present chapter on institutional climates is concerned.

Otto, S. and Orford, J. (1978) Not Quite Like Home: Small hostels for alcoholics and others. Chichester: Wiley.
  This book is in two parts. The first reviews work on institutions and on small hostels for the mentally ill, offenders, and people with drinking problems in particular. The second part describes in detail a research study of two particular hostels for problem drinkers. It covers a great deal of important ground but is probably not so easy to read as some of the other books suggested.

Rutter, M., Maughan, B., Mortimore, P. and Ouston, J. (1979) Fifteen Thousand Hours: Secondary schools and their effects on children. London: Open Books.
  Here is a recent account of a detailed research project concerning the organization of a number of London secondary schools and their effect on the pupils' achievement and behaviour. The research is detailed and painstaking and the book is probably not easy to read, but for those who find statistics heavy going it contains some valuable passages about differences in school organization.

Tizard, J., Sinclair, I. and Clarke, R.V.G. (eds) (1975)
Varieties of Residential Experience. London: Routledge &
Kegan Paul.
    This book is an important collection of chapters written
    by different authors describing a variety of studies of
    residential institutions of one kind or another, mostly
    for children or adolescents. Particularly important are
    the first chapter in which the editors criticize the
    simplicity of Goffman's approach in 'Asylums', and the
    chapter by Barbara Tizard in which she shows how
    residential nurseries can be run in very different
    ways.

Towell, D. and Harries, C. (1979) Innovations in Patient
Care. London: Croom Helm.
    These authors describe how changes were brought about
    in the running of a mental hospital. Particularly
    inspiring in my view is chapter 2 which describes how
    significant change was brought about in an acute
    psychiatric ward and on a long-stay ward.

Walter, J.A. (1978) Sent Away: A study of young offenders
in care. Farnborough, Hants.: Teakfield.
    Walter's book describes his detailed observations and
    results of interviews at one Scottish List D school (the
    equivalent of the English Community Home or, as it use
    to be called, Approved School). It is a racy, easy to
    read account, concentrating particularly on the overall
    ideology or philosophy of the school and its effect upon
    staff and boys.

15

Ageing and social problems
Peter G. Coleman

**What is it
to be old?**

The study of ageing and problems associated with it is now
recognized as important. This is not surprising, for older
people have become the major clients of the health and
social services. They also have a lot of free time at
their disposal. If there is to be an expansion in adult
education and opportunities for creative leisure activities, the benefits should go especially to retired
people.

What is surprising is that it has taken so long for
the social sciences to pay attention to ageing and old
age. So many young professionals are called on to devote
their attention to the needs of people at the other end of
the life span, yet they are likely to have received little
in the way of stimulating material about the distinctive
psychological features of old age.

Professional people do nevertheless have to be
introduced to the subject of ageing, and it is interesting
to note how that introduction has come to take on certain
standard forms over the last ten years. There are two very
popular ways, almost obligatory it seems, to begin talking
or writing about ageing. The first way is to present the
demographic data about the increasing numbers of elderly
people in the population; the second way is to discuss the
negative attitudes people have about working with the
elderly.

The common introduction to ageing
In important respects old age as we know it today is a
relatively modern phenomenon. Though there may have been
individual societies in the past where a comparably large
part of the population was old, it is clear that there has
been a dramatic change in developed countries since the
turn of the century. At that time in Britain those over
the age of 65 constituted one in 20 of the population;
today they constitute one in seven.

In recent years much more use is being made of the
statistic 'over the age of 75', since it has become clear
that this is the group in the population which makes the
largest demands on the health and social services. This

has highlighted the worrying news for service planners in a time of economic constraints that, while the total number of those over 65 will not increase very much in the coming years, the population of those over 75 has already passed 5 per cent of the total population and will reach 6 per cent by the end of the 1980s.

However, expressing concern simply at the number of elderly people in the population is misleading. Why after all should it be a problem that 15 per cent rather than, say, 10 per cent or 5 per cent of the population is over the age of 65, or that 6 per cent rather than 4 per cent or 2 per cent is over the age of 75? A lot of the issues have to do with economics. The State must find the means to continue paying adequate and perhaps even improved pensions, and to provide welfare services to larger numbers of people.

Yet perhaps the more fundamental issues are the availability and willingness of people, whether relatives, neighbours, professionals or volunteers, to give assistance to large numbers of disabled people in the population. For ageing, as any introduction to the subject makes abundantly clear, is associated with an increasing likelihood of developing chronic disability.

Global estimates of disability in daily living (in getting around the house and providing for oneself) indicate that the need for assistance is present in 15-20 per cent of the age group 65-74, rising to 35-40 per cent in the 75-84 age group and to over 60 per cent in those above 85. If one adds on the number of people living in institutions (hospitals and old people's homes), which is about 4-5 per cent of the total elderly population, one can conclude that about 30 per cent, nearly one in three, of all people over the age of 65 are disabled and in need of help.

A typical introduction to ageing then goes on to present further numerical data on the social position of the elderly. Almost one-third of people over 65 have been found to live alone and large numbers are lonely. Many live in poor housing, lack basic amenities and so on.

The need for a life-span perspective

Large numbers of elderly people, large numbers of disabled elderly people, and large numbers of elderly people living in deprived circumstances; such is a typical introduction to old age. But there are vitally important perspectives missing. No wonder indeed that we should be concerned with attitudes, with finding enough people prepared to work with the elderly, enough geriatricians, enough nurses, enough social workers and so on, when the only image we present of old age is a negative one. If the only perspective we emphasize is one of endless problems, often insoluble because of irremediable physical and mental deterioration, we cannot expect many people to have the courage to become involved.

Old people are people like the rest of us. What is special about them is not that they may be mentally deteriorated, disabled or isolated. The majority, after all, is none of these things and many people reach the end of their lives without suffering any disadvantages. What is special about old people is that they have lived a long time. They have had all the kinds of experience we have had and many, many more. They are moving towards the end of life it is true, but it is every bit as important how one ends one's life as how one begins it.

The perspective on ageing that is needed is one which takes into account the whole life span. The discovery any student of old age has to make is not only that old people have a long life history behind them but that their present lives, their needs and wishes, cannot be understood without an appreciation of that life history.

If we really talk to old people all this will become evident. But how often do we do this? A most eloquent testimony of our neglect is a poem (88 lines long) that was found in the hospital locker of a geriatric patient. (It can be found in full, quoted in the preface of the Open University Text, Carver, V. and Liddiard, P., 1978, 'An Ageing Population', Hodder & Stoughton.)

> What do you see nurses
>   What do you see?
> Are you thinking
>   When you are looking at me
> A crabbit old woman
>   Not very wise,
> Uncertain of habit
>   With far-away eyes
> ....
> Then open your eyes nurse,
>   You're not looking at me.

The writer emphasizes the continuity between her identity as an old person and her identities at previous stages in the life cycle. She is still the small child of ten with a large family around her, still the 16 year old full of hopes and expectations, still the bride she was at 20 and the young woman of 30 with her children growing up fast. At 40 her children are leaving home, and she and her husband are on their own again. But then there are grandchildren for her to take an interest in. Years pass and she has lost her husband and must learn to live alone. She is all of these people. But the nurse does not see them.

Psychological changes with old age

It is only proper to admit at the outset that the main activity of psychologists interested in ageing, with some exceptions, has not been of a life span perspective. Their work has mainly been concerned with trying to establish

251

what psychological changes, usually changes of deterioration, occur with advancing age, with understanding the
bases of such changes and finding ways of compensating for
them. These are obviously important questions.

Cognitive deterioration

It would be wishful thinking to deny that there is any
deterioration with age. Physical ageing is a fact which is
easy to observe, though it may occur at different rates in
different people. Performance in everyday tasks in which
we have to use our cognitive ability to register things we
see or hear, remember them and think about them also dete
iorates. Absent-mindedness is one of the most common
complaints of older people in everyday life.

In more recent cross-sectional studies of the performance of different age groups on experimental tasks, psychologists have tried their best to control for obvious
factors which might produce differences in their own
right, like education, illness, sensory impairment and
willingness to carry out the tasks in question. Of course,
certain question marks remain over differences in attitude
and perceived role: for instance, whether older people see
the purpose of such tasks in the same way as younger
people. Nevertheless, certain conclusions can be drawn
about the abilities which seem to change the most as one
grows older. In the first place, older people take much
longer to carry out tasks and this is not only because
their limb movements are slower. In tasks in which they
have to divide their attention ('try to do two things at
once'), decline with age is very marked and is already
evident in those over 30. Ability to remember things we
have seen or heard declines, as does the ability to hold
associations in mind.

However, in some older people decline is not evident
at all. Particular experiences, for example particular
occupational backgrounds, may develop certain abilities in
an individual to such an extent that they remain well
developed throughout old age. Retired telephone operators
who have no difficulty in dividing attention between a
number of messages are a case in point. The prominence of
so many older people in public life where they reap the
fruit of years of experience in political dealings is also
an obvious illustration. Moreover, it seems to be true
that in some old people deterioration does not, in fact,
occur. There are studies which indicate that the cognitive
ability of a sizeable minority of elderly people, perhaps
as many as one in ten, cannot be distinguished from that
of younger people.

This, then, is evidence that age itself is not the
important thing. Indeed it seems better to view age simply
as a vector along which to measure the things that happen
to people. Some things that happen with age are universal.
They occur at different times, but they are unavoidable.

These things we can, if we like, describe as 'age' changes. But a lot of the things we associate with old age are not due to ageing processes and are not universal. There is a great variation in the extent to which people are hit by physical and social losses as they grow old. Some people are fortunate, some people are unfortunate.

From the point of view of cognitive ability, the most unlucky are those people who suffer from the various forms of dementia or brain diseases which lead to a progressive deterioration in mental functioning. But health is by no means the only extrinsic factor influencing mental state in old age. A lot of research has been done recently on the psychological effects of such brain-washing treatments as isolation and sensory deprivation. Disorientation and confusion are common results. Yet we are often slow to recognize that old people may be living in circumstances where by any ordinary standards they are extremely isolated and deprived of stimulation. No one calls to see them, to engage them, to remind them of their names, roles and relationships. Disorientation in time and space, and confusion about identity and relationship with others, can be a natural result. From our own experience we know how time can lose meaning after one has been ill in bed for a day or two, away from the normal daily routine.

Other social and psychological factors play a role too. Motivation to recover or maintain abilities is obviously a crucial factor, and a number of studies have shown that amount of education remains one of the major factors in cognitive ability and performance throughout life.

Personality and life style
Scientific work on personality and style of life in old age does not match the amount that has been done on cognitive functioning. The evidence we do have, however, relates both to change and stability.

One clear finding from research is that introversion or interiority increases with age. This means that as people grow old they become more preoccupied with their own selves, their own thoughts and feelings and less with the outside world. This change is only relative, of course, but it is evident both from responses to questionnaires and also from projective tests, where people are asked to describe or react to stimuli they are presented with, such as pictures of family and social situations.

The term disengagement has been used to describe such a change in orientation; a decreased concern with interacting with others and being involved in the outside world and an increased satisfaction with one's own world of memories and immediate surroundings. However, critics have been quick to point out the dangers of exaggerating the extent to which disengagement is a 'natural' development in old age. Most of the decreased interaction and involvement of older people is forced upon them by undesired physical and social changes: disability, bereavement, loss of occupational roles and so on. Moreover, there is also clear evidence that old people are happier when there is a good deal of continuity between their past and present activities.

Indeed, in contrast to any change in personality that may occur, the stability that people show in their characteristics and style of life over a period of time is far more striking. Longitudinal studies show that people continue to enjoy the same interests and activities. When striking negative changes occur in a person's interests or familiar mode of activities, or ways of coping with life in old age, for no obvious reason, this is often a sign of psychiatric illness, especially depression.

Some of the most valuable studies on personality in old age are, in fact, those which have shown how important it is to take into reckoning a person's life style, for instance in explaining why people react differently to changes and losses such as retirement, bereavement and living alone, or a move to a residential home. Any research finding about old people usually has to be qualified by reference to life style. This is mentioned again when talking about adjustment to relocation.

Growth and development

Though deterioration has been the main perspective of psychological research on ageing up to now, it is not the only one. Certainly in literature old age has been treated much more generously. The works of Nobel prize winners, such as Patrick White ('The Eye of the Storm', 1973), Saul Bellow ('Mr Sammler's Planet', 1969) and Ernest Hemingway ('The Old Man and the Sea', 1952), present vivid and compelling pictures of old age that, like King Lear, have to do with deterioration and change but also with growth in understanding and the values of existence.

Indeed, a characteristic theme in literature is of old age as a time of questioning; of one's own achievements, of the meaning of one's life, of the values one lived by and of what is of lasting value. It is as if an old person, freed from the strait-jacket of society, suffering losses in his ability to function and in his social position - perhaps indeed precisely because of them - is, somehow, let free to question life. Psychologists have only begun tentatively to approach these issues, but have devoted considerable attention to the meaning of life.

Adaptation to loss in old age

From what has already been said it should be clear that old age is a time of great inequality. It is a time when losses occur, loss of physical and mental abilities, loss of people who were close to one, loss of roles and loss of activities. These losses are not inevitable; they do not

occur in the same degree to everyone; but adapting to loss
is a characteristic feature of old age.

Attitudes to health and well-being

Severe disability is one of the major losses of old age
and its central importance in shaping the rest of an
individual's life is one of the most common findings to
emerge from investigations on social aspects of ageing.
People who are disabled have more problems in maintaining
their desired styles of life and are more dissatisfied
than people who are not disabled. This is not surprising.

What is more surprising, or at least not logically to
be expected, is the fact that, in general, levels of well-
being do not decline with age. This is despite the fact
that the incidence and severity of disability tend to
increase with age and have a great influence on well-
being. The key to understanding this comes from studies on
subjective health.

The clear evidence from both longitudinal and cross-
sectional studies is that whereas objective health and
physical functioning of elderly people tend to deteriorate
with age, the same is not true in regard to how they feel
about their health. The most likely explanation has to do
with expectations. People expect to become somewhat more
disabled with old age. If they do, they accept it. But if
their physical functioning remains stable they may in fact
experience this as a bonus and feel better as a result.
Only if their health deteriorates beyond the expected norm
are they likely to feel badly about it.

This argument applies strictly only to feeling well,
but it has a wider implication for well-being generally
and for reactions to other losses in old age. Expectation
is a very important aspect of reaction to loss. It is what
people expect and what people find normal that determines
how they react to things and how satisfied they feel with
their situation. This kind of consideration also leads one
to reflect how different things could be if old people's
expectations changed. This is in fact not so unlikely.
Future generations of elderly people may be far less
accepting of lower standards of health and also, for
instance, of income. They may expect things to be a good
deal better for them. And if things are not going to be
better they are going to be less happy as a result.

Adjustment to relocation

Another misfortune often following from disability is that
people can find themselves being obliged to move, sometimes quite unexpectedly and against their will, to
different environments, particularly institutional
settings, where they often have to remain for the rest of
their lives. Though this is usually done to them 'for
their own good' (they are judged incapable of looking
after themselves in their own homes), the end result may

be much worse than leaving them alone: for instance, further deterioration and loss of interest in life.

There has been growing realization of the extent to which environmental changes can contribute to physical illness and psychiatric disorders. Even where it is voluntarily undertaken and has otherwise favourable effects, there are indications that rehousing can undermine a person's health. There is also a great deal of variation between individuals in their reactions, so it is important to discover which factors might predict the ability to adjust easily to new surroundings.

Among psychological factors cognitive ability is clearly crucial. There appear to be two major reasons why cognitively impaired old people react worse to relocation. In the first place, their lack of ability to anticipate and prepare means that they experience more stress on making the move. Second, because of their poor short-term memory and orientation abilities it may take them a long while to understand their new surroundings.

Personality is important too. We are not sufficiently sensitive to the fact that the institutional environments we provide may be fine for one kind of elderly person but not for another. American studies have shown the importance, for instance, of rebellious and aggressive traits, as opposed to passive and compliant ones, in predicting survival and lack of deterioration after relocation to institutional settings. Vital as well, of course, are attitudinal factors concerned with what a move means to the persons concerned, whether they want to go, and how they see their own future in a new setting.

Self-esteem and its sources: the lynchpin of adjustment?
Disability and environmental change have been picked out for consideration as two of the negative changes associated with old age. There are others, of course. Bereavement requires a major adjustment which seems to follow certain definite stages. Grieving is a normal, healthy part of the process, and the support and understanding of those around in allowing bereaved people to express themselves may be very important to it. Loss of occupational role with retirement is another big change. Indeed, adjustment to it is often thought of in the same terms as adjustment to the old age role itself. Most people make good adaptations, but not all, and retirement can be a major precipitating factor in the onset of late life depression.

Then again, a very significant loss for many people as they grow older is that of income: they must adapt to making do with less. There has been almost no psychological investigation of this kind of adaptation. From what one can see it would seem that a lot of old people positively take pride in stretching their money. This, of course, may also have a lot to do with their experience of deprivation in the past.

Naturally, in all these adaptations much depends on the characteristics of the individual person involved, and one is led to ask whether there are any general ways in which one can conceptualize how a person adapts to the various losses and changes that occur with old age. Some authors talk in terms of the individual possessing particular qualities: for instance, 'coping ability'. But the most valuable index of adjustment in old age is that of self-esteem.

Maintenance of positive attitudes to oneself seems to be one of the key issues in old age. An especially important component of self-image is a sense of being in control of one's own life. Development in childhood and adulthood is associated with an increasing sense of effectiveness and of impact on the external world. In old age this sense may well be taken away.

Intrinsic to this conception of self-identity is the notion that it must have roots outside itself. Therefore, if individuals are to maintain self-esteem they have a continuing need of sources from which they can define acceptable self-images. For some people these sources can exist in past relationships and achievements or in an inner conviction about the kind of person one is, but in the main they depend on the present external circumstances of their lives; their roles in the family, in relation to other people, in work and in other activities.

When these circumstances change, as they often do in old age, individuals may have to find alternative sources to maintain positive views of themselves. Here again it is vital to understand a person's life history. A person whose sense of self has been based on one particular kind of source, for instance relationships with close family members, is going to suffer especially if such family contacts are lost through death.

One way to investigate sources of self-esteem is to ask people directly what makes them say that they feel useful or feel useless, for instance. Not surprisingly, lack of infirmity and contact with other people including the family emerge as the major sources of self-esteem. Especially in disabled people, being able to do things for oneself, and in particular to get around, appear to be key factors; also being a source of help and encouragement to others is very important.

In this context it is worth putting in a good word for residential care and other types of grouped housing schemes. In a previous part of this section it was noted that a move to an institutional setting can be damaging for certain types of individual, but a good institutional setting can also be of great benefit to certain people. This is possible when sources of self-esteem are likely to be strengthened rather than weakened by the move.

257

For instance, some people could be said to be 'living independently in the community'. But in reality they may be extremely isolated and totally dependent on the services being brought to them. Once they have moved to a genuine communal setting the burden of infirmity and consciousness of being alone can be diminished. Precisely because they are better able to cope for themselves in the new environment and to be of importance to others, they may gain a new lease of life.

Helping old people

Not all the loss and trauma of old age can be countered from an individual's own resources. The modern welfare state provides a range of services for the elderly; housing, health and social services. These are, of course, limited, subject to decisions about what level of services the country can 'afford'. We do not know what a perfect service for the elderly would be like, but we certainly do know that what we provide at present falls a long way short of it.

However, the achievement of the present level of services needs to be respected if we are to develop further, and it is important that people in the various caring professions who carry out these services remember their responsiblities. One of the real dangers is taking the operation of a service for granted and applying it automatically or mindlessly. The people on the receiving end then cease to be considered as individuals.

A key element in any work with elderly people is the individual assessment, and it is here that the psychological perspective has a vital role. We need a good assessment not only of people's physical condition and capabilities and of their social situations, but also of their individual needs, their abilities and interests, which should include a good picture of how they used to be.

Besides helping in assessment, psychology can also play a role in the actual provision of therapeutic interventions both to old people themselves and to those around them. Applied psychology should be able to show the best way: for example, to help recover abilities that seem to be lost or to mend social relationships that have become tense.

Maintenance of interests, activities and functioning

One of the most tragic images we have of old age is that of an old person with shoulders sunk, sitting collapsed in a chair, totally uninvolved in the world around. In a previous section the question of 'disengagement' in old age was raised, and let us repeat the point made there that, although some decline in activity may be an intrinsic part of growing old, most of such decline is the result of physical disability and environmental trauma.

When there is a dramatic decline in a person's activities for no obvious reason, we need to alert ourselves to the possibility that the person may be depressed. Loss of well-established habits and activities and lack of interest or anxiety about trying to regain them may be symptoms of the kind of depression which will respond to treatment, even though the person may not admit to having depressed feelings. But, of course, there also has to be some activity and interests for the person to go back to. Particularly if someone is disabled there may be few possibilities available, and the person is then likely to decline again. It is also quite clear that prolonged inactivity has deleterious effects both on physical and psychological functioning. Skills that are not exercised tend to atrophy.

In recent years a lot of new initiatives have been taken in geriatric hospitals in providing opportunities for patients to engage in different types of activity, arts and crafts, music discussion and so on. Generally, staff report improvements in elderly people who do take part in such activities, which can be seen in their personal appearance, in their physical and mental functioning and in their contact with others.

An even greater challenge is offered by people who are mentally deteriorated. In the first place it is very important to distinguish elderly people who really have irretrievable brain disease from those who only appear to have because they are depressed. Indeed, it may be symptomatic of someone's depression that he thinks his brain is rotting. It may be no easy matter to distinguish this, because it is difficult to motivate someone who is depressed actually to demonstrate his abilities. With the right treatment and support depressed people can be encouraged to regain their old abilities.

However, elderly people who clearly are deteriorating mentally should not be abandoned to their fate. Tests have shown that such people, given encouragement and help, can still acquire and retain new information and maintain skills. But the effort needed from outside is great. A good example is the use of so-called 'reality orientation', where people around the elderly person, either informally through-out the day or in concentrated formal classes, systematically try to help remind the person of time, place and season, of names of people, of objects, and of activities and so on.

Psychologists have a lot to do applying findings from the study of learning and memory to help old people. The trouble at present is that such people are often left alone, and this only exacerbates their condition. Dementia is a progressive illness, but what happens between its onset and death is important. If in the future we find medical means of slowing down its progress, it will become an even more urgent matter to find means as well to allow people to maintain their optimum potentialities in the time that remains left to them.

Family relationships

Another vital issue is the relationship between disabled elderly people and their families. Many more of such people are supported by their families than live in institutions for the elderly. For instance, in the case of severe dementia, there are four to five times as many suffering from such a condition living in the community as live in residential homes or hospitals. Yet often families who are doing the caring get pitifully little in the way of support services.

If they become overburdened by the stress of their involvement, both they and their elderly relatives suffer. The old person's mental condition may well be aggravated by tired and irritable relatives, and if there is a breakdown in care and there is no alternative but to take the old person into an institution, the family members are likely to suffer greatly from feelings of guilt. They often want to care for a relative until that person dies, but need help in carrying it out.

It is an important principle to accept that work with families is an integral part of work with elderly people. Family ties after all usually form a substantial part of an individual's identity. If those ties are damaged, so is the person's identity. The physical and mental deterioration that affects many people as they grow older and their ensuing state of dependency can put a strain on many relationships. Men, for instance, usually do not expect to outlive their wives. They can encounter great problems if they find instead that they have to spend their old age looking after a physically or mentally deteriorated wife, especially if in the past it was their wives who ran the household. Children too often find difficulty in taking over responsibility for ailing parents.

The actual symptoms, particularly of mental disturbance in old age, can be very disturbing. In some forms of dementia (probably dependent on the part of the brain that has been affected) the behavioural changes that can occur, caricaturing the person's old personality, increasing aggression or leading to a loss in standards of cleanliness, can be very painful for relatives to bear. It may be difficult for them to accept that the patient is not simply being difficult or unreasonable.

Families need counselling about the nature of the illness and, in the case of dementia, of its progressive nature, and preferably, too, promise of continued practical support. Group meetings held for relatives of different patients by doctors, social workers or other professionals can also be useful in allowing relatives to share common experiences and problems. Groups for the bereaved, particularly husbands or wives, can also play their part. The last years of their lives may have revolved around the care of a sick spouse and they must now find new meaning in life.

The future

In discussing ageing and social problems it may seem strange to end with a note about the future. But from what has been said it should be obvious that great improvements need to take place, both in society's provision for the elderly and in the attitudes of each and every one of us to the elderly people we live among.

For most people old age is not a particularly unhappy time, though for some it is. In part that may be, as we have suggested, because old people have low expectations. They quietly accept a society that treats them meanly and as somehow less important. In the future that may all change. We may see new generations of elderly people, foreshadowed in today's Grey Panthers in America, who will mobilize their potential power as a numerically important part of the electorate and pressurize society to give them a better deal.

On the other hand, old people may continue to remain on the sidelines. They may refuse to see their own material and other interests as being of central importance to society, in which case the rest of the population must see they are not forgotten.

The most important changes indeed are the attitudinal ones. We must recognize that old people are ourselves. They are our future selves. There is a continuity in life both between their past and present and between our present and future.

Old people remain the same people they were. Indeed, if we really want to know about a person's needs and wants and how they could be satisfied, the best introduction would be to let them tell us about their life history. Whatever new steps are taken in the future must follow on from this and make sense in relation to it.

Better provision would follow from such a recognition. If we really respected people's individuality we would provide them with choice about the circumstances and activities with which they end their days, not just enforce certain standard solutions. In short, we must allow people to grow old in ways that suit them, perhaps to explore new avenues of development in order to make the most of the years that remain. Also, when we consider those who need our help, who suffer in old age and perhaps are dependent upon us, we should not forget these wider perspectives.

References

Birren, J.E. and Schaie, K.W. (eds) (1977)
Handbook of the Psychology of Ageing. London: Van Nostrand Reinhold.
Brearley, C.P. (1975)

Social Work, Ageing and Society. London: Routledge & Kegan Paul.

Bromley, D.B. (1974)
The Psychology of Human Ageing (2nd edn).
Harmondsworth: Penguin.

Carver, V. and Liddiard, P. (eds) (1978)
An Ageing Population (Open University text). Sevenoaks Hodder & Stoughton.

Chown, S.M. (ed.) (1972)
Human Ageing. Harmondsworth: Penguin.

Dibner, A.S. (1975)
The psychology of normal aging. In M.G. Spencer and C.J. Dorr (eds), Understanding Aging: A multi-disciplinary approach. New York: Appleton-Century-Crofts.

Gray, B. and Isaacs, B. (1979)
Care of the Elderly Mentally Infirm. London: Tavistock.

Kastenbaum, R. (1979)
Growing Old - Years of Fulfilment. London: Harper & Row.

Kimmel, D.C. (1974)
Adulthood and Ageing. An interdisciplinary developmental view. Chichester: Wiley.

Miller, E. (1977)
Abnormal Ageing. The psychology of senile and presenile dementia. Chichester: Wiley.

Neugarten, B.L. and associates (1964)
Personality in Middle and Later Life. New York: Atherton Press.

Questions

1. Discuss the view that old people do not differ from young people except in the number of years they have lived.
2. What factors influence mental performance in old age? What evidence do we have on their relative importance?
3. How important is a knowledge of life style or personality type to understanding how people react to change and stress in old age?
4. Are the changes we observe in old people's behaviour related more to the physical and social losses they incur or more to intrinsic processes of ageing?
5. Do old people show genuine developmental changes as well as changes of deterioration?
6. Analyse the relationship between well-being and health in old age with particular regard to increasing occurrence of disease and disability.
7. Discuss the role of 'expectations' in adaptation to loss in old age.
8. What behavioural and other psychological techniques are there available to help people to recover interests and customary activities that they may have lost in old age?

9. Social and psychological factors are more responsible for mental deterioration in old age than are physical disorders of the brain. Discuss.
10. 'Too many of our views on the psychology of ageing are restricted by the limits of our own society.' Discuss the value of a cross-cultural approach to the psychology of ageing.

Annotated reading

Brearley, C.P. (1975) Social Work, Ageing and Society. London: Routledge & Kegan Paul.
A book written for social workers, bringing together a wide range of material from medicine, psychology and sociology.

Bromley, D.B. (1974) The Psychology of Human Ageing (2nd edn). Harmondsworth: Penguin.
Written by a British psychologist, it gives a very thorough coverage of subjects such as changes in performance and cognitive skills with age, and is good on the methodological issues involved in doing research on ageing.

Carver, V. and Liddiard, P. (eds) (1978) An Ageing Population (Open University Text). Sevenoaks: Hodder & Stoughton.
A collection of readings for the Open University course. The papers have been drawn from a variety of sources to provide a multidisciplinary perspective on the needs and circumstances of the elderly.

Gray, B. and Isaacs, B. (1979) Care of the Elderly Mentally Infirm. London: Tavistock.
A specialized book on the elderly mentally infirm also intended for social workers, written jointly by a geriatrician and a social worker.

Kastenbaum, R. (1979) Growing Old - Years of Fulfilment. London: Harper & Row.
A short introduction to the subject written by an American psychologist. He presents a balanced approach to old age, giving due weight to positive perspectives. The book is also attractively illustrated.

16

Dying and bereavement
A.T. Carr

Demographic trends

If you had been born at the beginning of this century, your life expectancy at birth would have been 44 years if you were male or 48 years if you were female. If you were born today, your initial life expectancy would be 70 years or 76 years respectively. These figures reflect an ageing of the population that has occurred in all western industrial societies over the past 80 years. Although we all will die, most of us will do so at a relatively advanced age. Although we all will be bereaved, most of us will not suffer this until we are young adults or until we are in our middle years.

The fatal conditions of the present day, once hidden by the mass diseases, are those associated with longevity. In 1978, almost 590,000 people died in England and Wales and 85 per cent of these deaths were attributable to only three categories of illness: diseases of the circulatory system (heart and blood circulation), neoplasms (cancer) and diseases of the respiratory system (OPCS, 1979). Also, more than two people in every three now die in institutions of one form or another.

In the absence of any radical changes of events, the vast majority of us will die aged 65 years or over, in an institution of some sort and as a result of a disease of our circulatory system, or respiratory system, or of cancer. This underlines an important feature of dying and death at the present time: they have become unfamiliar events that take place in unfamiliar surroundings, watched over by unfamiliar people. We all know that we will die and that we may be bereaved, yet we have very little relevant experience upon which to develop our construing or anticipation of these events and states.

Telling

The majority of fatally ill people realize, at some point, that they will not recover, even if they have not been informed of the nature of their illness. However, it would appear that only about half of all fatally ill people appreciate their condition before significant changes in health force the conclusion 'I am dying'. This is almost certainly an under-estimate: there will be some people who know that they will not recover but who do not communicate this.

Although about one-half of terminally ill people appear to appreciate the seriousness of their illness, this awareness is usually achieved independently, informally and indirectly. No more than 15 per cent of terminally ill cancer patients are told of their prognosis either by their general practitioner or by a hospital doctor (Cartwright, et al., 1973). This contrasts markedly with the experiences of their close relatives. Almost 90 per cent of the close relatives of terminally ill patients are aware that the patient's illness is terminal and most of them are informed of this by a general practitioner or by a hospital doctor. There are several implications of these data, the two most obvious being that fatally ill people and their principal carers often do not share the same information about the illness, and that doctors usually are unwilling to tell patients when they have a disease that will kill them. Perhaps the most serious consequence is that one or more of the familial participants has to cope with the demands of this most stressful period without adequate support.

It is remarkable how little emphasis is placed upon the wishes of the patient. Most people, including doctors, whether they are young or old, ill or well, say they would want to know if they had a fatal illness or that they are glad they do know. Several studies have examined this issue and the results are consistent in showing that more than 70 per cent of all the samples used say they would want to be informed if they had a terminal disease. It is clear that most people say they would want to be informed of the seriousness of their illness and most doctors say that they would want to be told; yet the majority of fatally ill patients are not told. Also, the existence of a real threat to life does not reduce the very high proportion of people who want to know if they have a fatal illness.

In general, learning that one has a fatal illness is followed by a period of disquiet, even grief, although the emotional response may be concealed from others. It is worth noting that some patients do not 'hear' or at least appear not to remember, what they have been told regarding their prognosis. Although it has been proposed that the defence mechanism of denial is a ubiquitous response to learning of a fatal prognosis (Kubler-Ross, 1969), there are other more mundane possibilities. The first is the use of terminology that may have very precise meanings for a professional but which may mean nothing, or something very different, to the patient. To inform a patient of 'malignant lymphoma' or 'secondary metastases' may not constitute communication. Even when the words that are used are understood reasonably well, they may not convey what was intended. For some individuals, the knowledge of their impending death will be extremely distressing; in such cases the person may be quite unable to accept what is plain to everybody else. They may become distraught as their bodies show increasing signs of impending death while they continue to deny that they are dying. Such extreme responses, as a terminal illness progresses, correspond to denial as elucidated by Kubler-Ross (1969). However, it would be inappropriate to regard as denial a person's failure to comprehend or to recall initial statements about prognosis. Quite apart from the communication problems mentioned above, if people have no prior suspicions that their conditions may be terminal it is probable that they will be unable to accept a fatal diagnosis. It is not that they REFUSE to accept such information but they are UNABLE to accept it. It demands a radical revision of their view of the world and such a major psychological adjustment takes time. Initially, such news is not disbelieved, but on the other hand, it cannot be fitted into a person's perception of the world: it cannot be accommodated. The revised view of the world will need to be tested, amended and confirmed in the light of further information. The person will seek such information in what people say, how they behave and how his body feels. It is only when the revised view of the world 'fits', in the sense that it is not violated by new observations or new information, that the person is able fully to accommodate the 'truths' that have been offered. Individuals who have prior suspicions about the seriousness of their illnesses have already constructed, at least in part, a view of their world that includes themselves as dying individuals.

Our aim must be to maintain dignity, to alleviate suffering and to help people live as fully as possible for as long as they are able: they should be told what they are prepared to hear at a time when they are prepared to listen. The same principle might be kept in mind when dealing with relatives. There are indications that those who are told with care show improved family relationships, less tension and less desperation during their terminal illnesses than those who are not (Gerle et al., 1960). Helping a person towards fuller awareness of, and adjustment to, a fatal prognosis is the beginning of a communication process which is itself an integral part of caring for the terminally ill.

Terminality and dying

The two words terminality and dying are being used to draw a distinction that can have important implications for the way in which fatally ill people are managed and treated. The main implication is that of regarding someone as terminally ill, but nevertheless as living and with some valuable life remaining, rather than regarding the person

as dying with all the negative attitudes this provokes.
Once illnesses have been diagnosed as terminal we need to
regard patients as living and possibly living more
intensely than the rest of us, until they clearly are
dying. Terminality, then, begins when a terminal diagnosis
is made but dying starts later, usually when death is much
closer and when individuals are prepared to relinquish
their biological life in the absence of valuable,
functional life.

Sources of distress

Effective and appropriate care of the fatally ill requires
an awareness of potential sources of distress so that distress can be anticipated and thus be avoided or allevi-
ated. Of course, distress is not confined to the patient:
effective care and support for those who are close to the
patient is merited not only on humanitarian grounds, but
also because of the exacerbation of the patient's suffering that can result from the distress of relatives and
friends. Table 1 summarizes some of the most common
sources of distress for patients and those who are close
to them.

The listing contained in table 1 is by no means
exhaustive, but it illustrates a number of points. First,
given some capacity for empathy on the part of the sur-
vivor(s) there is little that the terminally ill person
must endure that the survivor can avoid. This commonality
of the sources of distress argues strongly for the need to
attend to the welfare of survivors before they become
bereaved. Second, it is clear that almost all the potential sources of distress are psychological in nature. Even
some of the physical symptoms such as incontinence or
smells are distressing because of our values and expectations. Also, pain itself is an experience that is subject
to psychological factors rather than a sensation that is
elicited by an appropriate stimulus.

Although we cannot examine in detail the physical distress of terminal illness, our discussion would be incomplete without a summary of this. Cartwright et al. (1973)
and Ward (1974) identified retrospectively the physical
symptoms experienced by their samples of terminal cancer
patients, 215 and 264 individuals respectively. These data
are summarized in table 2.

It is striking that the rank order of symptoms is the
same for both samples and a significant proportion of
patients in each sample experienced each of the symptoms
listed. Other common physical symptoms were breathing
difficulties, 52 per cent; coughing, 48 per cent (Ward);
and sleeplessness, 17 per cent (Cartwright et al.).

Distress and coping

An examination of tables 1 and 2 points to a number of
psychological processes that predispose people to react

Table 1

Common sources of distress

Fatally ill person (P)	Those who love P
Awareness of impending death	Awareness of impending bereavement
Anticipation of loss	Anticipation of loss
Physical sequelae of disease process, e.g. tumours, lesions, nausea, incontinence, breathlessness, unpleasant smells	Empathic concern, aversion, etc.
Frustration and helplessness as disease progresses	Frustration and helplessness as disease progresses
Uncertainty about the future welfare of the family	Uncertainty about the future welfare of the family
Anticipation of pain	
Empathic concern	Caring for P, night-sitting, tiredness
Changes in roles with family, friends, etc.	Changes in roles with family, friends, etc
Changes in abilities as illness progresses	Empathic concern
Changes in appearance as illness progresses	Empathic concern, aversion, etc.
Uncertainties about dying	Empathic concern
Dying	Empathic concern
	Discovery of death, directly or indirectly
	Practicalities, funeral, etc.
	Grief
	Role changes
	Reconstruction of life

Table 2

Symptoms suffered by terminal cancer patients

Symptom	Per cent in sample of Cartwright et al.	Per cent in sample of Ward
Pain	87	62
Anorexia	76	61
Vomiting	54	38
Urinary incontinence	38	28
Faecal incontinence	37	20
Bedsores	24	13

with depression and anxiety during a terminal illness. Current approaches to depression emphasize the role of loss and helplessness as aetiological factors. Loss refers to the real or imagined loss of a valued object, role, activity, relationship, etc. The individual relevance of the concept of loss lies in the individual differences of our value systems. For example, a person who highly values physical abilities, physical appearance, etc., is likely to be more at risk for depression as a result of physical debility, tiredness and deterioration in appearance, than someone for whom such attributes are low in a hierarchy of values.

Helplessness describes a state that is characterized by an awareness that one's behaviour is unrelated to the events which impinge upon oneself. When a person is subjected to aversive events whose occurrence, intensity, duration, etc., is quite independent of behaviour, a characteristic state may ensue. This state, which occurs in the majority of subjects tested, is known as learnt helplessness. There are individual differences in suscepti- bility to learnt helplessness, but the more aversive the events and the more frequently they are experienced as independent of behaviour the more likely it is to develop. It is a generalized state characterized by apathy, dys- phoric mood, psychomotor retardation (i.e. slowness in thought and action), and feelings of hopelessness. Many clinical depressions are explained most fully in terms of the development of helplessness and there is evidence that sudden death is not an uncommon consequence of learnt

helplessness in laboratory animals. There can be little
doubt about the relevance and importance of helplessness
to our consideration of the welfare of the terminally
ill.

Let us now return to the sources of distress summarized in tables 1 and 2. It is clear that some of these are
intrinsically uncontrollable, and others duplicate the
procedures that are used in experimental work to induce
helplessness in that they are aversive, uncontrollable and
repeated: for instance, urinary incontinence and vomiting.
Furthermore, many patients undergo physical investigations
and treatments that they do not understand, that they find
unpleasant or painful and about which they feel they have
little choice other than to accept them passively. It is
not surprising to find that depression is commonly encountered in the terminally ill. A significant minority of
fatally ill people and their next-of-kin become moderately
or severely depressed (about one in five people in each
group). Those most at risk are adolescents, young parents
with dependents, those who have many physical symptoms
and those who experience lengthy hospitalization.

The reciprocal interaction of physical and psychological processes must not be overlooked. We have already
considered the depressive role of repeated, unpleasant
physical symptoms. However, the interaction also proceeds
in the other direction: adverse emotional states such as
depression and anxiety augment pain and other physical
discomforts. The essential point is that pain is not a
simple response to an appropriate physical stimulus such
as tissue damage: it is an experience that is compounded
of the stimulation and the person's response to that
stimulation. The motivational and emotional state of the
person acts, as it were, to colour the sensation and to
produce the experience we call pain. Without such 'colouring' and evaluation the sensation may be perceived but not
experienced as painful.

It is the experience of most who work in terminal care
that the relief of anxiety or depression through appropriate support, communication and practical help reduces
the pain of patients and, not insignificantly, reduces the
need for medication. The point is not that attention to
the psychological state of the patient removes the need
for relevant medication but that it reduces the dosages
that may be required to bring relief. There are many
obvious advantages that derive from this, not the least of
which is the ability to alleviate pain without resorting
to medications that render the patient confused, drowsy or
comatose.

Anxiety arises when a future event is appraised as
threatening. This appraisal is the evaluation of an event
in terms of its harmful implications for the individual,
harm being the extent to which continued physical and
psychological functioning is endangered. Threat appraisal

is a highly subjective process that depends upon the
subjective likelihood of an event - that is, how probable
the person feels the event to be - and the degree of harm
that will result, this again being subjectively assessed.
So terminally ill people are anxious to the extent that
the events that they anticipate are both likely and
harmful in their own terms: if events are not perceived as
likely or harmful then they will not provoke anxiety.

Anxiety is an essentially adaptive emotion, in that it
motivates us to initiate behaviours that prevent the anticipated harm being realized. To the extent that individuals accept that they are dying and are unable to reduce
or eliminate the harmful consequences of this process,
they are liable to remain anxious. An inspection of tables
1 and 2 reminds us that there are many potential types of
harm that the fatally ill person is motivated, by anxiety,
to alleviate. It is reassuring to note that the intense
panic that is such a common feature of clinical anxiety
states occurs rarely in terminal illness except, perhaps,
in those who continue to deny the imminence of death as
the end approaches and those for whom breathing is difficult. However, moderate anxiety is by no means uncommon
in the terminally ill. This is not only an extra burden of
suffering for the person but it also exacerbates other
discomforts including pain.

There are few systematic reports of anxiety in
terminal illness but from the data that do exist it is
clear that moderate anxiety is experienced by between one-
quarter and one-half of patients. The anxiety may be
readily discerned in those people who are able to verb-
alize their fears, and who are given the opportunity to do
so, but it may be less obvious in those who communicate
less well verbally. However, the physiological and behavioural concomitants of anxiety are good indicators of the
presence of unspoken fear. Often it is difficult to
distinguish between physiological signs of anxiety such as
gastric upset, nausea, diarrhoea, muscular pains, etc.,
and symptoms of the disease process or side effects of
treatment. Nevertheless, the possibility that a patient
might be persistently anxious should not be overlooked.

Given the subjective nature of threat appraisal, the
causes of an individual's anxiety can be surprisingly idiosyncratic, but there are a few consistencies that may provide some clues. Younger adults expect to be distressed by
pain and parting from the people they love, whereas the
elderly fear becoming dependent and losing control of
bowel and bladder functioning. Hinton (1972) reports that
almost two-thirds of his patients who died aged 50 years
or less were clearly anxious but this was true of only one-
third of those aged 60 years and over. There is a clear
and understandable trend for young parents of dependent
children to be more anxious than other groups. Perhaps it
is not insignificant that younger patients also tend to

experience more physical discomfort during their terminal illnesses.

According to Hinton (1963), anxiety is more common in people with a lengthy terminal illness. He found more than 50 per cent of those who had been ill for more than one year to be clearly anxious, but only 20 per cent of those who had been ill for less than three months showed similar levels of anxiety. Although anxiety levels fluctuate during a patient's terminal illness, there is no general trend for anxiety to increase as the person draws closer to death. Some people become more apprehensive as their illnesses progress, but others become more calm during the last stages of their lives.

Some specific experiences of illness may be potent sources of anxiety. Prior episodes of intolerable pain can provoke great anxiety when they are recalled or when their return is anticipated. Difficulties in breathing are commonly associated with anxiety and a tendency to panic. Also, in the context of a mortal illness there are a number of sources of distress that are intrinsically uncontrollable and uncertain, such as the final process of dying, death and the nature of the world in which one's dependent survivors will be living. When anticipated harm remains and individuals perceive it as beyond their ability to influence, they become liable to the state of helplessness. If this is severe they may become depressed, as we have discussed: if less severe, then they may exhibit the resignation that has been termed 'acceptance' (Kubler-Ross, 1969). If they persist in their attempts to control and influence events that are beyond their reach they are likely to remain anxious and even to become more anxious as they approach death.

For the fatally ill child under five or six years of age, anxiety takes the form of separation anxiety, loneliness and fears of being abandoned. The young child does not appear to fear death and its implications, but fears are aroused by those aspects of illness and hospitalization which elicit fear in most ill children who require hospital treatment.

Between the ages of six and 10 or 11 years, separation fears persist, but the child is increasingly prone to anxiety over painful treatments and bodily intrusions. Such fears of mutilation and physical harm are intensified in the absence of familiar, trusted adults. Some children in this age group, because of differing prior experiences or more advanced cognitive development, are also aware of the cessation of awareness and bodily functioning consequent upon death.

Although there is some dispute as to whether the child under ten years of age can be aware of impending death at a conceptual level, there is little doubt that many young children perceive that their illness is no ordinary illness. This is a frequent clinical observation and there is

272

a good deal of evidence that it is so whether or not the diagnosis is discussed with the child (Spinetta, 1974). Of course there are many cues that may indicate to the child that something very serious and threatening is happening, quite apart from the numerous tests, treatments and visits to hospital. Most children are finely tuned to detect meaningful and subtle signs in the verbal and non-verbal behaviour of adults: the things that are not talked about, tone of voice, eye contact, posture, etc. Also, there are many cues that the child would find it hard to overlook: whispered conversations, unusually frequent and intense bodily contact, unusual generosity and freedom of choice with regard to presents and treats, and so on.

Parents and others usually begin to grieve for the fatally ill child soon after they accept the prognosis. Their ability to cope with this grief is an important determinant of their effectiveness in supporting the child. Since familiar adults and siblings are likely to be the child's greatest potential source of comfort and reassurance, it is important that time and attention is devoted to these significant others for the sake of the child's welfare. There are indications of a high incidence of psychological difficulties in family members, particularly siblings, during the terminal illness of a child. Clearly parents, who are themselves struggling with their own emotions, may have difficulty sustaining the other children in the family, let alone in providing comfort and reassurance to the one who is ill.

Adolescents and some younger children will be aware of the finality of death. Although dependent upon adults in a functional sense, they may perceive themselves as having important roles to play in the welfare of others and thus be subject to fears for the well-being of their survivors in much the same way as adults with dependents. Very young children may endure a terminal illness with striking calmness and acceptance of their lot, provided that their separation fears are allayed, but once they are past the age of six or seven years they become prone to a wide range of fears that exceed those of their 'normally ill' counterparts with severe, chronic, but non-fatal illness. Although children may be reluctant to express their fears, or may express them unclearly and indirectly, they should be anticipated in all aspects of care.

We have examined the range of potential sources of distress in terminal illness and the most common types of distress that result from these. Pain, anxiety and depression are sufficiently frequent and severe to merit attention when services are being planned and delivered. However, a majority of fatally ill people do not become severely anxious, deeply depressed or suffer from unrelieved pain. This does not minimize the awful suffering of the large minority or the pressing need for improvements in care to which this suffering testifies. It indicates only that, with whatever help they receive, most people who endure a terminal illness cope reasonably well, keeping their levels of distress within limits that are acceptable to themselves and to those who care for them.

The responses of people who are faced with impending death show sufficient uniformity to enable observers to write of stages, phases and patterns of coping (e.g. Kubler-Ross, 1969; Falek and Britton, 1974). Quite apart from doubts about the uniformity and progressive nature of stages of coping in terminal illness (e.g. Schulz and Aderman, 1974), it cannot be assumed that any particular individual NEEDS to negotiate these stages in order to cope most effectively with impending death. The emotional responses and their dependent behaviours are indicators of the difficulties, and triumphs, experienced by people in their attempts to cope. The absence of a specific emotion does not mean that the person has omitted a necessary stage of the 'normal' coping pattern and that this omission detracts from the person's adjustment. Provided we do not equate 'typical' with 'ideal' or 'necessary', an awareness of the emotional stages or phases that are commonly encountered in terminal patients can help us to understand the problems they face, to provide the types of help and support that might be beneficial and to improve our ability to cope with the emotions that their behaviours arouse in relatives and in ourselves.

However, there are a number of general points that can be made about a stage model of terminal illness. The responses delineated, including denial, anger, bargaining, depression and acceptance (Kubler-Ross, 1969), are not specific to people who are facing death; they have been observed in many other stressful situations that involve loss and uncontrollable harm, such as bereavement, amputation and imprisonment. The generality evidenced by these observations does not confirm the progression of the stage model: it highlights the normality of disbelief, anger, sadness, etc., in the face of irretrievable and severe loss.

Often it is difficult to decide which stage or phase a person is in. Without reasonable certainty in the identification of stages, the predictive value of a stage model is severely impaired. This predictive aspect of the model is also reduced if the stages are not ubiquitous and if they are not successive. Clinical observation suggests that the emotion displayed by a person is responsive to many internal and external events. Perhaps all that can be said with any certainty is that some responses, when they occur, are likely to predominate earlier in a terminal illness, for example denial, and some are more likely to appear later, for example depression and acceptance.

We must take care not to lose sight of the individual in anticipating responses to a terminal illness. Fatally ill people bring with them their own particular views of themselves, their families, their futures, doctors, death, etc. The importance of individual differences during the terminal phase of life is well illustrated by the work of Kastenbaum and Weisman (1972). They found that their patients could be divided into two broad groups, both of which were aware of the imminence of death but which differed markedly in their behavioural styles. One group gradually withdrew from their usual activities and social contacts, remaining inactive until their final illness. The other group was characterized by involvement: patients in this group remained busily engaged in everyday activities until death occurred as an interruption in their living.

Dying

The relationship between a patient's reactions to a terminal illness and dying is not only that these are the psychological context within which the final process occurs, but also there are increasing indications that they influence the timing of death (see Achterberg and Lawlis, 1977). Whereas blood chemistries reflect on-going or current disease status, psychological factors are predictive of subsequent disease status and longevity. Poorer prognosis and shorter survival occurs in patients who, typically, show great dependence upon others, who deny the severity of their conditions, who have a history of poor social relationships and who do not have access to, or do not utilize, supportive social relationships during their illnesses. These patients tend to become more withdrawn, pessimistic and depressed as their illness progresses. Longer survival is associated with patients who maintain good personal and social relationships in the context of an existing network of such relationships. They can be assertive without hostility, asking for and receiving much medical and emotional support. They may be concerned about dying alone and seek to deter others from withdrawing from them without their needs being met. These patients also experience less pain, or at least complain less about pain and discomfort.

Dying is a process rather than an event that occurs at one point in time. This final process that constitutes the transition from life to death is usually of short duration, a matter of hours or days. For the vast majority of people it is not dramatic. Most people, both ill and well, express a desire to die peacefully or to die in their sleep. There is little doubt that this wish is fulfilled in most cases. Although there are a few people for whom pain or breathlessness may increase near the end, most slip knowingly or unawares into the unconsciousness that continues until their dying is finished.

After a terminal illness lasting some months, most patients are tired and wearied by their experiences. During their last days, apart from having their needs tended, patients may wish to be alone or to avoid news and problems of the 'outside world'. They may well become less talkative and prefer shorter visits. Communication tends to shift increasingly towards the non-verbal. In terms of interaction they may want little more than somebody to sit with them in silence, perhaps holding hands. It is clear from those who wish to talk briefly in their last hours of life that there is an experience of 'distance' from life. As Saunders (1978) so aptly puts it, 'They were not frightened nor unwilling to go, for by then they were too far away to want to come back. They were conscious of leaving weakness and exhaustion rather than life and its activities. They rarely had any pain but felt intensely weary. They wanted to say good-bye to those they loved but were not torn with longing to stay with them.'

Euthanasia

Euthanasia, meaning a gentle and easy death and the act of bringing this about, has been a source of discussion and controversy for many years. The level of current interest is evidenced by the large number of recent publications on the topic in the professional literature and the increasing support of the public for such organizations as the Voluntary Euthanasia Society in the UK and the Euthanasia Education Council in the USA.

The public support for euthanasia is probably based upon an expectation that death will come as a result of a lengthy illness, an illness that may well be prolonged unduly by the application of current medical knowledge and techniques. It is based upon fears of the physical and psychological incompetence, dependence, indignity and pain that may result from a chronic or terminal illness. Even those professionals who oppose euthanasia on ethical, religious or practical grounds readily concede that such fears are not unjustified for many people. We have already examined the potential distress of terminal illness but, for many people, support for euthanasia is prompted by thoughts of an unwanted, useless existence where biological life is maintained artificially and against their wishes in a hospital, nursing home or geriatric ward. Sadly, such thoughts are all too often reinforced by cases that Saunders (1977) rightly describes as 'truly horrendous'. As a society we cannot escape the reality that far too many elderly people end their days in loneliness, isolation and degradation. Even when the physical care provided is good, the psychological distress can be great. The prima facie case for euthanasia appears to be strong.

The many logical, philosophical and ethical arguments relating to the legalization of voluntary euthanasia, both active and passive, have been well stated several times (e.g. Rachels, 1975; Foot, 1978), and space precludes their consideration here. However, these arguments frequently take little account of relevant practical and psychological issues. In drawing up the necessary guidelines for the legalization of voluntary euthanasia there are major problems in guarding against error and potential abuse, both by relatives and professionals. Nevertheless, many of these problems could be surmounted by the use and recognition of the Living Will. This document, as distributed by the Euthanasia Educational Council, is signed and witnessed when the person is in good health. Its aim is to avoid an existence in dependence, deterioration, indignity and hopeless pain.

Doctors spend their lives preserving the lives of others and alleviating their suffering. It can be argued that, in recent years, the pendulum has swung too far in the direction of the maintenance of life at the expense of the relief of distress, but the activities of doctors make demands upon their energies and their personal time that few other professions would tolerate. This degree of commitment is consistent with, and continually reinforces, a value system that places a very high priority upon the preservation of life and actions that serve this end. For individuals in whom such values relate closely to their self-concepts, the active termination of life may be damaging to their self-regard and to their concept of their own worth as individuals. Although there is little difference between active and passive euthanasia on moral and logical grounds, for individual doctors the difference may be vast and unbridgeable in terms of their own psychology. It would be quite unjustifiable to place such men in a position where society expected them to implement active euthanasia.

From the patient's point of view, the availability of euthanasia has a wider potential than the avoidance of further suffering. People who are given control over aversive and painful stimulation, by having the facility to terminate, reduce or avoid it in some way, are better able to cope with the experience. Even though the available control is rarely exercised, the aversive stimulation is better tolerated and provokes less distress. Provided that patients are quite sure that their lives can be terminated when they wish, and only when they wish, they are likely to cope better with the effects of their illness or condition and to be less distressed.

To allow patients to die in order to release them from hopelessness and irreducible suffering, while continuing to treat their current distress, is thoroughly compatible with the humanitarian principle of care. Whether or not one wishes to describe this as passive, voluntary euthanasia is a matter of personal choice. There are grounds for a more widespread recognition of this compatibility and for more weight to be given to the wishes of patients and their families. Of course, the same grounds demand that more effort, time and resources should be devoted to improving the quality of care that is offered. All such improvements weaken the case for regarding death as a desirable release from suffering, as a release that is needed so frequently that its use should be regularized. In the long term, and certainly in the shorter term, there are likely to be some people for whom death is the preferred option. It is a problem that will become more acute as our society continues to age and as the life-preserving techniques of medicine continue to develop.

Bereavement

Bereavement is a state characterized by loss. The main focus of interest is upon the loss occasioned by the death of a significant person but people are bereaved by other losses such as loss of role, loss of status, separation and amputation. The state of loss serves as the stimulus for the bereavement response, a response that is manifested culturally and individually. The cultural response constitutes mourning and is a pattern of behaviour that is learnt from and supported by one's immediate culture as appropriate following bereavement. Grief is the individual response and is the main area of concern for researchers and clinicians alike. In that grief typically follows a reasonably consistent course over time, ending ultimately in its resolution, it can be regarded as an individual process that occurs in response to individual loss.

The nature of grief

Although the major features of grief are known to most of us either intuitively or through personal experience, the chief findings of the many descriptive studies can be summarized broadly as follows:

* grief is a complex but stereotyped response pattern that includes such physical and psychological 'symptoms' as withdrawal, fatigue, sleep disturbance, anxiety and loss of appetite;
* it is elicited by a rather well-defined stimulus situation, namely the real or imagined loss of a valued object or role, and it is resolved when new object relations are established;
* it is a ubiquitous phenomenon among human beings and appears in other social species, especially higher primates;
* it is an extremely stressful response both physically and psychologically, but grief-related behaviour is often antithetical to the establishment of new object relations and hence to the alleviation of the stress. For example, fatigue and withdrawal make it much more difficult for the bereaved person to develop new roles and new personal relationships in place of those lost through bereavement.

The complexity and stress of grief is readily appreciated when the number and nature of its components are considered. Hinton's (1972) description of grief adumbrates the most commonly observed characteristics: shock, denial, anxiety, depression, guilt, anger and a wide variety of somatic signs of anxiety. Other components include searching behaviour, suicidal thoughts, idealization of the lost person, panic, a heightened vulnerability to physical illness and to psychological disorders.

The nature of grief as a process is emphasized by the designation of stages by many observers and authors. Although there is a sequential character to the process it would be incorrect to anticipate an orderly progression through the stages in all people. As with the notion of stages in dying that was discussed earlier, the component responses of the various stages overlap and merge into one another. Also, there are frequent 'regressions' to earlier stages. Again, it is better to think in terms of components, some of which will predominate earlier in the process and others that will predominate later. In general, three stages or phases have been delineated and labelled according to inclination: perhaps the best descriptive labels are shock, despair and recovery.

Initially there may be a period of numbness and detachment depending, to some extent, on the unexpectedness of the news of the death. During this immediate response people may appear stoical and calm. Normal routines may be maintained especially where domestic or other factors structure the situation. Alternatively, people may appear dazed and quite unable to comprehend the reality of the news; they may be unresponsive to their environment and in need of care and support during this period. Whatever the specific initial reaction in a particular instance, it can last from a few minutes to two weeks or so, with the stoical reaction being the more likely to persist longer. The bereaved person is less able than the terminally ill to deny successfully the reality of the situation: sooner or later, and in many different ways, powerful and pointed signs of the reality of loss occur, such as the empty place at table, the empty bed or chair, the funeral or the silent house when friends and relatives depart. As with the news of terminal diagnosis, people need time to assimilate and to accommodate to a new state of the world. Whether the period of shock and disbelief is long or short, a sense of unreality or even disbelief is likely to return periodically for several months.

As awareness of the loss develops people may express anger at themselves, at staff or at God for not preventing the death. Whether or not anger is present, the phase of acute grieving or despair is the most painful. Lindemann (1944), in his pioneering study of bereavement, observed the following 'symptoms' as common to all individuals suffering acute grief: somatic distress lasting between 20 minutes and one hour at a time, feelings of tightness in the throat, choking with shortness of breath, muscular weakness and intense subjective distress described as tension or psychological pain. This specific response, which appears to be unique to bereavement, occurs against a background of stress, anxiety and sadness or depression, together with the somatic concomitants of these emotions.

Behaviourally, grieving persons may be unable to maintain goal-directed activity, appearing disorganized and unable to make plans. They may be restless, moving about in an aimless fashion and constantly searching for something to do. They may find themselves going, unwittingly, to the places where the dead person might be found if still alive. A preoccupation with the lost person creates a perceptual set that leads to misinterpretations of ambiguous sights and sounds as indicative of his being alive. Some grieving people report seeing the dead person with a clarity that goes beyond illusion and misperception. Such experiences can occur long after the phase of acute grieving is past. Obviously, the physical and psychological demands of this period are heavy and it is not surprising that irritability is common, especially when the person is eating and sleeping poorly. Anger, frustration and resentment may be directed at friends and neighbours irrespective of merit. Such feelings may also be directed against the dead person for abandoning the survivor.

The intense anguish of the despair phase can be unremitting, rising to peaks of distress with thoughts of the loved one who has died. Most bereaved people seem unable to prevent themselves from thinking and talking about the one who has died even though this usually exacerbates their distress. Whether this is conceptualized as 'grief-work' or as repeated exposure leading to habituation, it appears to be necessary to recovery from grief. A reduction in the frequency and intensity of periods of peak distress may be the first sign that the process of recovery is beginning. Although estimates vary, the acute despair phase of grief typically lasts for three to ten weeks.

The process of recovery from grief is a process of reconstruction. Although some aspects of the person's private and public 'self' may survive bereavement relatively unchanged, it is necessary to develop new roles, new behaviours and new relationships with others. Whatever else may or may not be changed by bereavement, the survivor must live without one important and potentially crucial personal relationship that had existed previously: the loss of this relationship is the loss of the psychological and practical advantages, and disadvantages, that it conferred. Socially, the survivor is now a widow or a widower rather than one of a married couple: he is now a boy without a father, or she is now a mother without a child, etc. Apart from the direct, personal impact of such changes, they also influence the way survivors are viewed and treated socially. The bereaved person has to develop a new private and public self that enables him to live in a changed world.

Although a reduction in the frequency and intensity of periods of extreme distress may herald the process of recovery, it cannot begin in earnest until there are periods in which the person is not overwhelmed with despair nor preoccupied with thoughts of the one who has died. Many bereaved people recall with clarity the moment when they realized that they had not been preoccupied with their loss: when, for a brief period at least, their thoughts had been directed elsewhere and their emotions had been less negative, even positive. These moments of 'spontaneous forgetting', together with improvements in sleeping and appetite, provide people with some opportunity to reconstrue and to reconstruct themselves and their futures. With less exhaustion and a lightening of mood, decisions and actions become more feasible and people can begin the active process of reviving previous relationships and activities, perhaps in a modified form, and of developing new ones. This period of active readjustment may never be complete, especially in the elderly, but it usually lasts for between six and 18 months after the phase of acute grief and despair.

Determinants of grief
Strictly speaking, it is inaccurate to talk of determinants of grief for the available data do not allow us to identify the causative factors that lead to variations in the response to bereavement. However, it makes intuitive sense to talk of determinants and is in keeping with other literature on the topic. Parkes (1972) groups the factors of potential importance according to their temporal relationship to the event of death, that is, antecedent, concurrent and subsequent determinants. Among antecedent factors, the most influential appear to be life stresses prior to bereavement, relationship with the deceased and mode of death. On the whole, an atypical grief response with associated psychological problems is more likely when bereavement occurs as one of a series of life crises, when the death is sudden, unanticipated and untimely, and when the relationship with the deceased had been one of strong attachment, reliance or ambivalence.

A number of demographic variables (concurrent) relate to the nature of grief. In particular, being young, female and married to the deceased increases the likelihood of problems arising after bereavement. Of course, these factors are not unrelated to such antecedent factors as strong attachment, reliance and untimely death. Other concurrent factors with adverse implications are susceptibility to grief, as evidenced by previous episodes of depression, an inability to express emotions, lower socio-economic status and the absence of a genuine religious faith.

The presence of religious faith might be placed more appropriately with subsequent determinants, for its role is likely to be one of supporting the bereaved person during the stressful period of grief. Also, someone with an active belief system probably will be associated with a supportive social group, and there is little doubt that a network of supportive social relationships is the most advantageous of the subsequent determinants. Other subsequent factors that have positive implications are the absence of secondary stresses during the period of grief and the development of new life opportunities at work and in interpersonal relationships, for instance. Again, these are more probable when a good network of supportive social relationships exists. It is worth recalling our earlier conclusion about the value of such relationships in a person's adjustment to impending death.

Among the wide range of factors that have implications for a person's reaction to bereavement, there is most con-troversy about the importance of anticipatory grief. As the term implies, this refers to grief that occurs in anticipation of an expected death, particularly the death of a child or a spouse. Overall, it can be concluded that younger widows experience more intense grief, with associated problems, than those aged 46 years or over. Sudden death exacerbates the severity of the grief response for young widows but not for the middle-aged or the elderly. For the latter two groups there appears to be a small effect in the opposite direction: that is, some symptoms of grief, especially irritability, are greater after a prolonged illness prior to death. It should be noted that the potentially beneficial effects of antic-ipatory grief are not confined to conjugal bereavement but also mitigate the response to other losses, such as that of a child. Also, it seems possible that there is an optimum period for the anticipation of death, perhaps up to six months, after which the lengthy duration of illness may increase stress and exhaustion and increase the likelihood of adverse reactions in subsequent grief.

Illness and death after bereavement
There are clear data that reveal an elevated mortality risk after bereavement. At all ages, bereaved persons experience a higher risk of dying than married people of corresponding sex and age. The increase in risk is greater for bereaved males than females, and for both sexes, the increase is greater at younger ages.

The elevated risk of death is concentrated particularly in the first six months after bereavement especially for widowers, with a further rise in the second year for widows. The predominant causes of death are

coronary thrombosis and other arteriosclerotic or degen-
erative heart diseases. Most of these causes can be seen
as a result of continued stress and a lack of self-care.
In general, when the data from replicated studies in the
UK and the USA are taken together, the risk of dying is at
least doubled for widows and widowers at all ages for a
great variety of diseases.

Having briefly examined the possible psychological and
physical consequences of bereavement, and having considered relevant predictive factors, it is important to
remember that we are talking only of probabilities. A
person may be at great risk of problems following bereavement, in the statistical sense, and yet survive the
experience well. Another person with only favourable
indicators may suffer badly and experience severe physical
or psychological problems.

The vast majority of bereaved people, with a little
help from their friends, cope well with the experience and
reconstruct lives that are worth while in their own terms.
There are no persuasive grounds for considering the
provision of professional services for the bereaved. The
most useful strategy is to maintain some form of non-
intrusive follow-up after bereavement with ready access to
an informal support group if this should be necessary. The
bereaved need somebody who will listen when they want to
talk, somebody who will not try to push them into things
before they are ready: somebody who will support them
emotionally and practically when appropriate and just by
showing that they care. This demands an informal response
rather than a professional one. However, professional care
and concern should not end with the death of a patient:
the newly bereaved person still has a long way to go and
every effort should be made to ensure that they will have
access to whatever social support may be needed.

References

Achterberg, J. and Lawlis, G.F. (1977)
Psychological factors and blood chemistries as disease
outcome predictors for cancer patients. Multivariate
Experimental Clinical Research, 3, 107-122.

Cartwright, A., Hockey, L. and Anderson, J.L. (1973)
Life Before Death. London: Routledge & Kegan Paul.

Falek, A. and Britton, S. (1974)
Phases in coping: the hypothesis and its implications.
Social Biology, 21, 1-7.

Foot, P. (1978)
Euthanasia. In E. McMullin (ed.), Death and Decision.
Boulder, Co: Westview Press.

Gerle, B., Lunden, G. and Sandblow, P. (1960)
The patient with inoperable cancer from the psychiatric
and social standpoints. Cancer, 13, 1206-1211.

Hinton, J.M. (1963)
The physical and mental distress of the dying. Quarterly
Journal of Medicine, 32, 1-21.

Hinton, J.M. (1972)
Dying. Harmondsworth: Penguin.

Kastenbaum, R. and Weisman, A.D. (1972)
The psychological autopsy as a research procedure in gerontology. In D.P. Kent, R. Kastenbaum and S. Sherwood (eds), Research Planning and Action for the Elderly. New York: Behavioral Publications.

Kubler-Ross, E. (1969)
On Death and Dying. London: Tavistock.

Lindemann, E. (1944)
Symptomatology and management of acute grief. American Journal of Psychiatry, 101, 141-148.

Office of Population Censuses and Surveys (1979)
Mortality Statistics. London: HMSO.

Parkes, C.M. (1972)
Bereavement. London: Tavistock.

Rachels, J. (1975)
Active and passive euthanasia. New England Journal of Medicine, 292, 78-80.

Saunders, C. (1977)
Dying they live. In H. Feifel (ed.), New Meanings of Death. New York: McGraw-Hill.

Saunders, C. (1978)
Care of the dying. In V. Carver and P. Liddiard (eds), An Ageing Population. Sevenoaks: Hodder & Stoughton.

Schulz, R. and Aderman, D. (1974)
Clinical research and the stages of dying. Omega, 5, 137-143.

Spinetta, J.J. (1974)
The dying child's awareness of death. Psychological Bulletin, 81, 256-260.

Ward, A.W.M. (1974)
Telling the patient. Journal of the Royal College of General Practitioners, 24, 465-468.

Questions

1. How has the pattern of dying changed in the UK since t turn of the century? What has caused these changes and what are their consequences?
2. Who should be informed of a patient's fatal prognosis? Give reasons for your answer.
3. Summarize the most common sources of distress of the terminally ill and their families: what are the implications of these?
4. Why do terminally ill people become depressed and how large a problem is this?
5. How common is anxiety in terminal illness and why does it arise?
6. What psychological problems might arise for a fatally ill six-year-old child and his family? What steps could be taken to mitigate these problems?
7. Why should there be growing public support for the legalization of voluntary euthanasia and why is this not

reflected in professional attitudes?
8. What is the bereavement response and what causes it?
9. What factors are important in influencing the nature of grief?
10. Construct a stereotypic, but detailed, character sketch of the person most likely to cope badly with a terminal illness: do the same for the person most likely to cope well. Justify your answer.

Annotated reading

General

Kastenbaum, R.J. (1977) Death, Society and Human Experience. St Louis, Mo.: Mosby.
> Written by a psychologist, but for a general readership, this book provides broad coverage of the psychological and social aspects of death at a level that is readily understood, without being unduly simplistic. Relevant data are cited together with many illustrative examples. A good deal of space is given to concepts of death, from childhood to old age, and there are sections on bereavement and suicide. A few exercises for students are also included.

Terminal illness and dying

Hinton, J. (1972) Dying. Harmondsworth: Penguin.
> This is an eminently readable book by a psychiatrist with much practical experience of caring for the terminally ill and the dying. This experience enables Hinton to write with some authority on practical considerations and to place research findings in perspective. Relevant data are cited appropriately throughout the text and the book contains a good deal of useful information. The best sections are upon dying and the care of the dying and there is a concluding section on bereavement.

Doyle, D. (ed.) (1979) Terminal Care. Edinburgh: Churchill-Livingstone.
> This is a collection of papers arising from a multidisciplinary conference. Accordingly, it provides useful reading for a wide range of health-care professionals including nurses, social workers and ministers of religion. In addition to examining the roles of different professions there are chapters on grief, domiciliary care and primary care.

Euthanasia

Glover, J. (1977) Causing Death and Saving Lives. Harmondsworth: Penguin.
> This is a clear and concise consideration of the ethical and practical problems associated with most aspects of taking life, from abortion to euthanasia. For those who want a brief but careful consideration of euthanasia and

285

those who are seeking to place euthanasia in a wider context, this is a most valuable book.

Russell, R.O. (1977) Freedom to Die. New York: Human Sciences Press.
Although the author examines arguments for and against the legalization of voluntary euthanasia, the tone of the volume is clearly in favour of this. The value of the book lies in its uncomplicated style, broad coverage and extensive appendices. In addition to examining the relevant arguments, the author traces the development of public awareness of euthanasia and attempts that have been made to promote the practice. The appendice include an example of the Living Will and various legislative proposals and bills that have been proposed in the UK and USA.

Bereavement

Parkes, C.M. (1972) Bereavement. London: Tavistock.
This volume appeared in Pelican Books in 1975 and, although it is now beginning to age, it is probably the best single source of information on bereavement. The reader is taken progressively through the response to bereavement in its many manifestations and is provided with a clear account of grief, the factors that influence this and the nature of recovery. Illustrative examples and research findings are used throughout the text and the book concludes with a substantial section on helping the bereaved.

Smith, K. (1978) Helping the Bereaved. London: Duckworth
This is a short and unpretentious book aimed at a general readership. It is valuable for its reliance on the statements of bereaved people to convey powerfully the experience of grief and the range of emotions and events that commonly occur. The examples help one more accurately to empathize with the bereaved.

17

Psychopathology
David A. Shapiro

'Psychopathology', literally defined, is the study of disease of the mind. Our society entrusts most of the care of individuals whose behaviour and experience are problematic or distressing to medical specialists (psychiatrists).
Being medically trained, psychiatrists see their work as requiring diagnosis and treatment of 'patients'. Psychologists, on the other hand, have sought alternative means of understanding abnormal behaviour, and the aim of this chapter is to outline the progress that has been made in this direction.

The varieties of psychopathology

A good way to appreciate the great variety of problems we are concerned with is to examine the system of classification used by psychiatrists, summarized in table 1. Readers requiring more detailed descriptions of these should consult a psychiatric textbook. In the NEUROSES, the personality and perception of reality are fundamentally intact, although emotional disturbances of one kind or another, usually involving anxiety or its presumed effects, can make life very difficult for the individual. The PSYCHOSES, on the other hand, are characterized by gross impairments in perception, memory, thinking and language functions, and the individual is fundamentally disorganized, rather than merely emotionally disturbed. However, there is no clear-cut brain disease, and so the disorder cannot be explained in purely biomedical terms. The layman's conception of 'madness' is based on the symptoms of schizophrenia, including delusions (unshakeable, false beliefs), hallucinations (such as hearing 'voices') and thought disorder (manifested in 'garbled' speech). The third category of table 1, PERSONALITY DISORDERS, comprises deeply ingrained, motivational and social maladjustments. Table 1 also includes ORGANIC SYNDROMES, which are behaviour disorders associated with identified brain disease. Not included in the table are the important group of PSYCHOSOMATIC illnesses. These are characterized by physical symptoms whose origins are in part psychological (emotional). They include asthma, high

Table 1

Major category: NEUROSES (milder disturbances)

Illustrative syndromes	Characteristic symptoms
Anxiety state	Palpitation, tires easily, breathlessness, anxiety, nervousness
Obsessive-compulsive disorders	Intrusive thoughts, urges to acts or rituals
Phobias	Irrational fears of specific objects or situations
Conversion reactions	Physical symptoms, lacking organic cause
Neurotic depression	Hopelessness, dejection

Major category: PSYCHOSES (severe non-organic disturbances)

Illustrative syndromes	Characteristic symptoms
Affective disorders / Schizophrenia	Disturbances of mood, energy and activity patterns / Reality distortion, social withdrawal, disorganization of thought, perception and emotion

Major category: PERSONALITY DISORDERS (antisocial disturbances)

Illustrative syndromes	Characteristic symptoms
Psychopathic personality / Alcoholism and drug dependence	Lack of conscience / Physical or psychological dependence

Major category: ORGANIC SYNDROMES

Illustrative syndromes	Characteristic symptoms
Epilepsy / Severe mental handicap	Increased susceptibility to convulsions / Extremely low intelligence, social impairments, impairments

blood pressure, gastric and duodenal ulcers. More generally, psychological stress is increasingly implicated in many physical illnesses.

The medical model of psychopathology
Before describing psychological approaches to behaviour disorder, it is necessary to examine critically the predominant medical approach. This makes three major assumptions, which are considered in turn.

The diagnostic system
The first assumption of the medical model is that the various kinds of abnormal behaviour can be classified, by DIAGNOSIS, into SYNDROMES, or constellations of SYMPTOMS regularly occurring together. This diagnostic system has already been summarized in table 1. It has a number of disadvantages. First, some disorders appear to cut across the boundaries of the system. Thus an individual whose severe anxiety is associated with fears of delusional intensity may defy classification as 'neurotic' or 'psychotic'. Second, scientific studies of the ability of psychiatrists to agree on the diagnosis of individuals have suggested that the process is rather unreliable, with agreement ranging from about 50 per cent to 80 per cent depending upon the circumstances (Beck et al., 1962). Third, research also suggests that the diagnosis given to an individual may bear little relationship to the symptoms the individual has (Zigler and Philips, 1961). Fourth, the diagnosis of psychiatric disorder is much more subjective and reflective of cultural attitudes than is the diagnosis of physical illness; one culture's schizophrenic might be another's shaman; similar acts of violence might be deemed heroic in battle but psychopathic in peacetime. Careful comparisons of American and British psychiatrists have shown that the two groups use different diagnostic criteria and hence classify patients differently.

Despite these limitations, the psychiatric classification persists. This is largely because no better descriptive system has been developed, whilst improvements have been obtained in the usefulness of the system by refining it in the light of earlier criticisms. For example, agreement between psychiatrists has been improved by standardization of the questions asked in diagnostic interviews and the use of standard decision-rules for assigning diagnoses to constellations of symptoms. But it is still necessary to bear in mind that the diagnostic system is not infallible and the 'labels' it gives individuals should not be uncritically accepted.

Physiological basis of psychopathology
The second assumption of the medical model is that the symptoms reflect an underlying disease process, physiological in nature like those involved in all illnesses,

causing the symptoms. Three kinds of evidence are offered in support of this. First, the influence of hereditary factors has been assessed by examining the rates of disorder among the relatives of sufferers. To the extent that a disorder is heritable, its origins are considered biological in nature. For example, comparison between the dizygotic (non-identical) and monozygotic (identical) twins of sufferers suggests that there is some hereditary involvement in schizophrenia, anxiety-related disorders, depression and antisocial disorders, with the evidence strongest in the case of schizophrenia (Gottesman and Shields, 1973). Studies of children adopted at birth also suggest that the offspring of schizophrenic parents are more liable to suffer from schizophrenia than other adopted children, despite having no contact with the biological parent. On the other hand, the evidence also shows that hereditary factors alone cannot fully account for schizophrenia or any other psychological disorder. Even among the identical twins of schizophrenics, many do not develop the disorder. Both hereditary and environmental influences are important.

The second line of evidence for a 'disease' basis of psychopathology concerns the biochemistry of the brain. This is a vastly complex subject, and one whose present methods of investigation are almost certainly too crude to give other than an approximate picture of what is going on. Over the years, a succession of biochemical factors have been suggested as causes for different forms of psychopathology. Unfortunately, the evidence is not conclusive, as biochemical factors found in sufferers may be consequences rather than causes. Hospital diets, activity patterns or characteristic emotional responses may influence the brain biochemistry of disordered individuals.

Despite these problems, there are some promising lines of biochemical research. For example, it has been suggested that schizophrenia may be caused by excess activity of dopamine, one of the neurotransmitters (substances with which neurons stimulate one another: see Snyder et al., 1974). This suggestion is supported by the similarity in molecular structure between dopamine and the phenothiazine drugs which are used to alleviate schizophrenia, suggesting that these drugs block the reception of dopamine by taking its place at receptors which normally receive it. These drugs also cause side effects resembling the symptoms of Parkinson's disease, which is associated with dopamine deficiency. Although this and other evidence supports the dopamine theory of schizophrenia, some research has failed to support it, and so the theory has yet to be universally accepted. In sum, biochemical evidence is suggestive, and consistent with presumed physiological origins of psychopathology, but it is not conclusive, nor can such evidence make a psychological explanation redundant. It is best seen as an important part of our understanding of psychopathology, whose causal significance varies from disorder to disorder.

The third line of evidence for the physiological basis of psychopathology concerns disorders with clear organic causes. Disease or damage to the brain can result in severe disturbance of behaviour. A classic example of this is 'general paresis of the insane', whose widespread physical and mental impairments were discovered in the last century to be due to the syphilis spirochete. This discovery encouraged medical scientists to seek clear-cut organic causes for other psychological abnormalities. A large number of ORGANIC BRAIN SYNDROMES have been established, in which widespread cognitive and emotional deficits are associated with damage to the brain by disease, infection, or injury. EPILEPSY, in which the individual is unusually susceptible to seizures or convulsions, is associated with abnormal patterns of brain activity measured by the electro-encephalogram (EEG) even between seizures. Many individuals with severe MENTAL HANDICAP (Clarke and Clarke, 1974), who attain very low scores on tests of general intelligence and show minimal adaptation to social requirements and expectations, suffer from clear-cut organic pathology, often accompanied by severe physical abnormalities.

On the other hand, all of these disorders are affected by the person's individuality, experience and environment. For example, similar brain injuries result in very different symptoms in different individuals. Those suffering from epileptic seizures can make use of their past experience to avoid circumstances (including diet and environmental stimuli) which tend to trigger their convulsions. Most mentally handicapped people do not have clearly identifiable organic illnesses. Even among those who do, the environment can make a big difference to the person's ability to learn the skills of everyday living. Psychologists have found that special training can help mentally handicapped people who might otherwise appear incapable of learning.

Medical treatment of psychopathology

The third assumption of the medical model concerns how psychopathology should be managed. Physical treatments are offered in hospitals and clinics to persons designated 'patients'. It is beyond our present scope to describe the extensive evidence supporting the effectiveness of drugs and electro-convulsive therapy (ECT), the major physical treatments currently employed. However, there are several reasons why psychologists are often inclined to question the support this evidence gives to the medical model. First, individuals differ in their responsiveness to physical treatments, and nobody really understands why some individuals are not helped. Second, the fact that abnormal behaviour can be controlled by physical means does not prove that its origins are physical. Third, the physical treatments often lack a convincing scientific rationale to explain their effects.

The medical model: conclusions

In sum, the medical model gains some support from the evidence, but is sufficiently defective and incomplete to warrant the development of alternative and complementary approaches. Although the diagnostic system is of some value, it must be used with caution. Although hereditary influences, biochemical abnormalities and organic pathology have a part to play in our understanding of psychopathology, they cannot explain its origins without reference to environmental and psychological factors. The apparent efficacy of physical treatment does not establish the physical origins of what they treat. The remainder of this chapter is concerned with five alternative approaches developed by psychologists and social scientists, and assesses their contribution with respect to some of the most important kinds of psychopathology. The evidence presented is, of necessity, very selective, and a full appreciation of these approaches can only follow more extensive study. It should also be borne in mind that the present emphasis on origins of disorder entails a relative neglect of research on treatment.

The statistical model

The statistical model identifies individuals whose behaviour or reported experience is sufficiently unusual to warrant attention on that basis alone. Abnormal individuals are those who greatly differ from the average with respect to some attribute (such as intelligence or amount of subjective anxiety experienced). For example, according to Eysenck (1970), people who score highly on dimensions known as 'neuroticism' (very readily roused to emotion) and 'introversion' (quick in learning conditioned responses and associations) are likely to show what the psychiatrist calls 'anxiety neurosis'. Although this approach is commendably objective, it is not very helpful alone. Not all unusual behaviour is regarded as patho-logical. Exceptionally gifted people are an obvious case in point. Some statistically abnormal behaviours are obviously more relevant to psychopathology than are others, and we need more than a statistical theory to tell us which to consider, and why. But the model is of value for its suggestion that 'normal' and 'abnormal' behaviour may differ only in degree, in contrast to the medical model's implication of a sharp division between them.

The psycho-dynamic model

The psychodynamic model is very difficult to summarize, based as it is on theories developed early in the century

292

by Freud, and revised and elaborated by him and subsequent workers within a broad tradition (Ellenberger, 1970). Like the medical model, it seeks an underlying cause for psychopathology, but this is a psychological cause, namely, unconscious conflicts arising from childhood experiences. Freudians have developed a general theory of personality from their study of psychopathology. Freud viewed the personality as comprising the conscious EGO, the unconscious ID (source of primitive impulses) and partly conscious, partly unconscious SUPER-EGO (conscience). The ego is held to protect itself from threat by several defence mechanisms. These are a commonplace feature of everyone's adjustment, but are used in an exaggerated or excessively rigid manner by neurotic individuals, and are over-stretched to the point of collapse in the case of psychotic individuals.

For example, neurotic anxiety is learnt by a child punished for being impulsive, whereupon the conflict between wanting something and fearing the consequences of that desire is driven from consciousness (this is an example of the defence mechanism known as REPRESSION). According to this theory, pervasive anxiety is due to fear of the person's ever-present id impulses, and phobic objects, such as insects or animals, are seen as symbolic representations of objects of the repressed id impulses. Dynamic theory views depression as a reaction to loss in individuals who are excessively dependent upon other people for the maintenance of self-esteem. The loss may be actual (as in bereavement) or symbolic (as in the misinterpretation of a rejection as a total loss of love). The depressed person expresses a child-like need for approval and affection to restore self-esteem. In psychotic disorders such as schizophrenia, the collapse of the defence mechanisms leads to the predominance of primitive 'primary process' thinking.

Despite its considerable impact upon the ways in which we understand human motivation and psychopathology, psychodynamic theory has remained controversial. Most of the evidence in its favour comes from clinical case material, as recounted by practising psychoanalysts, whose work is based on the belief that unconscious conflicts must be brought to the surface for the patient to recover from the symptoms they have engendered. Whilst this method often yields compelling material which is difficult to explain in other terms (Malan, 1979), it is open to criticism as insufficiently objective to yield scientific evidence. It is all too easy for the psychoanalyst unwittingly to influence material produced by the patient, and the essential distinction between observations and the investigator's interpretations of them is difficult to sustain in the psychoanalytic consulting-room. The abstract and complex formulations of psychodynamic theory are difficult to prove or disprove by the clear-cut scientific methods favoured by psychologists, and the patients studied, whether in Freud's Vienna or present-day London or New York, are somewhat unrepresentative.

There is some scientific evidence which is broadly consistent with psychodynamic theory; for example, the defects in thinking found in schizophrenia are compatible with the dynamic concept of ego impairment, and loss events of the kind implicated by dynamic theory are associated with the onset of depression. Although psychologists hostile to dynamic theory can explain these findings in other terms, there is little doubt that the theory has been fruitful, contributing to psychology such essential concepts as unconscious conflict and defence mechanism.

The learning model

The learning model views psychopathology as arising from faulty learning in early life, and conceptualizes this process in terms of principles of learning drawn from laboratory studies of animals and humans. The most basic principles are those of Pavlovian or 'classical' conditioning (in which two stimuli are presented together until the response to one stimulus is also evoked by the other), and 'operant' conditioning (whereby behaviour with favourable consequences becomes more frequent). According to proponents of the learning model, the symptoms of psychopathology are nothing more than faulty habits acquired through these two types of learning. The 'underlying pathology' posited by the medical and psychodynamic models is dismissed as unfounded myth.

For example, it is suggested that phobias are acquired by a two-stage learning process; first, fear is aroused in response to a previously neutral stimulus when this stimulus occurs in conjunction with an unpleasant stimulus; then the person learns to avoid the situation evoking the fear, because behaviour taking the person away from the situation is rewarded by a reduction in fear. Another learning theory is that schizophrenic patients receive more attention and other rewards from other people, such as hospital staff, when they behave in 'crazy' ways, thereby increasing the frequency of this behaviour. Again, depressed people are seen as failing to exercise sufficient skill and effort to 'earn' rewards from situations and from other people; a vicious circle develops and activity reduces still further in the absence of such rewards.

In general, the learning model provides a powerful set of principles governing the acquisition of problem behaviour. But it has severe limitations. For example, the fact that fears and phobias can be established by processes of conditioning in the laboratory does not prove that this is how they come about naturally. The theory cannot readily explain how people acquire behaviours which lead to such distress (it is hardly 'rewarding' to suffer the agonies of depression or anxiety, and learning theorists acknowledge their difficulty over this fact by referring to it as the 'neurotic paradox'). Recently, learning theorists have examined the important process of imitative learning or modelling, whereby the behaviour of observers is influenced by another's actions and their consequences. Fear and aggression can be aroused in this way, with obvious implications for the transmission of psychopathology from one person (such as a parent) to another. But human thinking is considered by many psychologists too complex to be understood in terms of these relatively simple learning theories. Hence the development of the cognitive approach, to which we now turn.

The cognitive model

The cognitive model focusses upon thinking processes and their possible dysfunctions. 'Neurotic' problems are seen as due to relatively minor errors in reasoning processes, whilst 'psychotic' disorders are held to reflect profound disturbances in cognitive function and organization.

For example, it is well known that depressed people hold negative attitudes towards themselves, their experiences and their future. According to cognitive theory, these attitudes give rise to the feelings of depression (Beck, 1967). Although an episode of depression may be triggered by external events, it is the person's perception of the event which makes it set off depressed feelings. Experiments in which negative beliefs about the self are induced in non-depressed subjects have shown that a depressed mood does indeed follow. But whether similar processes account for the more severe and lasting depressive feelings of clinical patients is another matter, although the promising results of 'cognitive therapy', in which the attitudes of depressed patients are modified directly, may be taken as indirect evidence for the theory.

Cognitive theory also embraces people's beliefs about the causation of events (known as ATTRIBUTIONS). For example, it has been suggested that the attributions one makes concerning unpleasant experiences will determine the impact of those experiences upon one's subsequent beliefs about oneself; thus, if a woman is rejected by a man, this is much more damaging to her self-esteem if she believes that the main cause of the event is her own inadequacy, than if she attributes the event to the man's own passing mood. An attributional approach suggests that failure experiences are most damaging if individuals attribute them to wide-ranging and enduring factors within themselves. Consistent with this, depressed people have been found to attribute bad outcomes to wide-ranging and enduring factors within themselves, whilst they attribute good outcomes to changeable factors outside their control.

Psychologists have devoted considerable efforts to precise descriptions of the cognitive deficits of schizophrenic patients through controlled laboratory experiments. For example, schizophrenics have difficulty performing tasks requiring selective attention to relevant information and the exclusion from attention of irrelevant information. Schizophrenics are highly distractable. This may help to explain how irrelevant features of a situation acquire disproportionate importance and become interpreted as part of their delusional systems of false beliefs, or how speech is disorganized by the shifting of attention to irrelevant thoughts and mental images which other people manage to ignore.

The cognitive approach is of great interest because it combines the systematic and objective methods of experimental psychology with a thoroughgoing interest in an important aspect of human mentality. It is a very active 'growth area' of current research, and shows considerable promise. It is perhaps too soon to evaluate many of its specific theories, however, and it does carry the risk of neglecting other aspects of human behaviour.

The socio-cultural model

The final model to be considered attributes psychopathology to social and cultural factors. It focusses upon malfunctioning of the social or cultural group rather than of an individual within that group.

In terms of the socio-cultural model schizophrenia, for example, has been considered both in relation to the quality of family life and to larger socio-economic forces. Within the family, behaviour labelled schizophrenic is seen as a response to self-contradictory emotional demands ('double binds') from other family members, notably parents, to which no sane response is possible. Although graphic accounts have been offered of such patterns in the family life of schizophrenic patients, there is no evidence that these are peculiar to such families. If anything, the research evidence suggests that abnormalities of communication within the families of schizophrenics arise in response to the behaviour of the patient, rather than causing the disorder. Looking beyond the family, the higher incidence of schizophrenia amongst the lowest socio-economic class, especially in inner city areas, is attributed to the multiple deprivations suffered by this group. Episodes of schizophrenia are triggered by stressful life events, some of which are more common, or less offset by social and material supports, amongst lower-class people. On the other hand, cause and effect could be the other way round, with persons developing schizophrenia 'drifting' into poverty-ridden areas of the city. Indeed, schizophrenic patients tend to achieve a lower socio-economic status than did their parents.

296

The socio-cultural approach is of undoubted value as a critical challenge to orthodox views, and has generated useful research into social and cultural factors in psychopathology. Its proponents have also made valuable contributions by bringing a greater humanistic respect for the personal predicament of troubled individuals, and to the development of 'therapeutic communities' and family therapy as alternatives to individually-centred treatments. However, many of its propositions concerning cause-effect relationships have not stood the test of empirical research.

The psychology of illness

It is well known that certain physical illnesses are related to psychological factors. These 'psychosomatic disorders' include ulcerative colitis, bronchial asthma and hypertension. It is not so widely appreciated, however, that psychological factors may be involved in any physical illness. This is because the physiological changes associated with stress (for instance, the release of the 'stress hormones' such as adrenalin) can suppress immune responses and so increase the individual's susceptibility to many diseases, ranging from the common cold to cancer (Rogers et al., 1979). Many aspects of a person's life have been implicated in ill-health, presumably because of their effects on such physiological mechanisms. These include physical stresses such as noise, highly demanding and/or repetitive jobs (whether physical or mental), catastrophic life events (such as accidents, illness or bereavement) and major emotional difficulties (such as marital discord).

However, for physical illness as for psychopathology, the cause-effect relationship is not simple. Some individuals are more constitutionally stress-prone than others, it appears. Some people live in congenial and supportive surroundings, enabling them to withstand pressures which might otherwise lead to illness. Most of the events implicated in psychological distress and ill-health are in part the results of the individual's own state and behaviour. For example, marital conflict may reflect prior strains felt by the individuals involved. Furthermore, the impact of a stressful event or circumstance depends on the individual's appraisal of it. For example, noise is less distressing if we know we can silence it should it it become unbearable. Thus consideration of psychological factors in ill-health demonstrates clearly the interaction between features of individuals and of their surroundings. For physical illness as for psychopathology, we must realize that there are many interacting causes rather than imagine that any one factor is alone responsible for the problem at issue.

Conclusions   Each of the approaches surveyed has contributed to our
understanding of psychopathology. The evidence presented
for each can only illustrate the massive amounts of
research which have been carried out. Nonetheless, several
clear themes emerge which have profound implications for
our present and future knowledge of psychopathology.

First, the system of classification is inadequate, and
research shows that different people within the same broad
diagnostic group (such as schizophrenia) behave very differently; it therefore follows that different causes may
be found for the difficulties experienced by these sub-
groups of people.

Second, the different approaches could profitably be
integrated rather more than they have been in the past.
For example, elements of the medical, statistical, socio-
cultural and cognitive approaches have been combined in
recent work on schizophrenia, in which the vulnerability
of an individual to the disorder is seen as reflecting
both heredity and environment; this vulnerability
determines whether or not a person experiences schizophrenia when faced with stresses which are too much to
cope with (Zubin and Spring, 1977). The fact that
psychopathology generally has multiple causes lends
particular urgency to the need to construct broad theories
incorporating the facts which were hitherto regarded as
supporting one or another of the competing approaches.

Third, the different approaches have more in common
than is often acknowledged. In relation to schizophrenia,
for example, the breakdown of ego functioning described by
psychodynamic theory resembles the inability to process
information identified by cognitive theory.

Fourth, the limitations of existing models have encouraged the growth of alternative approaches. For example,
the 'transactional' approach emphasizes the importance of
the individual's active part in bringing about apparently
external stressful events and pressures (Cox, 1978). This
approach views the individual as neither a passive victim
of circumstances, nor as irrevocably programmed from birth
to respond in a particular way. Person and environment are
seen as in continuous interaction, so that one-way cause-
effect analysis is inappropriate. For example, harassed
executives and mothers of small children bring some of the
stress they suffer upon themselves as they respond sharply
to colleagues or children and thus contribute to a climate
of irritation or conflict. Research using this approach
has only recently begun, but it holds considerable hope
for the future.

Finally, what can this psychological study of psychopathology offer the professional? There are as yet no
certain answers to such simple questions as 'What causes
schizophrenia?' or 'Why does Mrs Jones stay indoors all
the time?' If and when such answers become available, they
will not be simple. They will involve many interacting

298

factors. Meanwhile, the psychological approach teaches us a healthy respect for the complexity of the human predicament, and is a valuable corrective to any tendency to offer simplistic or unsympathetic explanations of human distress. Furthermore, professionals will often find it illuminating to apply some of the approaches outlined here to help understand distressed individuals they encounter in their daily work.

References

Beck, A.T. (1967)
Depression: Clinical, experimental and theoretical aspects. New York: Harper & Row.

Beck, A.T., Ward, C.H., Mendleson, M., Mock, J.E. and Erlbaugh, J. (1962)
Reliability of psychiatric diagnosis II: a study of consistency of clinical judgments and ratings. American Journal of Psychiatry, 119, 351-357.

Clarke, A.M. and Clarke, A.D.B. (1974)
Mental Deficiency: The changing outlook (3rd edn). London: Methuen.

Cox, T. (1978)
Stress. London: Macmillan.

Ellenberger, H.F. (1970)
The Discovery of the Unconscious. London: Allen Lane/Penguin.

Eysenck, H.J. (1970)
The Structure of Human Personality. London: Methuen.

Gottesman, I.I. and Shields, J. (1973)
Genetic theorising and schizophrenia. British Journal of Psychiatry, 122, 15-30.

Malan, D.H. (1979)
Individual Psychotherapy and the Science of Psychodynamics. London: Tavistock.

Rogers, M.P., Dubey, D. and Reich, P. (1979)
The influence of the psyche and the brain on immunity and disease susceptibility: a critical review. Psychosomatic Medicine, 41, 147-164.

Snyder, S.H., Banerjee, S.P., Yamamura, H.I. and Greenberg, D. (1974)
Drugs, neurotransmitters and schizophrenia. Science, 184, 1243-1253.

Zigler, E. and Philips, L. (1961)
Psychiatric diagnosis and symptomalogy. Journal of Abnormal and Social Psychology, 63, 69-75.

Zubin, J. and Spring, B. (1977)
Vulnerability - a new view of schizophrenia. Journal of Abnormal Psychology, 86, 103-126.

Questions

1. What problems are raised by the diagnostic system used by psychiatrists? Can it be improved?
2. What can the study of twins tell us about psychopathology?

3. Outline the evidence for a biochemical basis for schizophrenia.
4. How useful is the medical model of psychopathology? Does it have any disadvantages?
5. Outline the statistical approach to psychopathology, indicating its value and limitations.
6. What is wrong with psychoanalysis as a scientific method of investigating psychopathology?
7. Is psychopathology simply behaviour which has been learned because it produces rewards?
8. Which of the models of psychopathology do you prefer? Give your reasons.
9. How can psychological factors affect susceptibility to physical illness?
10. Which forms of psychopathology would be particularly disabling to a person employed in your profession, and why?

Annotated reading

Davison, G.C. and Neale, J.M. (1977) Abnormal Psychology: An experimental clinical approach (2nd edn). New York: Wiley.
> The chapter can provide no more than an introduction to psychopathology. This is the best of the textbooks available: it is readable, comprehensive and, in general, accurate. It is useful in teaching, and has been drawn upon extensively for drafting the chapter. If you want to follow up any aspect of the chapter in more detail, look up the topic in the Index of this book.

Hilgard, E.R., Atkinson, R.L. and Atkinson, R.C. (1979) Introduction to Psychology (7th edn). New York: Harcourt Brace Jovanovich (chapters 14, 15 and 16).
> Intermediate in length between the present chapter and the Davison and Neale book, this group of chapters gives a good general account. Chapter 14 reviews conflict and stress in terms of both experimental and psychoanalytic work; chapter 15 gives a good outline of much of the ground covered in this chapter; and chapter 16 discusses methods of treatment.

Spielberger, C. (1979) Understanding Stress and Anxiety. New York: Harper & Row.
> A very readable and well-illustrated introduction to experimental and clinical work on stress and anxiety, recommended for the student wishing to look further into these aspects.

Seligman, M.E.P. (1975) Helplessness: On depression, development and death. New York: Freeman.
> Seligman presents his theory of learnt helplessness in a very stimulating and engaging book. Although the theory was based on laboratory studies with animals,

Seligman has injected a great deal of 'human interest'
into this account. Students who are especially
interested in the theory of depression should note,
however, that Seligman's ideas have moved on since the
book was written to incorporate attributional concepts.

Stafford-Clark, D. and Smith, A.C. (1979) Psychiatry for
Students (5th edn). London: Allen & Unwin.
The present chapter does not attempt to do full justice
to psychiatry. This is the most readable of the general
textbooks on psychiatry, written for students rather
than practitioners. It is a good source for more details of psychiatric symptoms, disorders and treatments.

Inechen, B. (1979) Mental Illness. London: Longman.
This reviews the field from a sociological viewpoint,
and covers a good deal of research on social factors in
psychopathology.

Bannister, D. and Fransella, F. (1980) Inquiring Man (2nd
edn). Harmondsworth: Penguin.
A persuasive account of George Kelly's personal
construct approach to psychology and psychopathology,
written by two of its leading exponents.

18

Interviewing
Russell P. Wicks

If there is one universally applied technique to be found
in behavioural research it is 'interviewing'. If there is
one technique basic to all professional practice it is the
interaction between people that is called 'interviewing'.
It is the nature of this interaction between people which
is the concern of this chapter. It is to be hoped that
what is said can be applied not simply to 'the interview'
in 'an interview situation' but to all purposive contacts
between individuals; the critical feature, it is claimed,
being the purposive nature of the encounter. The participants bring hopes, fears, expectations, misconceptions
and many other cognitions to the situation, most times in
the hope that their wishes will be met, fears reduced and
so on. Customarily this view is found in the characterization of an interview as a 'conversation with a purpose'.
So it is, but ALL those participating in an interview have
their purposes and not simply, for example, the
interviewer. In the complex transactions of getting and
giving information we observe effort aimed at achieving
purposes. Thus the psychologist testing a client by means
of, say, the Wechsler Adult Intelligence Scale is
conducting an interview as defined. The purpose from one
point of view is to help the client in some way, from the
other to be helped. In the exchange of information each
has purposes and expectations that they hope will be met.
Each may be optimizing their strategies towards fulfilling
these purposes. Roles will be assumed constraining and
shaping behaviour. If participants in interviews can
become more skilful and aware of the processes involved
there is some hope of raising levels of satisfaction. It
is, therefore, the aim of this chapter to examine such
interview processes with this goal in mind. For this
purpose a simple model of an interview is described (see
figure 1) and for illustrative purposes reference made to
three particular interview situations; occupational
counselling, job interviews and research interviewing.

Initiation

The view that it is the purposive nature of the interview
that is crucial leads us to consider the motives of the

Figure 1

Model of an interview

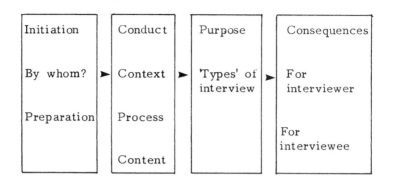

Initiation	Conduct	Purpose	Consequences
By whom? ►	Context ►	'Types' of ► interview	For interviewer
Preparation	Process		For interviewee
	Content		

participants. An individual approaching a counselling situation may be motivated by a complex of needs, and voluntary or compulsory attendance may be crucial in structuring these needs. Whether these needs are shared and whether they can be fulfilled is another matter. It may well be the case that some frequently voiced criticisms of interviews arise, in part, from a failure to make explicit the needs and expectations of the parties involved. Nowhere is this more important than in those situations with a high level of emotional involvement. Two people may look back on an interview as a total failure because each had different expectations which unfortunately were not fulfilled. We all, interviewers and interviewees, bring hopes and fears to the task. Just as Orne (1962) draws our attention to the 'demand characteristics' of the experimental situation as a result of which subjects perform as they believe they are expected so to do, so participants in interviews will seek a role that they perceive as being appropriate. Not always, unfortunately, do they choose correctly.

In analysing an interview it follows, therefore, that attention to preliminaries and preparation is vital. Many writers on interviewing stress the physical preparations needed, literally setting the scene. Here, 'cognitive' scene setting is judged to be more important; for example, in employment interviewing paying attention to providing information about the organization, or providing an adequate job description. Considering the contribution of application forms and references, together with other 'scene setting' activities, will go a long way towards minimizing the cognitive gap that may occur. Furthermore, such preparations are in fact part of the information exchange that lies at the heart of an interview. In general, preparation from the interviewer's point of view means careful planning of all aspects of the situation.

Briefing oneself, rehearsing the interview, anticipating needs; all contribute to an efficiently managed, worthwhile encounter.

Recently, increasing attention has been given to preparation on the part of the interviewee, especially for those about to be interviewed for a job. For example, a great deal of work stemming from careers work with young people has resulted in programmes aimed at developing 'life skills'. There is clear evidence that all can profit from paying attention to the activities and skills involved in job seeking. The material included in such programmes varies widely but may cover:

* where to get job information;
* work experience;
* how to reply to advertisements;
* how to become more self-aware;
* how to be interviewed.

The techniques employed range from self-instructional material to the use of video-recording of role-play situations. In general, however, the emphasis is on providing guidelines, improving social skills, self-presentation and making people more aware of the processes of social interaction.

Conduct

Context

What effect on the behaviour of the participants in an interview might the following environments have: a police station; a doctor's surgery; a street corner; a psychology laboratory? Clearly the effect can be dramatic. We have the clearest evidence here for the importance of the frame of reference, role expectations and construal of the situation upon behaviour in an interview. Indeed, the subtlety of the rules of the 'games' played out in different contexts is such that we spend our lives refining and editing our private rule books. Within each context there may be a range of indicators signalling to us how to behave, how to address people, what to say and what not to say, an obvious example being dress, particularly a uniform which may be anything from a pin-stripe suit to a white coat. What is the experience of people who customarily wear a 'uniform' when they discard it? What might people say to a priest in mufti that they would not say if he donned his clerical garb? Thus our perception of the interview context is an essential part of the scene setting previously discussed. Most interviewers, being aware of this, go to some trouble to ensure that the physical setting signals what they wish it to: they dress in a particular style, arrange the seats appropriately, adjust the lighting, ensure that interruptions do or do not occur. They try to ensure that the interview is conducted in a 'good mannered' way.

A further aspect is that participants bring substantial resources to the task: their background knowledge, and skills expectations. Whilst these resources may bring benefits to an interview, they sometimes create problems. Such difficulties have been extensively investigated by Rosenthal and his co-workers (e.g. Rosenthal and Rosnow, 1969) in studies of the character- istics of 'volunteers' in research and studies of the expectations of subjects in experiments, as well as the experimenters. Avoiding bias and error arising from these factors is a major concern of investigators; thus one should be aware that volunteers for survey research tend to be better educated; if male, they score higher on IQ tests; and they are better adjusted than non-volunteers. Such factors should be taken into account in evaluating data. Similarly, the survey interviewer asked to find a sample of five people, even though certain characteristics of the sample are specified, may unwittingly choose those they feel it would be 'nice' to interview.

Process

A great deal of what we know about interpersonal communi- cation has been learnt by systematic study of interviews, especially the face-to-face two-person encounter. What is offered here, however, is a general communication model which may be used to analyse an interview (see figure 2). The utility of this model as a tool for examining inter- personal behaviour rests upon the conceptualization of communication as a system; the model is dynamic because it has independent parts with provision for feedback.

Figure 2

A communication model

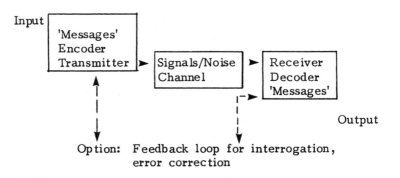

Such a model could stand for many communication sys- tems: radio or television transmission; a nervous system; or, in this case, an interview. A useful procedure arising from the 'system' model is that we can examine its integrity. In other words, we can see what happens when one part of the system is distorted or eliminated.

In this model, 'message' is taken to stand for that which we wish to transmit. Embedded in this is the difficult problem of meaning, and an obvious use of the model is to compare inputs and outputs according to some criterion of meaningfulness. Such a comparison is the basis of a hilarious game in which the distortion occurring when a 'message' is passed along a line of people by word of mouth is examined. Bartlett (1972) showed in his method of serial reproduction the simplifications and intrusions which occur in this process.

Within the interview, 'meaning' arises at a number of levels. First, it arises at the level of verbal content. What was the question and what is the answer? Much has been written about asking the right sort of question in an interview, whether to use direct or indirect questions, the appropriate form of words, and the dangers of certain questions such as leading or multiple forms. Skilful interviewers do not seem to be constrained by rigid rules but show flexibility, constantly probing and following up interesting leads. They tend to ask: 'Tell me', 'When was that?', 'How was that?', 'What did you do?' and perhaps the most difficult question of all, 'Why?'

Second, the question of meaning arises at the level of recording the interview material. What gets lost or distorted when an interviewer distils a reply into notes or makes a decision? Third, a consideration arising especially in the research interview is: what has happened to the original meaning when a response is coded, probably into a pre-determined category, and is lumped together with others when the study is reported?

However, the verbal content of the message is only a small part of the signal. Many researchers assert that the non-verbal component of a signal is of greater importance. Argyle (1973, 1975) in particular has drawn our attention to the role of non-verbal communication factors such as:

* bodily movements: body language: gestures;
* facial expression;
* eye movements and eye contact;
* personal space: proximity.

Socially skilled performers are simultaneously transmitting signals using all these components together with verbal material whilst reacting to similar signals constituting feedback from their partners.

Utilizing and decoding this complex of information involves us in consideration of interpersonal perception, a key area in the analysis of interviewing. How we form judgements about other people is at the heart of interview decisions: the substantial literature on this topic, for example Cook (1979), suggests that the information we use includes:

* a person's actions;
* the situation in which the person is observed;
* appearance (including facial expression, physique, speech characteristics and dress style);
* non-verbal cues mentioned previously.

The powerful influence of some cues is seen most clearly in the study of stereotypes. Picking up one piece of information and building often unwarranted assumptions upon it is the classic error in judging others. Reacting to a regional accent, to hair colour, to ethnic origin or any other isolated item is all too common. Such a reaction, especially to irrelevant information, is usually dubbed the 'halo effect'. Since the judge or interviewer is striving for cognitive consistency, information is often interpreted in such a way that it fits this single judgement. Thus favourable material or even attributions will be ascribed to a liked person. Contrariwise, undue weight may be given to negative indications in the case of dislike. Clearly, interviewers must be constantly on their guard against introducing bias of this kind. Awareness of their prejudices and the sorts of errors we make in judging others will help.

It is the process component of interviewing which has received most attention in the training of interviewers. Such training commonly takes the form of general social skills training together with exercises directed at the specialization of the interviewer; for example, obtaining clinically relevant material in the hospital setting. Just how effective training may be is not easy to assess. Largely this is so because published studies of interview training tend to use different criteria, thus making comparisons difficult. The benefits to the trainee probably come from receiving informed feedback in role-playing or group tasks about their performance together with enhanced self awareness.

Content

The point has been made that the absence of a shared common aim or the lack of a clear plan in an interview leads to many difficulties. Specifically, criticisms in terms of interview decisions tend to the view that they may leave much to be desired. It is claimed, for example, that the research literature points overwhelmingly in this direction. Without wishing to dismiss the many studies leading to this conclusion, it must be pointed out that they cover a wide range of interview outcomes made by many interviewers at different levels of experience and training with their decisions based on imprecise criteria. The message of these studies seems to be that all concerned with interviews should be aware of the shortcomings and take steps to overcome them. Apart from errors arising from factors already mentioned in describing context and process aspects at an interview, the principal source is often the lack of a clear plan for an interview; in other words, content must be tailored to the particular aim in mind, each interview requiring careful planning with preparation related to a desired outcome. By way of illustration let us consider the content of interviews within the three professional contexts of counselling, job interviews and research interviewing.

Counselling: Occupational guidance

What is the aim of an occupational guidance procedure? At one time the approach was modelled upon the notion of talent matching: specify the job, specify the person and attempt to match the two. On the job side of the equation techniques of task analysis, job description and content specification were developed whilst evidence of congruent relevant behaviour was sought from the interviewee. It is no coincidence that the heyday of this approach coincided with the early boom in psychological test production. Aptitude tests, occupational interest guides, and tests of specific skills were all produced to aid the matching. Today, with the application of computer-based matching procedures, the approach is enjoying a revival. The role of the interview in this model was largely to establish the congruence of job and applicant profiles by comparison through discussion. From this approach evolved the contemporary developmental model, with an emphasis on career decision making as a process over time, starting in the early years with educational counselling, proceeding to occupational counselling and then to career development counselling, with perhaps counselling for retirement in later years. Thus there may be many interviews within this model each with a specific aim, the sum aimed at the overall development of the individual. Among the subgoals of this process we can recognize the following:

* self-appraisal: equipping the client to achieve realistic self-assessment;
* self-perception: providing frames of reference, categories of occupationally significant behaviours;
* job perception: acquiring the skills required to assess the world of work in terms of job content, values, role and life style;
* reality testing: matching aspirations and goals with opportunities within one's limitations;
* setting goals and objectives: specifying attainable goals and precise objectives;
* hypothesis generation: helping the client to generate occupational 'theories';
* interaction of the person and the job environment:

examining the complexities of the person/work situation interaction;
* sharing information: providing the client with educational and occupational information, and providing the counsellor with perceptions of the client;
* task setting: translating immediate goals into discrete tasks, such as finding an address, seeking information, reading a pamphlet, etc.

The task of the interviewer/counsellor therefore becomes that of achieving these goals at the appropriate time and in a manner which meets the client's needs. Flexibility, wide background knowledge and the ability to relate to the client are clearly prerequisites on the part of the counsellor. Similar goals are shared by modern staff appraisal schemes and staff development procedures.

Job interviews
Being interviewed for a job, for promotion or for annual assessment is probably the most commonly experienced form of interview. It has certainly attracted a substantial body of folk-lore, myth, jokes and hard-luck stories. That this is so is, in itself, of considerable psychological significance. The job interview comes in many varieties, not least the panel interview. Here especially the crucial importance of planning an interview is seen. The justifiable criticism of such encounters is frequently due first to poor interviewing skills on the part of the individual board members, and second to the lack of an agreed role for each.

Whilst not normally included under the heading of interviews, such behavioural observation techniques as role-playing by candidates, group discussions, problem-solving exercises and others raise the same problems previously mentioned of reliable and valid judgements about other people. Two examples of interview plans used in job interviews will be presented here: one is a general approach commonly employed, namely, the biography; the second a well-known technique called the Seven-Point Plan.

THE BIOGRAPHY: the majority of job interviews employ this approach, often, however, in an undisciplined fashion, hunting and pecking at a person's history. However, a simple structure which can be readily shared consists of establishing landmarks within relevant areas; commonly times of change such as leaving school. Bearing in mind the selectivity of recall, in itself an important indicator within an interview, and that the recent past may be more accessible, one should not expect uniform coverage of a life history. This raises the problem of breadth and depth within the interview in relation to the relevance of the information. Too often an interviewer will spend time on an irrelevant area, missing the opportunity to explore a significant point in detail.

However, a plan such as that shown in figure 3 provides a secure frame of reference for interviewer and interviewee. Not least, the interviewee can be assembling information and anticipating questions; the task is not unlike talking through a curriculum vitae. A final benefit of this approach is that it enables the interviewer to check dates, spot gaps in the account and draw out the inter-relationships between events. This approach is underpinned by application forms and curricula vitae, which are customarily set out in biographical order.

Figure 3

	Education	Interests	Home	Work
The past	Dates			
Land marks				
The present				

THE SEVEN-POINT PLAN: probably the best known of all assessment and interview formats, the plan was originally developed by Alec Rodger within the framework of the talent matching approach to occupational guidance. It was intended to apply to both candidates and jobs, to obtain relevant information about people and, by asking the same questions of a job, to facilitate matching.

The plan was rapidly adopted for job interviewing and has undoubtedly been highly influential in so far as it provides the unskilled interviewer with a robust, easily understood framework within which to work. Over the years a number of modifications have been suggested to the original plan. Similarly based schemes have been published, but what is essentially the original is presented here (Rodger, 1974).

1. Physical characteristics:
   Physical abilities of occupational importance.
   State of health. Vision, hearing. Appearance. Speech.
2. Attainments (and previous experience):
   Educational background, achievements. Occupational and professional training. Experience. How well has this person done? Personal achievements in any area: sports, pursuits, etc.
3. General ability:
   Especially general intelligence and cognitive skills - words, numbers, relationships.
4. Special aptitudes:
   Particularly occupationally applicable talents -

scientific, mechanical, mathematical, practical, literary, artistic, social skills.
5. Interests:
    Often the core information: type of interests, how they are pursued, to what effect. Intellectual, practical, physical, social and artistic interests may be occupationally significant.
6. Personality:
    What is this person like? Especially in terms of self-perception. Social relationships, behaviour indicative of self-reliance, dependability.
7. Circumstances:
    The context of the person's life in so far as it affects aspirations. Family circumstances, financial background, current problems.

The first six points apply particularly to the study of jobs. What physical characteristics, what attainments and so on are required for this job? It should be added that Rodger emphasized the importance of paying attention to individual likes and dislikes, to difficulties or distastes mentioned by people, and to the individual's strengths and weaknesses when applying the plan; in particular, stressing the importance of negative information in making selection decisions and the noting of danger signs.

Finally, in considering job interviews it should be noted that advice and preparation for interviewees is widely available in relation to the job interview. Social skills training and self-presentation courses are examples.

Research interviews

The place of the interview in social research is central. Its contribution ranges from preliminary information gathering to a place as the principal research tool. Clearly it takes many forms but the main dimension along which it varies is that of being unstructured/structured, from free to semi-structured to structured. Here, the highly structured form typically found in market research and surveys is considered, the characteristics of the unstructured form being similar to counselling interviews. For the structured approach a unique feature is the use of an interview schedule: in effect, a carefully prepared script meticulously adhered to by the interviewer. A great deal of thought is put into preparing the schedule in order that question form and content, question order, response mode, use of response aids and other factors can be taken into account.

Customarily these factors are checked by conducting pilot studies. Another feature of research interviewing is the attention paid to teaching interviewers how to present a particular schedule, together with supervision of their work in the field. Finally, since it is often the case that large numbers of respondents are involved, it is usual to design the schedules with data analysis in mind: for example, the coding of responses by interviewers for data entry.

As an example of research interviewing the approach of the Government Social Survey is now described. The Social Survey began work dealing with wartime problems of the 1940s. It is now a Division of the Office of Population Censuses and Surveys carrying out a wide range of studies of social and economic interest for public departments. A detailed description of the practices and procedures it employs is to be found in the handbook for interviewers (Atkinson, 1971).

Steps in producing such surveys include:

*   identifying research question: decide on form and content of survey, consider costs;
*   draft proposals: content of schedule, sampling of respondents;
*   pilot stage: explore degree of structure appropriate, such as free to highly. Coding of replies. Analyse pilot material;
*   brief and train interviewers: careful training including practice on schedule. How to contact the public. Identifying the person to be interviewed (e.g. by age, sex, role). Putting over the purpose of the survey; problem of refusals or lack of co-operation. Conducting the interview: defining the roles of interviewer and informant;
*   timetable: prepare addresses, number of interviewees, target dates;
*   carry out field survey: interviewers adhere to research officers' instructions on each question. Comprehend the purpose of each question: (i) factual information; (ii) expression of opinion; (iii) attitude measures.
    Deploy response modes without distortion: open questions with free response, closed/forward choice questions with pre-coded or scaled responses. Interviewers practise use of response aids: prompt cards for scaled responses, self-completion scales, repertory grids, examples of products in market research.
    Interviewers pay particular attention to prompting and probing.
    Guard against distortion in recording data: both precoded and open response items are susceptible;
*   coding: check schedules and categorize response;
*   computing: produce tables, analyse data;
*   conclusion: write report.

Purpose At this stage in the discussion of our model of an interview it must be clear that so many varieties exist as to demand careful consideration of each in terms of purpose. The variety of purposes has been mentioned, and also that the approach may vary from structured to unstructured according to purpose. Thus a number of recognizable forms of interview have emerged to meet particular needs. Examples include:

* non-directive counselling, client-centred therapy;
* psychotherapeutic encounters of many kinds;
* depth interviews emphasizing motivational factors;
* group interviews involving a number of respondents in a discussion group type format;
* psychological testing, especially individual tests such as WAIS (Wechsler Adult Intelligence Scale);
* problem-solving interviews such as individual role-playing for a variety of purposes.

Consequences Accepting the purposive nature of the interview implies that outcomes are important for all concerned and that their nature depends on the situation, and not least how the situation is perceived. For the interviewer, this will involve achieving the particular aims which have been identified together with maintenance of professional competence; for example, in the research interview maintaining the validity, reliability and precision of data with errors eliminated as far as possible.

For the interviewee or respondent one might ask: what do they get out of the experience? All too often what might be called the public relations aspect of interviewing is ignored. Symptoms of this include fears on the part of correspondents regarding the confidentiality of data, or that in some way they are being threatened. Such considerations appear to bring us full circle, for if attention is paid to the initiation stage of the proceedings by way of setting the scene such alarms can be reduced. Nevertheless, the sometimes necessary use of subterfuge in research needs to be handled with great care, a minimum requirement being the provision of an adequate explanation after the event or an account of the research.

References **Argyle, M.** (1973)
Social Interaction. London: Tavistock.
Argyle, M. (1975)
Bodily Communication. London: Methuen.
Atkinson, J. (1971)
A Handbook for Interviewers (2nd edn). London: HMSO.
Bartlett, F.C. (1932)
Remembering. Cambridge: Cambridge University Press.

Cook, M. (1979)
Perceiving Others. London: Methuen.
Orne, M.T. (1962)
On the social psychology of the psychology experiment.
American Psychologist, 17, 776-783.
Rodger, A. (1974)
Seven Point Plan. London: NFER.
Rosenthal, R. and Rosnow, R.L. (1969)
The volunteer subject. In R. Rosenthal and R.L.
Rosnow (eds), Artifact in Behavioral Research. New
York: Academic Press.

Questions

1. 'The interview is a wide-band procedure with low fidelity'. Discuss.
2. Assess the contribution of the study of social skills to the improvement of job selection interviewing.
3. 'Interviewing is the most commonly used selection tool'. Why do you think this is and what else are its strengths and weaknesses?
4. What future do you see for the interview?
5. Discuss the significance of role expectations for the conduct of an interview.
6. Write an account of the function of non-verbal communication in the interview.
7. Critically assess the form of an interview in a counselling situation with which you are familiar.
8. What are the advantages and disadvantages of using a scheme such as the Seven Point Plan for job interviewing?
9. Identify common sources of error in research interviewing. How might these be eliminated?
10. Choose a particular type of interview and design an appropriate interviewer training course.

Annotated reading

Anstey, E. (1976) An Introduction to Selection Interviewing.
London: HMSO.
Originally prepared for staff training in the Civil Service, this practical guide is useful for the advice it gives on general preparation for selection interviewing as well as the conduct of interviews.

Bingham, W.V. and Moore, B.V. (1959) How to Interview (4th edn). New York: Harper & Row.
A classic work. An early attempt to offer general guidance for those engaged in selection, survey interviews and counselling. Rather general in its approach.

Cannell, C.F. and Kahn, R.L. (1968) Interviewing. In G. Lindzey and E. Aronson (eds), Handbook of Social Psychology, Volume 2 (2nd edn). London: Addison-Wesley.

A systematic account of the research interview. Tends towards a theoretical presentation; for example in its discussion of problems of reliability and validity and measurement. Includes discussion of interview technique, question form and the training of interviewers.

Cross, C.P. (1974) Interviewing and Communication in Social Work. London: Routledge & Kegan Paul.
A useful guide to the 'helping' interview. Represents the movement towards enhancing social skills of all involved in such encounters.

Sidney, E. and Brown, M. (1973) The Skills of Interviewing. London: Tavistock.
Aimed at managers, especially personnel staff. A generally acclaimed book, based on the extensive experience of the authors, it offers a very practical guide to the selection interview.

Sidney, E.; Brown, M. and Argyle, M. (1973) Skills with People. London: Hutchinson.
A guide for managers. Concerns itself with a wide range of topics: communication in general, social skills, interviews, meetings and committees, interpersonal skills and training in social skills.

Ungerson, B. (ed.) (1975) Recruitment Handbook (2nd edn). London: Gower Press.
Very useful guide to the context of job interviewing, preparing job specifications, advertising, references; all the supporting activities of selection are covered.

Index